BEYOND QUEER

THE FREE PRESS

NEW YORK LONDON TORONTO SYDNEY TOKYO SINGAPORE

BEYOND QUEER

CHALLENGING GAY LEFT ORTHODOXY

Edited by

BRUCE BAWER

A list of reprint permissions can be found at the back of the book.

THE FREE PRESS
A Division of Simon & Schuster Inc.
1230 Avenue of the Americas
New York, NY 10020

Designed by Carla Bolte

Manufactured in the United States of America

10 9 8 7 6 5 4 3 2 1

Library of Congress Cataloging-in-Publication Data

Beyond queer : challenging gay left orthodoxy / edited by Bruce Bawer.
p. cm.
ISBN 0-684-82766-2
1. Homosexuality—Political aspects—United States. 2. Gay liberation movement—United States. 3. Gays—United States—Political activity. I. Bawer, Bruce
HQ76.3.U5B49 1996 95–52264
305.9'0664—dc20 CIP

CONTENTS

CONTENTS

INTRODUCTION

Queer. Once—and still—an anti-gay slur, it's been reclaimed by a minority of gay people as a supposedly affirmative label. Yet it's an odd and problematic word, often less indicative of sexual orientation than of ideology. To be queer, by some people's definitions, is not so much to be homosexual as it is to be a socially marginal rebel, defined primarily by his or her sexuality, who is perpetually and intrinsically at odds with the political and cultural establishment. But you don't have to be all these things, as long as you think of yourself that way, or say that you do, or adopt a personal style that implies that you do. Or something like that.

Though many people who call themselves queer have accomplished good things, queer ideology itself is ultimately selfish and immature. It presents itself as revolutionary, but instead of making a serious attempt to understand underlying psychological causes of homophobia and address them, it assumes homophobia to be implacable and confronts it with pointless, often quite puerile posturing. It's not about substance, strategy, or sacrifice, but about style and self-image.

Queer ideology is essentially a legacy of the 1969 Stonewall riots in New York, which ushered in the modern gay rights movement. It informs the philosophy of Queer Nation, the now almost entirely defunct group whose name suggests a socially and politically separate dominion within each of the presumably "straight" countries of the world. Reflected in this organization's name is the distinctive notion that gays don't have any place in "straight" establishment institutions—for example, the military and the clergy—and that gays who do belong to those institutions are traitors to their brothers and sisters.

Wayne Dynes notes in a recent article, "It is not clear whether the label queer designates (a) gay/lesbian, (b) gay/lesbian/bisexual, (c) gay/lesbian/bisexual/transpeople, etc., or (d) almost everybody, in some mood or other. Thus, there is a range of definitions, from minimalist (a) to maximalist (d)." One proponent of the term, he adds,

> has remarked that the virtue of "queer" is its very uncertainty and flexibility. We have recently heard tell, it is true, of the advantages of "fuzzy thinking." But as a group of people who have suffered from the fuzziness and illogic of the fabrications of bigotry, gay men and lesbians should pause before embracing such imprecision themselves.

Dynes, a professor of history at Hunter College, further observes that while self-styled queers tend to espouse Marxist politics and to speak of solidarity with workers, Third Worlders, and other presumably oppressed groups, the adoption of the word *queer* is an "elite phenomenon" confined largely to upper-class and upper-middle-class white Americans. Indeed, Dynes remarks that the word *queer* "often functions as a wedge issue separating generations and classes (working-class and non-white gay men and lesbians have displayed little enthusiasm for it)." As Dynes points out, the groups with which self-styled queers routinely proclaim their shared interests tend to be far more anti-gay than members of the purportedly "oppressive" white ruling class of America and western Europe. (A dramatic illustration of this fact came during the 1995 Beijing Women's Conference, when a group of lesbians, most of them white upper-middle-class Westerners, were confronted by a hostile group of veiled Moslem women.)

A disproportionate number of those who work for gay political organizations, write for the gay press, and teach in university gay-studies programs call themselves queer. Collectively, these folks make up a "queer establishment" whose views have played a big part in shaping the way the news media view homosexuality (although, thankfully, the word *queer* has not replaced *homosexual* and *gay* in the mainstream press). "Queer" professors have also shaped the minds of many gay students, such as the undergraduate who, during the question-and-answer period following a lecture I gave about gay politics at a large Southern university, tendered the familiar academic argument that gay people who use the word *queer* thereby defuse it and rob homophobes of their power to hurt. "I wish you were right," I replied, "but human psychology doesn't work that way." I cited a book by John Lauritsen, in which he recalls a New York City forum on the question "Do you like being called 'queer'?" He writes:

> The only two panelists who approved of using the word "queer" were women, although until very recently "queer" was always clearly understood as applying to gay men, not to lesbians. Donna Minkowitz, the most vociferous advocate of "queer," was shocked and upset when asked whether she would mind being called a "cunt" or a "kike." And yet, what is the difference? Have African-Americans chosen to describe themselves as "niggers," or Jews as "kikes," or Asian Americans as "gooks"? What indeed *is* the difference?

Most gay men and lesbians, I feel sure, would agree with Lauritsen: what is the difference? Yet queer ideology, unfortunately, has an immense influence. Why unfortunately? Partly because the queer image is false: most gay people don't subscribe to this ideology. Partly because queer identity is confining: it imposes on individuals who happen to be gay a monolithic set of ideas about who they are or should be. And partly because queer politics is disastrously counterproductive: it insists on a narrow, prescriptive view of personal identity that ultimately serves the interests of those who would prefer not to see gay people become full, equal, and open participants in mainstream society.

The ineffectuality of the queer approach to social, cultural, and political questions grew increasingly obvious in the early 1990s as gay issues became more prominently featured in the news media. Gay-left figures were routinely called on to provide a "gay perspective" on these issues. What might have been valuable opportunities to educate straight people about homosexuality often served instead to reinforce in the public's mind the very stereotypes that the radical right *wanted* to see reinforced.

This spectacle impelled me to write a book—*A Place at the Table: The Gay Individual in American Society* (1993)—that proved to be only part of a groundswell of change. Even before its publication I began to meet writers (most but not all of them gay) who shared many of my concerns. Their essays were beginning to define a mature and practical-minded direction in thinking on gay issues, one that seemed to hold out a realistic hope of effecting real social change. As these writings appeared in increasing numbers, several of us realized that a collection of them might help both straight and gay readers to recognize that there is indeed a serious alternative to "queerthink."

The writers represented in this book are a varied group. We don't agree on everything, in the realm of gay issues or otherwise. Most of us are gay; some aren't. Some are practicing Christians or Jews, while some are unabashed atheists. Among our number are Los Angeles and Boston lawyers, a New York rabbi, a former Bush Administration staffer, a vice president of a Washington think tank, a poet and literary critic, a novelist, and columnists for the *Advocate,* the *Chicago Tribune,* Chicago's *Windy City Times,* and the *New York Native,* as well as the editor of the *New Republic.* Though many of us have been tagged in the gay press as "gay conservatives," few of us would be considered conservative by anyone who objectively examined our politics; we variously call ourselves liberals, moderates, libertarians, and communitarians—or we eschew such labels altogether as increasingly irrelevant in a post-ideological era.

What we do have in common is that we've all challenged received opinions about gay life and politics. Some of us have been described as saying to straight America, "We're just like you." This is not true; no two people are "just like" each other. Rather, most of us would reject the notion that gays are monolithically identical to one another and monolithically different from straights. Most of us would affirm that everybody, gay and straight, is a complex individual—two people who share an orientation may differ in many other ways, and two people who don't share an orientation may well share much else. Sexual orientation, in short, is neither utterly defining nor utterly differentiating. This puts us at odds with queer ideology, with its group-by-group notion of "diversity"—its vision of a society of ghettos, each with its own style and philosophy.

Most of the contributors to this book share a perception that the gay rights movement has reached a turning point, and that we need a new gay politics (though we certainly aren't in accord on precisely what form that politics should take). We agree that we need to write about who gay people *really* are, and to do so in a way that straight people can understand. Those of us who are gay, moreover, need to ask ourselves where we want to go in this society and how we can reasonably get there. We need to rethink the meaning of the word *activism,* and we need to put behind us the concept of monolithic otherness that is urged on us by many gay-left leaders, academics, and writers.

The essays in this book represent the authors' respective gropings toward this new politics. Together they depict what I think it's fair to call a school of thought—one of which many people are as yet unaware. Though many of the pieces have appeared in such prominent places as the op-ed pages of the *New York Times* and the *Washington Post,* the writers may well have been dismissed by some readers as isolated voices crying in the wilderness. Part of my aim in compiling this book is to make it clear that there is indeed a "new gay paradigm"—that there are writers with a wide range of professional backgrounds and political allegiances who are finding words for the ways in which most gay people think about themselves, their sexual orientation, their individual identities, and their relation to society.

Let me make one important point. The title of this book doesn't signify that the rest of us must in some way get "beyond" gay men and lesbians who call themselves queer. Rather, it signifies that all of us (whatever our orientation, and whatever labels we attach to ourselves) would do well, as a society, to progress beyond the narrow set of ideas represented by the word *queer.* It's time, in short, for the gay rights movement to grow up.

This book contains six sections. It moves from the public (queer activism, Section I, and conservative politics, Section II) to the private (family and marriage, Section VI), by way of considerations of prejudice and oppression, tolerance and acceptance, rights and responsibilities (Section III), sex and outing, gay identity, and gay culture (Section IV), and religion (Section V). This movement from public to private, from political to personal, is especially relevant here because this is the direction in which several of the writers represented here feel that gay rights efforts should be moving. Instead of concentrating exclusively on the national political scene, that is, we should be placing more emphasis on the grass-roots level—the level of family, neighborhood, workplace, and house of worship.

A December 1993 issue of the *New Republic* contained a long cover story entitled "Democracy and Homosexuality" by Paul Berman. Though essentially a review of several recent books on gay issues, the piece also provided a concise history of the gay rights movement, with its emphasis on identity politics and its romantic image of itself as representing "a radicalism beyound all radicalisms." Berman noted "that history has not yet said its last word about the gay movement, and there are newer people still to be heard from."

Well, here they are.

BEYOND QUEER

SECTION I

RAGE, RAGE

On an episode of "The Charlie Rose Show" devoted to the twenty-fifth anniversary of the Stonewall riots, the radical lesbian activist Donna Minkowitz told me: "We don't want a place at the table—we want to turn the table over." That line pretty well sums up the attitude of many leftist gay activists toward both "the system" and gays who seek to work within it.

For a generation, the gay rights movement was dominated by that attitude. Consequently, as Paul Berman has noted, the movement was riddled with potentially disastrous "embarrassments and misfortunes," among them

> the organizational chaos of the Gay Liberation Front in the months after the Stonewall riot, the calamitous notion of allying at home and abroad with every pirate and tyrant who ran up a revolutionary flag, the invention of a kitschy cultural identity on the basis of sex and the ensuing campaigns to eroticize art and culture, the snarly air of intolerance radiating from the radicals, the parading fetishists, the maneuverings of the flacks and the blackmailers and the conspiracy theorists.

2

RAGE, RAGE

In a 1993 issue of the *Saint Louis Lesbian and Gay News-Telegraph,* Jim Thomas lamented that too many gay activists are sympathetic to a "quasi-Marxist" ideological model that identifies heterosexuals as oppressors and gays as victims. He calls this model a dead end, because it posits that "if the system is the oppressor. . . . one is morally acceptable only if one is disenfranchised. Ironically, then, anyone who actually makes progress working with it is really only being co-opted and compromised." Thomas bluntly speaks up for a pragmatic gay politics: "If we are unable to entertain serious self-criticism to find out what works and, yes, what doesn't work, then we are lost." Similarly, in a 1995 *Advocate* column entitled "Leaving the Comfort Zone," I noted that gays who do try to work within the system are often "attacked by the queer establishment for 'getting into bed with our enemies.'" By contrast, the gay press celebrated a

> raucous busful of Lesbian Avengers who, on a recent Dixie bus tour, breezed from town to town, recklessly disrupting social circumstances they knew nothing about. Politically, of course, such "activism" does only harm, but because it's all pluses on a personal level (little physical or emotional risk and lots of opportunity for fun, adventure, self-affirmation, anger release, and gay solidarity), the queer establishment applauds it.

In a 1993 column called "The Trouble with Activists," Paul Varnell focused on a particularly distressing aspect of the movement:

> Local activism up until now—with honorable exceptions—has too often tended to attract the socially alienated, the under-employed, political wanna-be's and hangers-on, even marginally disturbed personality types. For such people, activism serves as a social activity, a kind of therapy, or even an opportunity for acting out free-floating hostility. We all know people in each of these categories and I, for one, am tired of pretending to take them seriously as activists.
>
> It is probably useless to try to train most of these naive and alienated peo-

> ple in the tactical skills, the political savvy and the ability to generate an appealing message to a broad range of legislators and public opinion. Such people's primary emotions seem to run a narrow gamut from petulance to anger. And most such people may very well lack the social skills necessary for lobbying, the patience to persuade, the perseverance to build slowly and effectively, the affability to recruit talented gays into the effort, and the confident self-possession to make a credible presentation to a journalist.

Though dissent from lockstep gay-left politics is not a new phenomenon, gay voices of opposition were, until recently, isolated and obscure. For example, Marshall Kirk and Hunter Madsen's 1989 book *After the Ball: How America Will Conquer Its Fear and Hatred of Gays in the 90's* effectively assailed the counterproductiveness of gay-left strategies and proffered an elaborate advertising campaign to correct the image of gay people. If Kirk and Madsen's book had insufficient impact, it is largely because gay people in 1989 were still too willing either to ignore gay politics or to be led by the gay left. It took the trauma of the gays-in-the-military controversy in 1993 to make some politically active gay people realize that standard left-wing assumptions needed to be examined, and to make politically inactive gay people become involved. So it was that gay people moved in greater numbers from both the quiet closets and the noisy ghetto barricades to what Carolyn Lochhead calls "the third way." Though the writers represented in this section don't agree on everything, the following essays could all be fairly said to exemplify that "third way."

BRUCE BAWER

To commemorate the twenty-fifth anniversary of the Stonewall riots, the New York Public Library sponsored a series of four lectures in the spring of 1994. I gave the last of those lectures, entitled "Common Humanity," on 17 May of that year; the following shorter version of that lecture appeared as the cover story in the 13 June issue of the *New Republic.*

NOTES ON STONEWALL

Twenty-five years ago, in the early morning hours of June 28, 1969, several patrons at the Stonewall bar in Greenwich Village, many of them flamboyant drag queens and prostitutes, refused to go quietly when police carried out a routine raid on the place. Their refusal escalated into five days of rioting by hundreds of people. Though it wasn't the first time anyone had contested the right of the state to punish citizens just for being gay, that rioting marked a pivotal moment because news of it spread in every direction and sparked the imaginations of countless gay men and lesbians around the world. It made them examine, and reject, the silence, shame, and reflexive compliance with prejudice to which most of them had simply never conceived a realistic alternative.

5

BRUCE BAWER

There is something wondrous about Stonewall, and it is this: that a mere handful of late-night bar patrons, many of them confused, lonely individuals living at the margins of society, started something that made a lot of lesbians and gay men do some very serious thinking of a sort they had never quite done before—thinking that led to action and to a movement. It was the beginning of a revolution in attitudes toward homosexuality. How odd it is to think that those changes could all be traced back to a drunken riot at a Greenwich Village bar on a June night in 1969. But they can. And that's why Stonewall deserves to be commemorated.

Today, however, Stonewall is not only commemorated but mythologized. Many gay men and lesbians routinely speak of it as if it was a sacred event that lies beyond the reach of objective discourse. They talk as if there was no gay rights activism at all before Stonewall, or else they mock pre-Stonewall activists as Uncle Toms. They recite the name *Stonewall* itself with the same reverence that American politicians reserve for the names of Washington and Lincoln. And indeed the word is perfectly suited to the myth, conjuring as it does an image of a huge, solid barrier separating the dark ages prior to the day that Judy Garland died from the out-loud-and-proud present. Every year, on what has long since become an all-purpose gay holiday—a combination of Independence Day, May Day, Mardi Gras, and, since the advent of HIV, Memorial Day as well—millions ritualistically revisit the raucous, defiant marginality of Stonewall in marches around the world. This year in New York, on the twenty-fifth anniversary, the ritual will reach a climax. For many, Stonewall has already become a Platonic model of gay activism—and, indeed, a touchstone of gay identity.

A few weeks ago, in a sermon about an entirely different subject, the rector of the Episcopal church I belong to in New York used the phrase "the politics of nostalgia." The phrase has stuck in my mind, for it seems to me that both sides of the gay rights struggle are trapped in what may well be characterized as a politics of nostalgia. Many of those who resist acceptance of homosexuality and reject equal rights for gay men and lesbians know on some level that they are wrong, but they cling to old thinking because a change, however just, seems to them a drastic departure from the comfortable world of "don't ask, don't tell." Some gay people, likewise, cling to what might be called the Stonewall sensibility, reacting defensively and violently, as if to some horrendous blasphemy or betrayal, even to the hint that perhaps the time has come to move in some way beyond that sensibility. Such people often declare proudly that they have been "in the trenches" for twenty-five years, which is to say that in a way they have been reliving Stonewall every day since June 1969.

Yet every day *can't* be Stonewall—or shouldn't. And in fact the time *has* come to move beyond the Stonewall sensibility. For, thanks largely to developments that can trace their inspiration to that barroom raid, some things *have* changed since 1969. Levels of tolerance have risen; gay rights laws have been passed; in the last quarter-century, and especially recently, gay Americans have come out of the closet in increasing numbers. As a result, it has become clear to more and more heterosexuals that gay America is as diverse as straight America—that many of the people who were at the Stonewall bar on that night twenty-five years ago represent an anachronistic politics that has largely ceased to have salience for gay America today. To say this is not to condemn people who consider themselves members of that fringe or to read them out of the gay community. It is simply to say that for gay America to continue to be defined largely by its fringe is a lie, and that this lie, like all lies about homosexuality, needs to be countered vigorously. The Stonewall sensibility—like the Stonewall myth—has to be abandoned.

On May 6 the *New York Times* described the arguments among gay leaders about the planning of Stonewall 25, the forthcoming

New York event that will culminate in a march on the United Nations. Some of these leaders worried that Stonewall 25 wouldn't focus enough on the fact that many of the Stonewall heroes were transvestite and transsexual hustlers. One woman wanted, in her words, to "radicalize" Stonewall 25. "Stonewall," she told the *Times,* "was a rebellion of transgender people, and this event has the potential to reduce our whole culture to an Ikea ad."

It is strange to read the words of those who speak, on the one hand, as if Stonewall, in and of itself, achieved something once and for all time that gay Americans are now free to celebrate, and, on the other, as if the kind of growing acceptance that is represented by the depiction of a middle-class gay couple in a furniture commercial on network TV is bad news, a threat to a Stonewall-born concept of gay identity as forever marginal. It would almost seem as if those leaders don't realize that Stonewall was only part of a long, complex process that is still proceeding, and that the best way to honor it is to build upon it by directing that process as wisely and responsibly as we can.

In the May 3 issue of the gay magazine the *Advocate,* activist Torie Osborn wrote that thirty-nine gay leaders, whom she described as "our community's best and brightest," had gathered recently to discuss the state of the movement and "retool [it] to match the changing times." The group, she wrote, "had a collective 750 years of experience in gay rights or other political work." But even as she wrote of seeking "common ground" and "common vision" among the gay leaders, Osborn reaffirmed the linking of gay rights to "other progressive movements with which many of us identify."

In other words, she embraced the standard post-Stonewall practice of indiscriminately linking the movement for gay equal rights with any left-wing cause to which any gay leader might happen to have a personal allegiance. That practice dates back to 1969, when radical activists, gay and straight, were quick to use the gay rights movement as a way to prosecute their own unrelated revolutionary agendas. Such linkages have been a disaster for the gay rights movement; not only do they falsely imply that most gay people sympathize with those so-called progressive movements, but they also serve to reinforce the idea of homosexuality itself as a "progressive" phenomenon, as something that is essentially political in nature. Osborn wrote further that she and the other gay leaders at the summit "talked about separating strategic thinking into two discrete areas: our short-term political fights and the long-term cultural war against systematic homophobia." And she added that "we have virtually no helpful objective data or clear strategy on the long-term war, which grapples with deep-seated sexphobia as well as heterosexism." Her conclusion (my emphasis): "*We need to start working on this problem.*"

With all due respect to Osborn and her fellow gay leaders, it seems to me more than a bit astonishing that in spite of their collective 750 years of experience, at least some of them have only now begun to realize that homosexuals should be giving thought to something other than short-term political conflicts. At the same time, those leaders still can't quite understand the long-term challenge as anything other than, in Osborn's words, a "war." Nor can they see that achieving real and lasting equality is a matter not of changing right-wingers into left-wingers, or of emancipating Americans from "sexphobia," but of liberating people from their discomfort with homosexuality, their automatic tendency to think of homosexuals in terms of sex, and their often bizarre notions of who gay people are, what gay people value, and how gay people live.

Perhaps, at the threshold of the second generation of the post-Stonewall gay rights movement, it behooves us to recall that, as I've noted, there *was* at least some species of gay activism prior to

Stonewall. Years before those patrons at the Stonewall bar hurled garbage, beer bottles, feces, and four-letter words at the policemen who had come to arrest them, a few small groups of men in business suits and women in dresses staged sober, orderly marches at which they carried signs that announced their own homosexuality and that respectfully demanded an end to anti-homosexual prejudice. Those people were even more radical than the rioters at Stonewall, and—dare I say it?—perhaps even more brave, given how few they were, how premeditated their protests, and how much some of them had to lose by publicly identifying themselves as gay. They were heroes, too; they won a few legal battles, and they might have won more. Sure, Stonewall was, without question, an important step—indeed, the biggest single step the gay rights movement has taken. But that's all it was: a step, the first big one in a long, difficult journey. It was a reaction to intolerance, and it set us on the road to tolerance. The next road leads to acceptance—acceptance not only of gay people by straight people, but an easier acceptance by young gay people of their own sexuality. It's a different road—and, in a way, a harder one.

First-generation post-Stonewall gay activists saw themselves as street combatants in a political war. Second-generation activists would better see themselves as participants in an educational program of which the expressly political work is only a part. Getting America to accept homosexuality will first be a matter of education. The job is not to shout at straight Americans, "We're here, we're queer, get used to it." The job is to do the hard, painstaking work of *getting* straight Americans used to it. This isn't dramatic work; nor is it work that provides a quick emotional release. Rather, it requires discipline, commitment, responsibility.

In some sense, of course, most straight Americans are used to the idea of people being gay. The first generation of the post-Stonewall gay rights movement has accomplished that. At the same time, it has brought us to a place where many straight Americans are sick and tired of the very word *gay.* They've heard it a million times, yet they don't understand it nearly well enough. They still feel uncomfortable, confused, threatened. They feel that the private lives of homosexuals have been pushed "in their faces," but they don't really know about those private lives.

And why should they be expected to? Yes, at Gay Pride Day marches, some gay men and lesbians, like the Stonewall rioters, have exposed America to images of raw sexuality—images that variously amuse, titillate, shock, and offend while revealing nothing important about who most of those people really are. Why, then, do some people do such things? Perhaps because they've been conditioned to think that on that gay high holy day, the definitively gay thing to do is to be as defiant as those heroes twenty-five years ago. Perhaps they do it because they can more easily grasp the concept of enjoying one day per year of delicious anarchy than of devoting 365 days per year to a somewhat more disciplined and strategically sensible demonstration designed to advance the causes of respect, dignity, and equality.

And perhaps they do it because, frankly, it is relatively easy to do. Just as standing up at a White House press conference and yelling at the president can take less courage than coming out to your parents or neighbors or employers, so taking off your pants or your bra for a Gay Pride Day march in the company of hundreds of thousands of known allies can be easier than taking down your defenses for a frank conversation with a group of colleagues at an office lunch about how it feels to grow up gay. For an insecure gay man or lesbian, moreover, explaining can feel awfully close to apologizing, and can open one up to charges of collaboration with the enemy by those who join the author Paul Monette in seeing America as the "Christian Reich" and themselves as members of the queer equivalent of the French resistance.

As a friend said to me recently, building acceptance of homosexuals is like teaching a language. When gays speak about themselves, they are speaking one language; when most straight people speak about gays, they are speaking another. Most heterosexuals look at gay lives the way I look at a page of German. I may be able to pick out a few familiar words, but I feel awkward when I use them, and if I try to put together a sentence I'm likely to find myself saying something I don't mean at all, perhaps even something offensive or hurtful. There's only one way to get past that feeling of confusion: tireless, meticulous dedication to study. You can't learn a foreign language overnight, and you can't teach it by screaming it at people. You teach it word by word, until, bit by bit, they feel comfortable speaking it and can find their way around the country where it's spoken. That's the job of the second generation of post-Stonewall gay activism: to teach those who don't accept us the language of who gay people are and where gay people live. Indeed, to the extent that professional homophobes have stalled progress in the movement toward legal and social parity for gay men and lesbians, it is not because those homophobes are so crafty, and certainly not because they are right. It is because they have spoken to straight America in its own language and addressed its concerns, whereas gay Americans, more often than not, out of an understandable fear and defensive self-righteousness, haven't.

Some reviewers in the gay press read the title of my book, *A Place at the Table: The Gay Individual in American Society,* as a sign that I, personally, long to sit at a dinner table with people like Pat Buchanan and Jerry Falwell—that this book is my attempt to indicate to them that I'm a nice, well-mannered gay man and that I, along with the other nice, well-mannered gay men, should be allowed at the table while the "bad," ill-mannered gays are excluded. Some other gay-press reviewers have understood that I don't mean that at all, and that I feel everyone should be welcome at the American table, but they have angrily rejected the idea: "Why," one critic wrote, "should *I* want to sit at that table?" A writer for the gay magazine *Out* dismissed the book in one line: "Bruce Bawer has written a book about the gay individual in American society entitled *A Place at the Table.* Some will prefer take-out."

What these reactions signify to me is a powerful tendency among some homosexuals to recoil reflexively from the vision of an America where gays live as full and open members of society, with all the rights, responsibilities, and opportunities of heterosexuals. Many gay people, indeed, have a deep, unarticulated fear of that metaphorical place at the table. This is understandable: gay people, as a rule, are so used to minimizing their exposure to homophobia, by living either in the closet or on the margins of society, that for someone—even a fellow gay person—to come along and invoke an image of gay America sitting openly at a table with straight America can seem, to them, like a hostile act. This sense of threat—this devotion to the margin—may help explain the gay-activist rancor toward the movie *Philadelphia.* But most gay men and lesbians were happy to see a movie that showed homosexuality as part of the mainstream, just as most are pleased by the new tendency to depict gay life, in everything from Ikea ads to movies like *Four Weddings and a Funeral,* in a matter-of-fact way, as an integrated part of society.

Am I attacking radicalism? No. I'm saying that the word *radical* must be defined anew by each generation. In the late twentieth century, when radicalism has often been viewed as a fashion choice, it's easy to lose sight of what real radicalism is. It's not a matter of striking a defiant pose and maintaining that pose over a period of years; it's not a matter of signing on to a certain philosophy or program and adhering to it inflexibly for the rest of your life. And it's not always a matter of manning barricades or crouching in trenches. It's a matter of honest inquiry, of waking up every morning and looking at the social circumstances in which you find yourself and having the vision to perceive what needs to be done and the courage to follow up on that vision, wherever it may take you. It's a matter of going to the *root* of the problem, wherever that root may lie.

And going to the root of this particular problem means going to the root of prejudice. It means probing the ignorance and fear that are responsible for the success of anti-gay crusaders. It means seriously addressing those opponents' arguments against gay rights, in which they combine a defense of morality and "family values" with attacks on homosexuality as anti-God, anti-American and anti-family. Too often, the first generation of the post-Stonewall gay movement has responded to such rhetoric by actually saying and doing things that have only reinforced the homophobes' characterization of homosexuality. The second generation of the movement would do well to respond not by attacking the American values and ridiculing the religious faith that these people claim as a basis for their prejudice, but by making it clear just how brutal, how un-American and how anti-religious their arguments and their prejudice are.

And there are a lot of untruths out there to overcome. More and more people understand that homosexuals are no more likely to be child molesters than heterosexuals are, but there remains on the part of many people a lingering discomfort about such notions, and anti-gay crusaders exploit that discomfort with ambiguous, dishonest rhetoric suggesting that homosexuals are (to quote a recent statement published in the *Wall Street Journal* by a group of religious figures calling itself the Ramsey Colloquium) a threat to the "vulnerabilities of the young." That's a lie. But how can homosexuals help heterosexuals understand it's a lie so long as some gay political leaders, in the best Stonewall tradition, feel more comfortable condemning the Log Cabin Republicans than they do condemning the North American Man-Boy Love Association?

Likewise, more and more people understand that homosexuals' lives are no more about sex than their lives are, but there are many who still *don't* understand that, and the anti-gay crusaders exploit their ignorance by saying (again in the words of the Ramsey Colloquium) that gay people "define" themselves by their "desires alone," that they seek "liberation from constraint," from obligations to the larger society and especially to the young, and from all human dignity. *That*'s a lie. But how can gays help straights understand it's a lie so long as a few marchers on Gay Pride Day feel the best way to represent all gay men and lesbians is to walk down the avenue in their underwear?

Anti-gay propagandists shrewdly exploit the fact that we live in times when there's ample reason for concern about children. American children today grow up in an often uncivil and crime-ridden society, and with a pop culture that is at best value-neutral and at worst aggressive and ugly. Altogether too many of those kids grow up inured to the sight of beggars sleeping on the sidewalk, of condoms and hypodermic needles in the gutter, of pornographic magazines on display at street-corner kiosks. Anti-gay propagandists routinely link homosexuality to these phenomena, seeing homosexual orientation, and gay people's openness about it, and gay people's desire for equal rights and equal respect, as yet more signs of the decline of morals, of the family, of social cohesion and stability and of civilization generally.

One of Stonewall's legacies is that gay leaders have too often accepted this characterization of the conflict and see any attempt to correct it as "sex-negative." The second generation of post-Stonewall gay activism has to make it clear that that's not the way the sides break down at all, and that when it comes to children, the real interests of parents and of gay people (many of whom are themselves parents, of course) are not unalterably opposed, but are, in fact, perfectly congruent. Gay adults care about children, too; and they know from experience something that straight parents can only strive to understand—namely, what it's like to grow up gay.

Homosexuals, of course, are *not* a threat to the family; among the things that threaten the family are parents' profound ignorance about homosexuality and their reluctance to face the truth about it. In the second generation of the post-Stonewall gay rights movement, gay adults must view it as an obligation to ensure that parents understand that truth—and understand, too, that according equal rights to homosexuals and equal recognition to same-sex relationships (and creating an atmosphere in which gay men and lesbians can live openly without fear of losing their jobs or homes or lives) would not threaten the institution of the family but would actually strengthen millions of American families.

It is ironic that, to a large extent, what perpetuates Stonewall-style antagonism between gay and straight are not our differences, really, but traits that we all share as human beings. We all, for instance, fear the unknown. To most straight people, homosexuality is an immense unknown; to gay people, a society that would regard sexual orientation indifferently and grant homosexuals real equality is also an immense unknown. But it is also our humanity that makes most of us long to know and live with the truth, even in the wake of a lifetime of lies. The greatest tribute we can pay to the memory of Stonewall is to work in our own homes and workplaces to dismantle, lie by lie, the wall of lies that has divided the families of America for too long.

BRUCE BAWER

The last page of each issue of the *Advocate,* the biweekly gay newsmagazine, contains a column on gay culture and politics called "Last Word." I began writing that column, in alternation with other writers, in 1994. The following column appeared on 20 September 1994.

THE ROAD TO UTOPIA

"Stonewall 25," exulted a friend after the march in June, "saw the last gasp of the radical gay left." Perhaps. Certainly things are changing dramatically. Left-wing gay groups are floundering; the Log Cabin Republicans grow apace. While the gay left seems increasingly barren intellectually and unable to distinguish tactics from strategy, moderate gay voices are being raised—and listened to. Unable or unwilling to address the important questions that openly gay moderates are raising, gay-left honchos have chosen instead to paint us—dishonestly—as a bunch of bigoted, reactionary, self-serving upper-class conformists.

Last spring in *Gay Community News,* Urvashi Vaid lodged a by-now-familiar complaint: "By aspiring to join the mainstream rather than continuing to figure out the ways we need to change it, we risk losing our gay and lesbian souls in order to gain the world." But nobody's "aspiring to join" the mainstream; the point is that most gays live in that mainstream. What Vaid apparently hasn't been able to reconcile to her worldview is the emergence from the closet—and from political silence—of increasing numbers of gays whose politics differ dramatically from her own. The more visible such people become, the clearer it will be how out of touch many gay-left leaders are with the majority of those whom they claim to represent.

Although Vaid and her philosophical allies routinely label gay moderates as members of a "new gay right," most of those so described would consider themselves politically liberal to middle-of-the-road. We've been described as wanting to exclude certain gay people. Wrong. Nor do we deny or disavow the heroic contributions of gay activists over the past three decades. What we are about is building on those contributions—and moving beyond certain ways of thinking that harm all of us.

Above all, the moderate gay rights movement is, quite simply, about gay rights. By contrast, gay-left leaders apparently view those rights as only one plank of a comprehensive socialist platform that all gays are inherently obliged to support. In a July 4 *Nation* essay titled "A Socialism of the Skin," Tony Kushner argued that socialism follows from homosexuality as night follows day. Speaking up for "solidarity," Kushner assailed what he sees as "assimilationism." But it's Kushner who's the assimilationist: far from wanting all gays to be themselves—free of pressure from anyone, straight or gay, to become something other than who they are—he wants us all to conform to his notion of what it means to be gay. When he applauds solidarity, he means solidarity on his terms. Yet as more of us come out, it becomes increasingly clear that few of us identify with his extreme ideology.

Kushner warned of "the emergence of increasing numbers of conservative homosexuals . . . who are unsympathetic to the idea of linking their fortunes with any other political cause." Put it this way: Most gays—liberal or conservative, libertarian or moderate—reserve the right to make their own linkages. Most would deny that their homosexuality obliges them to subscribe to the laundry list of far-left positions. Most feel, as I do, that what we're up against in this country is mainly the ignorance that makes many straight people fear homosexuality and consider it a threat to American society.

For Vaid and Kushner, however, the enemy is American society itself, and the gay rights movement is principally a means of attacking its foundations. Uninterested in such bourgeois goals as gay marriage and military service, they agree with Donna Minkowitz, who in an appearance on Charlie Rose's show a couple of days before Stonewall 25, declared that "we don't want a place at the table—we want to turn the table over." That sentiment is as philosophically alien to most gays as it is to most straight people.

In his *Nation* piece Kushner wrote that he "expect[s] both hope and vision from [his] politics." Yes, utopian hope and vision. He admitted his utopianism, citing Oscar Wilde's remark that "a map of the world that does not include Utopia is not worth even glancing at." But we've allowed ourselves to be guided for too long according to this map; it's time to replace it with a map of the real world. Kushner scorns gay people who, plotting their courses on such maps, patiently persevere in their attempt to change straight people's attitudes. "I am always suspicious," he complained, "of the glacier-paced patience of the right." Well, more and more gay people are impatient with the queer left's abiding fascination with aimless utopianism; we're impatient with models of activism that involve playing at revolution instead of focusing on the serious work of reform.

Kushner insisted that gay people require "a politics that goes beyond." Yes—beyond counterculture posturing and extreme ideological rhetoric. What we require is a politics that recognizes the real-world possibilities and limitations of politics—a realpolitik that stands a chance of effecting a genuine improvement in the lives of gay Americans, rather than a self-indulgent millenarianism full of sound and fury, signifying nothing.

PAUL VARNELL

Varnell, who writes the "Observer's Notebook" column for the *Windy City Times,* Chicago's weekly gay newspaper, has also contributed to *Reason,* the *Advocate, Lambda Book Report,* and Chicago's *Reader.* The following column appeared in the *Windy City Times* on 8 September 1994.

MEMO TO THE GAY MOVEMENT

Tim McFeeley, executive director of the Human Rights Campaign Fund (HRCF), is leaving that post. Peri Jude Radecic, executive director of the National Gay and Lesbian Task Force (NGLTF), is stepping down to return to her former position as director of public policy. William Rubenstein, head of the ACLU's Lesbian and Gay Rights Project, has announced his departure. Daniel Bross, executive director of the AIDS Action Council, has announced his resignation. As of this writing, the Gay and Lesbian Alliance Against Defamation has yet to designate a new national director.

If all this does not suggest the need for a little fundamental perestroika for our movement, at least it provides a nearly unparalleled opportunity for it. Perestroika—restructuring—would hardly be necessary if our movement as presently constituted had been a success. It hasn't.

Half of the states still have sodomy laws. Only eight states bar anti-gay discrimination, and at least two of those (Massachusetts and Minnesota) still have sodomy laws. Barely 100 cities—a few big ones and a large number of small university towns—ban discrimination.

A handful of cities have "domestic partners" provisions of one sort or another, but most are laughable in the pittance they offer gays. Gay men are still hunted down and beaten or killed by bored heterosexual youths. Gays in the military must live like capitalists in Stalinist Russia.

Our national organizations are pitifully small, with total budgets of less than $13 million (HRCF, $8 million; NGLTF, $3 million; others less than $2 million), with a total membership barely in excess of 100,000 (HRCF 80,000—counting anyone who has contributed to any HRCF program; NGLTF, 30,000; others far less). Most state and local gay organizations are minuscule and powerless. The largest nonerotic community publication has a circulation of barely 80,000—and regards that as an achievement.

In Congress, we have been able to obtain only brief hearings in one house on a stripped-down bill to ban discrimination in employment, and that was considered a breakthrough. Sixty-three craven votes in the Senate were cast for an amendment to block federal funds for school programs that might help young gays and lesbians lead less miserable lives.

When an openly gay or lesbian character turns up on television it is still regarded as a "breakthrough"—in other words, an anomaly.

I put all this as bluntly as possible because I think we need to face up to how little we have achieved in the last twenty-five years—and ask ourselves what that means. We achieve tiny victories, and we become exultant. We lose by less than we thought, and we proclaim a victory. We lose by a lot, and we praise how much organizing was done and how much "grassroots activism" was generated and how "energized" the community has become and how "empowered" people feel about their lives. Gag!

There are now real grounds to question whether we have the potential to be a large and effective political movement of the sort many envisioned, with national organizations of a half million to a million members employing skilled professionals, with savvy and effective local affiliates. The support simply may not be there. Why not? Are gays too scared? Or not scared enough? Or do most gays simply not think politically? If not, why not?

Mostly, they may believe that their small contributions will not make much difference in their own lives—in contrast with the marginal benefits of renting a few good films to watch on their VCR or buying a few more compact discs. It is not clear that they are wrong.

Maybe we are too impatient? After all, it has been more than 130 years since the Emancipation Proclamation, and black Americans still do not have full social equality.

But we have enormous advantages that blacks for a long time lacked: Many of us are well educated. We are at no enormous economic disadvantage and could fund substantial advocacy efforts. We have excellent means of internal communication, and we have surprisingly good newspapers to keep us informed. And we live in an era of mass literacy and mass communications with an extremely rapid circulation of ideas through the population.

If we are making actual progress so slowly, maybe we should scale back our expectations and expand our time frame. Somehow we have been led to expect far more rapid progress than we are seeing: a gay civil rights bill now, openly gay senators soon, and so on. They are not going to happen. Maybe the best we can do is not "Equality in Our Time" but "Equality in One Hundred Years." Or two hundred years. Or maybe only gradual progress asymptotically approaching equality—a domestic partners registry here, a favorable amendment there, legislative hearings over yonder, an occasional minor entertainment figure coming out once in a while.

But what would it mean for activists' energy and enthusiasm to simply dig in for the long haul—a very long haul? And what does it mean for us and our organizations to work as hard as they do for such small gains? How can we avoid chronic burnout and frustration among leaders and activists themselves? And how can we keep people interested and supportive if we constantly win so much less than we have been led to expect, less than we have led others to expect?

Almost surely we cannot. So maybe we should give up the whole thing and admit that the gay "movement" in any organized form is a failure. Maybe organizations have been, and are, entirely epiphenomenal: Maybe what progress we have seen would have happened anyway without any organized advocacy efforts on our part.

Maybe that progress has been fueled by social and economic trends no one controls—as younger, more tolerant baby boomers achieve positions of power and influence; with the increase in the number of people with college and postcollege education; with the growing presence of women in the workforce; with the social and cultural diversification of the country; with the growth of service and high-tech industries with their more individualist corporate climates.

So perhaps in the end we should conclude that the gay movement has been ineffective, useless, a waste of people's time and resources, and finally unnecessary. If so, we owe it to ourselves to face up to that fact. It is surprising to reach this conclusion, but given the logic of the situation, this is where the arguments lead. Perhaps someone else can explain why all this is wrong. We would all benefit from knowing if they can. Or cannot.

STEPHEN H. MILLER

Miller, a self-described "recovering progressive," writes the "Culture Watch" column for the *New York Native*. A contributing writer for *Christopher Street* and a former media columnist for *Genre,* he served for five years as a board member and the media committee chair for the Gay & Lesbian Alliance Against Defamation in New York. In the latter position he coined the organization's slogan ("Fighting for fair, accurate, and inclusive representations of gay and lesbian lives"), arranged meetings with national media executives, and coordinated responses to anti-gay hate. Miller subsequently broke with the organization over "political correctness" issues. The following essay appeared in the November/December 1994 issue of *Heterodoxy,* a conservative journal, under the title "Gay-Bashing by Homosexuals." It appears here under Miller's original title.

GAY WHITE MALES: PC'S UNSEEN TARGET

Let me be frank. I am a gay white male who was victimized by the gay and, especially, the lesbian left.

Here's my story. For more than five years, I chaired the media committee of the New York chapter of the Gay and Lesbian Alliance Against Defamation. I coordinated national media efforts responding to perceived defamation and wrote and placed numerous letters to the editor, opinion pieces, magazine and newspaper articles, and press quotes. I met with leading American media figures, including the president of CBS News and the managing editor of *Time* magazine. In 1990, I received a GLAAD Media Award for Outstanding Volunteer Services.

Then, in December of 1992, I was purged (there is no better word for it) because I challenged some of the left-wing, politically correct mantras constantly intoned by those who are involved in the "progressive" wing of the lesbian and gay movement.

To many readers of this magazine, GLAAD's mission itself may be suspect: "To fight for fair, accurate and inclusive representations of gay and lesbian lives in the media and elsewhere." Actually, I thought up this definition, which is still used by the organization to this day. But even if I hadn't, I would still maintain that this is a valid goal—responding to misinformation and stereotype with reasoned argument. Yet it is also a goal that has been greatly perverted (if there is a pun here, it is intended) as a result of the rise of political correctness and its censorious ways within the gay and lesbian movement. GLAAD/New York got off track when, in the early '90s, old-guard gay activists began to be supplanted by younger PC types. Militant lesbian feminists—using "diversity" as their battle cry—assumed positions of power and started attacking a new enemy: gay white men.

Ellen Carton, formerly head of National Abortion Rights Action League/New York, was hired by GLAAD toward the end of 1991. Shortly thereafter, a majority of the old board members, most of them suffering from burnout, drifted away. Carton, along with then-chair of GLAAD Mary Nealon and current chair Peggy Brady, was instrumental in packing the new board with many of their friends and political cronies. As in the universities and other venues where such a radical takeover has occurred, it soon became apparent that under this new regime, race and gender would be given precedence over individual merit when it came to hiring staff. Moreover, only leftists now seemed welcome. Discussions with the new staff were dominated by endless sensitivity sessions meant to inculcate political correctness, sessions that quickly identified white men (whatever their sexual orientation) as the oppressor class. In fact, the reconstituted and radicalized GLAAD staff (Carton especially) seemed far more passionate about combating the pernicious influence of patriarchal white males within the lesbian and gay movement than in focusing on anti-gay defamation from without.

As a political moderate who believed in dialogue with the straight world and a good-faith search for common ground. I found myself shunned by the new clique in charge of GLAAD. Finally, Carton announced she would no longer work with me because I didn't treat her with "sufficient respect." (That is, I disagreed with her occasionally!) Finding no support from the recently reconstituted board and unable to awaken the dormant membership about the PC fog that had descended over GLAAD, I felt I had no choice but to depart. (Board chair Peggy Brady, by the way, often pointed to the fact that I appeared to doze off during one of the organization's interminable all-day "diversity" retreats as proof of my prejudice against women and a "progressive" agenda.)

Carton and Brady like to claim that the organization is still controlled by white males. But as I will show in a minute, the dominance of GLAAD by radical lesbians couldn't be more evident.

At the same time Carton is complaining of ongoing white male domination, however, she tells *The Chronicle of Philanthropy,* "Now that we've become more diverse, we have a diversity of opinion." I hear this and wonder what left-wing African Americans, left-wing Latinos/Latinas, left-wing Asian feminists, and upper-middle-class left-wing white lesbians—all of whom think exactly alike—can possibly have a diversity of opinion about; perhaps, which group has been more victimized by gay white men?

Here's the point. To most conservatives, gays and lesbians may seem an undifferentiated radical bloc intent on subverting all the bourgeois norms that underlie the social order. (Especially when we seek the right to marry the person we love or to serve our country in the armed forces—both of which, somehow, get termed "special rights" when, in my opinion, they are basic equity issues, as opposed to the gay left's more sweeping and intrusive demands.)

What straight conservatives haven't acknowledged (or, for that matter, exploited) are the fault lines inside the gay and lesbian movement. These conservatives haven't seen the extent to which people who are gay but not otherwise politically radical have been targeted and scapegoated by the self-appointed gay-left and lesbian-feminist cliques that dominate the organized "lesbigay" political movement.

To those who can't fathom that gays could be victims of PC, here are some examples of how it happens:

The Quota Game. The national by-laws of the Gay and Lesbian Alliance Against Defamation now contain a convoluted quota requirement under which each chapter sends two delegates to the GLAAD/USA steering committee. But unless one of these delegates is a "person of color" and one is a woman, the chapter is penalized by getting only one vote instead of two. This sanction can be avoided only when one delegate is a lesbian of color (a "two-fer"), which allows the second to be a gay white male. (I said it was convoluted.)

For the new regime, quotas are cool. Ellen Carton, head of GLAAD/New York, proudly notes that her staff now is both 75 percent people of color and 75 percent female. There are currently no white men on staff. Even so, Carton says, "Lesbians have deep resentments of what they see as yet another conspiracy of white males at the top—even if they are gay white males."

It is no accident that gay white men have been shut out of all

GLAAD leadership positions since the adoption of the diversity agenda. The executive directors of the two coastal offices, GLAAD/New York and GLAAD/Los Angeles, are women, as is the national coordinator of GLAAD/USA. Nor is this quota system in effect only at GLAAD. Most of today's gay organizations are characterized by rigid gender and race quotas for staff and leadership (including weighted voting favoring women and people of color) and a disdain for professional expertise. This is evident in the penchant for labeling gay white men (especially gay white male professionals) as part of the "oppressor patriarchy" from which leadership must be wrested.

Organizers of the 1993 March on Washington for gay, lesbian, and bisexual rights mandated 50-percent "people of color" quotas in communiques with state organizing committees. Next came Stonewall 25, a march and rally in New York City on June 25, 1994, to commemorate the quarter-century anniversary of the Greenwich Village riots (set off by a police raid on a gay bar, the Stonewall Inn) that sparked the modern gay rights movement. The Stonewall 25 organizers seemed determined to go to the March on Washington one better. The event's executive committee conformed to a requirement for 50-percent gender parity and 25-percent representation by people of color. But since many of the regional delegations that filled out the larger national steering committee failed to achieve their quotas at a meeting in Milwaukee in August 1993, it was decided that women present could cast three votes apiece, and people of color, two. Mutterings of reverse discrimination were summarily dismissed by the event's "progressive" organizers with a lecture about the importance of diversity.

According to an editorial in San Francisco's *Bay Area Reporter,* the meeting "left one Minnesota white male furious that his policy vote was 'weighted down' and therefore did not equal the votes of women and people of color. 'I feel I don't count,' he said. And he was right, and that was wrong."

In knee-jerk fashion, those who challenge the new orthodoxy are deemed racist and sexist. (At a GLAAD/NY retreat, I was denounced as "someone who thinks white men are the main victims of discrimination" simply for raising the issue of gender and race quotas.) As a consequence, those sensing that hostility toward gay white men, rather than desire for equality and community, is the motive of radical gays and lesbians have learned not to express their opposition too openly.

The results are not unexpected. The March on Washington came off *despite* its organizers. In particular, the state organizing committees (with the 50-percent minority quotas) failed miserably at directing participants to lobby their Congress members while in town. Writing in the *New Republic,* Jacob Weisberg noted the event "was appallingly organized [and] failed to coordinate even a single time for a photo-op on the Mall." Similarly, the Stonewall 25 committee was beset by such mismanagement and internal turmoil that when the commemoration ended, the committee was over $300,000 in debt.

Call it another victory for left-wing organizational strategy, with its "appointment-by-quota, only-leftists-need-apply" mentality along with a fixation on "process" and consensus-based decision making (a demand for uniformity that, in effect, stifles democratic debate).

Male-Bashing in Extremis. Increasingly, it seems, radical feminists (lesbian and straight), influenced by academic feminist theory, propound a variant of neo-Marxism in which capitalists are replaced by white men (straight and gay) as the oppressor "class." Torie Osborn, a former executive director of the National Gay and Lesbian Task Force, blamed "straight white men talking in detached terms about our lives" for backing the military's ban on gays—failing to acknowledge that then–Joint Chiefs of Staff Chairman Colin Powell and other people of color were major players supporting the ban (or, for that matter, that two white men on the Senate Armed Services Committee, Carl Levin and the vigorously heterosexual Ted Kennedy, were outspoken ban opponents). A subsequent NGLTF fundraising letter signed by Martina Navratilova demanded power be taken from "white, Christian, heterosexual males"—apparently the configuration of vices representing the root of evil in the world.

But it's not just heterosexual white males who are targeted. NGLTF, having abandoned its former policy of alternating between male and female directors, now has appointed its third consecutive female top executive. And the Human Rights Campaign Fund, the nation's largest gay organization, recently joined NGLTF and GLAAD in appointing a female leader. So much for gay white male hegemony.

Leftist lesbian feminists who disproportionately influence the feminist movement have, to a large extent, taken charge of the "lesbian and gay" movement—leaving gay men who don't buy the militant feminist agenda out in the cold. At the 1992 Democratic Convention, for instance, signs demanding "Lesbian Rights" equaled in number the placards proclaiming "Lesbian and Gay Rights," while of course anyone urging "Rights for Gay Men" would have been hooted off the floor.

Gay men receive fundraising letters from the National Center for Lesbian Rights and numerous other women's and lesbian organizations. There is no National Center for Gay Male Rights to focus exclusively on gay male issues (such as defending a gay father's right to child visitation when his former spouse, backed by the courts, says no). Any attempts to form such a group would be condemned by lesbian feminists as "sexist and elitist."

Even the Gay Men's Health Crisis, a leading AIDS service and support organization, was pressured into creating a Lesbian AIDS Project with its own female executive director—despite the fact that women-to-women transmission of the virus remains so rare that whenever a case is documented, it makes headlines. At the same time they are insinuating themselves into the AIDS crisis, however, lesbian feminists, playing a game of "whose disease is more PC," often decry the fact that AIDS receives too much attention compared to breast cancer. And a left-wing Latino drag queen, one of the co-chairs of the Stonewall 25 rally, blasted gay men as sexist for wearing red AIDS ribbons but not pink breast cancer ribbons (a predominantly gay male tragedy alone, it seems, being unworthy of a special memorial).

If anything, male-bashing within the lesbian/gay movement is getting increasingly bizarre. At last year's Michigan Womyn's Music Festival, a largely lesbian affair, four postoperative male-to-female (MTF) transsexuals were thrown out of the event for violating the "womyn-born, womyn only" policy. As recounted in the *Washington Blade,* concerns were expressed over these transsexuals' socialization, privilege, and "male energy."

To assert that transsexual women had a high old time as part of the patriarchy is curious, to say the least. As one of the exiled transsexuals lamented, "I felt that I was a woman. I changed my body to correspond with my gender." Regardless, the womyn-born-womyn refused to consider compromising around a simple "no penis" policy. To have been once tainted by maleness was sufficient to be banished, even if the taint was subsequently removed with the surgeon's knife.

There's a context here that should be recognized. When an entire stratum of gay male movement leaders succumbed to AIDS, radical lesbian feminists, nurtured by the politics of the women's movement, moved in and fundamentally altered the nature of gay politics. Today's radically feminist "lesbian and gay" movement tends to incorporate lesbian feminism's critical attitude toward men, male sexuality, and "the patriarchy." Male solidarity, once a hallmark of gay liberation, is now anathema.

Radical feminists, of course, argue all this is necessary because of the greater discrimination faced by lesbians. In truth, a convincing argument can be made that American society as a whole is far more accepting of women loving women than of men loving men. Gay men are much more frequently victims of anti-gay violence than are lesbians. Even that paragon of PC, the *New York Times,* admitted recently that "people are much likelier to express animosity toward gay men than toward homosexual women."

But let facts not stand in the way of feminist victimology. It's now common for feminist lesbians to demand that they not only be welcome in gay male bars (few are ever turned away) but that there be something close to numerical parity among patrons—while also demanding the creation of more exclusively lesbian bars. This parallels in the social sphere the feminist lesbian dual political demand for their own "lesbian rights" in lesbian organizations funded not only by lesbian but also by gay male money and also guaranteed quotas for top leadership positions in all "lesbian and gay" organizations.

The issue of lesbian parity in gay bars was highlighted by a polemic titled "Brothers—Or Oppressors," which appeared in the *Bay Area Reporter.* Written by the women's caucus of San Francisco's Community United Against Violence organization, the diatribe complained of "the way women are made to feel less than welcome in the majority of bars" in the Castro district. "It will take a lot of conscientious hard work to get us out of this mess intact as a community," the CUAV women declared. In short, bring on the sensitivity trainers, and let's hear another round of white male guilt.

The growing hostility between white gay males and radical lesbians was shown in the response of one gay man to the CUAV piece in a letter to the editor. "I hope the authors remember the women-only Dyke March in June; the women-only music festivals up at Camp Mather, the women-only Dykes on Bikes . . . while they rage over their evil gay brothers." Another letter writer reported that when he marched in the political funeral of a lesbian, "A woman loudly complained about why all the men were there, and why they were not all in the back where we belonged. Presumably, if no men showed up at all, the complaints would have been about lack of 'community support.'" And a third noted that he had attended a meeting of the Harvey Milk Democratic Club at which one lesbian after another made disparaging remarks about gay white men: "A process was announced that basically told the GWM in the room to sit down and shut up. . . . Talk about disempowering people for who they are! After the meeting, when I expressed these concerns to the organizers, my commitment to a 'progressive agenda' was immediately questioned. . . . Having grown up in a small town where conformity was everything, I needed to be somewhere where I wouldn't be demeaned for who I am. Imagine my surprise to discover that in San Francisco being a male and having white skin, both of which—like being gay—I didn't choose, was something for which I would be ridiculed and insulted."

Now the mere right of gay men to socialize in a gay male environment is increasingly under attack—not by the religious right, but by the gay left. A recent AP wire story reported that a lounge in New Port Richey, Florida, became a gay bar and announced it would no longer employ female barmaids. Although the bar's manager insisted that his patrons preferred being served by other gay men, a statewide lesbian and gay rights group took up the heterosexual barmaids' cause, arguing the women were victims of sexual discrimination!

Lesbian feminists and their left-wing, "pro-feminist" gay male cohorts are determined to eliminate all gay male-only space, holding that a "lesbigay" culture should sanction autonomous space for women only, but that male space apart from women is an anti-female conspiracy. This siege against gay male culture by leftists seeking the obliteration of gender distinctions is no different than the attacks being waged against straight male institutions like the Citadel or all-male campus fraternities.

Playing the Race Card. A December 1993 *New York Times* op-ed piece by Donald Suggs of GLAAD and Mandy Carter of the Human Rights Campaign Fund (the nation's largest gay PAC) held gay white men responsible for black homophobia. Suggs and Carter, both African-Americans, began by asserting that "leaders of the gay and lesbian movement have given highest priority to the interest of their most powerful constituents—white men." And this has apparently led to gays of color being alienated from the gay rights movement, which, in turn, caused black churches to support the religious right. (Got that?)

The piece ended with the charge that "anyone who tries to widen the focus of gay activism is characterized in some gay publications as a white-male basher or is accused of caving in to political correctness." (This last reference may apply to me, since I wrote in the November 1993 issue of *Christopher Street* magazine that "support for greater inclusiveness in the gay and lesbian movement has been twisted into something altogether different—a rationale for bashing gay white men.")

One might ask Suggs and Carter to explain just what they think are the exclusively "gay white male" issues that have dominated the gay movement. Sodomy law repeal? Domestic partnership? Employment and housing discrimination? Gays in the military? AIDS? None of which, of course, solely concerns "gay white men."

When the foot soldiers of the Nation of Islam claimed Jewish racism was the cause of African-American anti-Semitism, that view was denounced by the Jewish community in no uncertain terms. But when lesbigay leftists promote the scurrilous ideal that gay pale males are responsible for homophobia in the black community, we gays are expected to nod our heads in shameful agreement.

The amount of knee-jerk agreement with this kind of thinking is quite amazing. "I think white gays and lesbians can never move forward until they acknowledge [their] racism," David Smith (he's white) of the National Gay and Lesbian Task Force told the *Washington Post* last June. Tony Summers of the D.C. Coalition of Black Lesbians and Gay Men and Bisexuals was quoted in the same story as expressing "concerns [that] black and Hispanic homosexuals as well as transvestites might not be well represented" at Stonewall 25. Just who was standing at the gates keeping them out? After all, the quota-minded Stonewall 25 crew appointed a Latino drag queen as a co-chair/spokesperson for the event, so if gays of color didn't participate in sufficient numbers perhaps they should blame themselves.

Speaking of baiting gay white males, Raan Medley, a lawyer and former member of ACT BLACK (the African-American caucus of ACT UP), wrote a June *Newsday* op-ed in which he gave as an example of gay white male supremacy (as well as the white gay community's "conspicuous consumerism") the IKEA commercial featuring a gay white male couple buying furniture. "That ad was the culmination of 25 years of . . . de facto segregation by one of the nation's best organized, most politically cohesive and, indeed, narcissistic minorities," Medley wrote in a sentiment that could put the worst gay-bashers in the country to shame.

In July, Eric Stephen Booth, who described himself as "a middle-class black gay man," wrote a letter to the *New York Times* in which he came to the astounding conclusion that "since AIDS, white gays have endured discrimination for the first time." He added that in terms of its bigotry "the upper-middle-class white gay community is no better than its straight counterparts."

In fact, there's not one gay organization that I know of which isn't devoting substantial time and energy to outreach efforts on behalf of gays and lesbians of color. But true "diversity" and "inclusion" isn't really what lesbigay leftists are after. They're seeking to disempower gay white men who are, by virtue of their race and gender, demonized into part of a class of oppressors—regardless of their individual histories, economic situations, or what have you. It is, in short, an ethos of collective guilt. And the remedy is quotas.

The result of all this radicalism in the gay and lesbian community is clear: polarization between moderates interested in gay rights and radical leftists and feminists bent on keeping gay white male professionals in their place—writing checks and making guilty self-criticism.

Gay conservative and libertarian dissidents, such as *A Place at the Table* author Bruce Bawer, are regularly excoriated in the leftist gay press. There has been a concerted attempt to silence these individuals. As lesbian feminist Sara Miles recently huffed in *Out* magazine, "Their criticisms of existing gay politics and subculture are rooted in the same backlash against feminism, multiculturalism, and affirmative action that fuels the broader neo-conservative movement."

It was my growing sense of unease with all this that eventually led me to step back from the gay rights organizations, and I'm far from alone. The majority of gay men and lesbians avoid active involvement in the movement per se (as opposed to AIDS causes). A big reason is that the politically correct ethos is so off-putting, especially with the new wrinkle of self-criticism sessions led by overpaid diversity consultants, where gay participants must confess their sexism and racism.

Fortunately, as in society at large, a growing number of gay people are now expressing resentment toward the leftist-feminist "oppression hierarchies" that scapegoat gay white men as privileged members of the patriarchy and belittle the bigotry we face. But many on the anti-PC right, rather than reaching out to gays and lesbians who are standing up to radical lesbigay PC, prefer to label all gay people as naturally subversive. These same conservatives have no trouble distinguishing between millions of moderate African-Americans, on one hand, and militant Afrocentrists on the other, or between moderate women and radical feminists. Yet when it comes to gays, we're all painted in a single shade with a broad brush.

There are electoral advantages that the conservative movement could reap by recognizing that all gays are not born leftists and are becoming alienated from the gender left in increasing numbers all the time. In its recent post-election "Portrait of the Electorate: Who Voted for Whom," the *New York Times* included a breakdown of voters across the country who identified themselves to exit pollers as gay, lesbian, or bisexual. In 1992, 23 percent of them had voted for Republican House candidates. This year the figure was 40 percent. (Surprised?)

The trend toward the GOP is even more pronounced in the nation's large metropolitan areas. Last year saw the election of Rudy Giuliani in New York and Dick Riordan in Los Angeles (when they were still perceived to be loyal Republicans!). Both ran as fiscal conservatives who were gay-friendly. Election day exit polling in New York showed Giuliani received 31 percent of the gay/lesbian vote, and Riordan got about a third of the vote in Los Angeles.

Recently in the radical publication the *Nation*, left-wing gay playwright Tony Kushner expressed his fear that gays would reject their self-appointed leadership's political radicalism. This makes my point for me. If gay leftists can see the handwriting on the wall and realize that the average gay person need not remain an unquestioning constituent of the far left, why can't straight conservatives read the same message?

JOHN WEIR

Weir is the author of a novel entitled *The Irreversible Decline of Eddie Rocket* and a writer at large for the *Advocate*. He lives in New York City. The following essay appeared in the *New Republic* on 13 February 1995.

RAGE, RAGE

My friend David Feinberg, the novelist and essayist who died of AIDS last November, has been memorialized as a kind of alternative North American martyr. He was not just homosexual, he was self-consciously "queer." His novel *Eighty-Sixed* was not just a brilliant monologue about male horniness, Jewish guilt and AIDS anxiety, it was "transgressive." He was not merely a regular ACT UP member who was routinely arrested at demonstrations, he was "countercultural." He did not die, he was "killed by government neglect."

In short, David has emerged postmortem as the kind of outsider who is sentimentalized by the left and demonized by the right. He is noted for being difficult because we expect difficulty from antagonists and sufferers. Mourners celebrate his jokiness, his irritability, his honesty about how much of his life he spent wanting, having, or not getting sex. If David was popular among heterosexual readers, I suspect it was in part because his writing satisfied certain preconceptions about homosexual men. Of course, gay men like to believe clichés about themselves, too.

David's writing is not clichéd. Rather, it is profoundly superficial. It works not because it goes deeply into any subject, but because it skirts so quickly and so hectically over the surface of things, accumulating so many details, fact upon fact, that it gives the effect of deep feeling. It has virtual depth. There is no comfort in his writing, only anxiety, humor, sentimentality, rage, and despair, as well as a lot of silliness. His genius was in being silly; he could make it feel like a meaningful connection. He was also an artful complainer. His last book, *Queer and Loathing: Rants and Raves of a Raging AIDS Clone,* which was published the week he died, is the least wisecracking and the hardest to read of all his work because it is the most unmitigated by irony. He used irony to distance himself from pain, but irony failed him in the end, and all that was left was his devastating fear and rage.

He was my closest friend for the past five years. As death approached, I was asked, "How do you feel about David's dying?" and I would answer, "If AIDS doesn't kill him, I will." People would laugh as if I were making a kind of Feinbergian joke, as a homage to him. What I didn't say is that shortly before he died, I stopped liking him. I stopped liking him not just then, but always. It was retroactive. He was so mean to me and to all of his devoted friends, so relentlessly and mindlessly and destructively angry, that I forgot, for a time, what I ever liked about him.

Yet he is being honored for his anger. Anger is the orthodoxy of the self-proclaimed AIDS activist community. It is the authority invested in the individual as well as the group. "Where is your anger?" people still ask, over and over, at ACT UP meetings, as if checking other people for ID. Rage bestows authenticity. Anger is seen as wholly reliable because it is so intensely felt. The fundamental sentimentality of ACT UP is the belief that emotions always tell the truth. The group's miscalculation is that feelings alone, directly and powerfully expressed, can change things.

I am speaking now as someone who has laid across pavement in subzero temperature in February, my arm hooked to David's arm through steel tubing, blocking the entrance to Hoffman-LaRoche, a big pharmaceutical company in New Jersey. For three hours we chanted, "Arrest the real criminal," while the four local police officers who bothered to show up watched us with bemused contempt. In Albany, in New Hampshire during primary season, in Washington, D.C., inside Grand Central Station, marching through the financial district in Manhattan, I held David's hand, or clenched my fists with his and raised them high to shout, "We'll never be silent again." When I ran across the set of the "CBS Evening News" during the height of the Gulf war, chanting, "Fight AIDS, not Arabs," I was doing it for David.

Like David, I thought that if I got angry enough, he would not have to die. I was wrong, and so was he. ACT UP was wrong. Anger is a useful strategy—so is foolishness—if it remains a strategy and does not become a faith. David was angry for a living. Not only did it not keep him alive, it kept him from whatever comfort he might fleetingly have felt when he was dying. I learned a lot about anger watching David die. The New Age premise that "finding your anger" is the key to health and strength turns out to be wishful thinking. Anger generates nothing but anger. It doesn't express truth, it glorifies ego.

The limitations of anger as a public cry to action were clear to me when I went with David last October to help him deliver what he called his "scathing diatribe" to ACT UP. He weighed 106 pounds that night, down from 150. He was three weeks from death. His body, which he was always careful to maintain in perfect shape, as if he might be called upon to use it as a weapon, had disintegrated. His skeleton showed everywhere. He clutched his trousers in an angry fist to keep them from sliding halfway down his thighs. Like King Lear back from the heath, he looked and sounded furious, raving, and crazy. There was, however, no catharsis in his rage. It was wasted on him, and it was wasted on the room.

There ought to be a sign hanging over New York's Gay and Lesbian Community Center on Monday nights—ACT UP nights—that says, "Abandon hope, all who enter here." The night David showed up, he was addressing an organization that no longer exists. So much anger was spent by so many people so quickly, to so little effect, that the residue of bitterness left most of New York's AIDS activist community burned out. A lot of people died. But many more were exhausted by the group's ineffectual ethos of collective, unquestioned rage.

It isn't poetry that makes nothing happen, it's anger. I don't remember much of David's speech. I remember he said *fuck* a lot. Like many ACT UP members, he had an adolescent's faith in the totemic power of the word *fuck*. He also used the word *anger.* He was angry about dying. He was angry ACT UP was not going to keep him alive. He was angry at everyone in the room, and everyone who had ever attended a meeting, living or dead. It was the kind of speech that has a long tradition in ACT UP, a purging cry of rage, meant to renew activist fervor. I couldn't listen. I thought the point was not that David wanted a cure for AIDS, but that he wanted a cure for him. For the past five years, he put all his faith and energy into a group that was supposed to be a community. In the end, however, David didn't care that his friends were dying, he cared that he was dying.

Many people in the room that night, and others who heard about what went on there, feel he had a perfect right to his self-interest. I don't. His death wasn't something that happened only to him. I was losing something, too. So were a lot of people. Apart from anger, one of the implicit faiths of ACT UP is selfishness. What ACT UP wants as a group is to provide an outlet for the personal gratification of each individual soul. The HIV-negative members want to be affirmed. The HIV-positive members want to be cured. David's speech was not courageous or inspiring, it was egotistical. What he finally said to the AIDS activist community was, "This is about *me.* Nothing matters now except saving *me.*"

I would have done anything to help him, but finally, what David wanted rescuing from wasn't AIDS. He hated AIDS, but more than that, he hated being human. Like a lot of AIDS activists, he thought that he alone was too special to die.

BRUCE BAWER

The following column appeared in the *Advocate* on 11 July 1995.

TRUTH IN ADVERTISING

Another Sunday in June, another bonanza for the religious right. To the gentle whir of Christian Broadcasting Network cameras, gay people in cities across America hold their annual Mardi Gras. In the middle of Main Street, men frolic in Speedos. Bare-chested women wave their fists. Activist leaders give speeches praising their audience's dedication, victimhood, and all-around fabulousness. Thousands dance from dusk till dawn. Then, exhausted by having made such a strenuous contribution to the cause, the participants go their separate ways. And in the ensuing weeks and months, while they're absorbed in their lives and careers, money from underpaid Iowa farmhands and dirt-poor Arkansas pensioners helps finance the conversion of raw parade footage into slick videotapes efficiently designed to prop up the misperceptions that undergird continued inequality.

More than anything else, Gay Pride Month symbolizes for me the ineffectuality of our movement in comparison with the religious right. A few years ago that movement's leaders decided they didn't want to remain a marginal subculture but wished instead to become a respected part of the political mainstream and to wield real secular power. They've succeeded—in fact, they've convinced a lot of moderate Christians that extreme reactionary fundamentalists speak for them and are socially and culturally closer to them than are most gays.

How have they managed this? By talking to Americans consistently about shared ideals and values, while gay leaders have too often focused on differences. By identifying themselves with God, America, and family, while gay leaders have too often derided all three. Perhaps most ironically, these people who have little interest in or knowledge of Western civilization have presented themselves as defenders thereof and have depicted gays as the greatest threat to it, while gay leaders—instead of reminding the world that homosexuals, of all groups, have made the most disproportionately large contribution to the great Western heritage of thought, art, and literature—have too often responded by attacking Western civilization as being homophobic.

Although its power base is rural, the Christian Coalition has learned how to exploit modern media with remarkable sophistication. Meanwhile, although creative gay people crowd the fields of publicity, advertising, and every branch of showbiz, our big annual media moment is always a public-relations nightmare, reinforcing the deplorable notion that gay people, as a group, represent some kind of bizarre revolt against nature. This, of course, is the entire thrust of queer ideology; we call ourselves "queer," then wonder why the world continues to think of us as, well, queer—and why parents of gay kids can't deal with the idea of their kids' being (to borrow from the Microsoft Word thesaurus) "odd, quaint, curious, eccentric, extraordinary, fantastic, freakish, peculiar, singular." Far from lending support to this damaging view, we should be helping heterosexuals to understand that what's natural to one individual isn't necessarily natural to another and that to affirm one's homosexual identity is not to defy nature but to embrace one's own true nature.

While we've got truth on our side—the truth that accepting one's emotional orientation is a socially positive act of honesty, wholeness, and self-respect—the Christian Coalition has lies: the lie of "choice," of "recruitment," of homosexuality as an undisciplined, carnally obsessive rebellion against all good things and an emblem of cultural collapse. The success of Pat Robertson's supposedly scripture-based arguments against gay rights rests entirely on his constituents' ignorance about homosexuality and their crude understanding of biblical interpretation; the more Christians can be educated about both, the more they'll recognize the mendacity of Robertson's anti-gay assertions.

Yet even as Robertson and company spread their lies expertly through such vehicles as "The 700 Club," many of us maintain, perversely, that it's not worth the effort to confront those lies and to set plainly before straight America the truth about who we are. To the extent that we take this view, our society will remain one that defines gay men and lesbians largely in the terms of religious-right propaganda and one that accordingly denies us equal rights and respect. Granted, there's a minority of pathological bigots whose hate will never be vanquished. But most of those who might well be written off as intractably rigid or zealous homophobes are in fact quite willing to hear what we have to say and are quite capable of changing their views once they've walked, as it were, in our shoes. I've met too many former homophobes who have become gay rights supporters to reject the possibility of wide-scale social change on this front.

The more of this kind of activism we can accomplish, the more we'll deserve our annual party. Celebrations are great, you know, once you've won a war; our problem is that we're still in the thick of battle—a battle that will be won only through a disciplined, determined effort to counter the Christian Coalition's falsehoods with the truth about who we are. When that victory's achieved, I'll enjoy a gay-pride event as much as anybody.

SECTION II

GAYS AND THE RIGHT

Until lately, gay party politics in America was an almost entirely Democratic affair. Gay-left political leaders painted a black-and-white picture: Democrats are friends; Republicans are enemies; our best hope lies in solid support for the the Democratic party. Recent events have challenged that view. Arguably, the most pro-gay governor in America is a Republican, William Weld of Massachusetts; Senate opposition to gays in the military was led by a Democrat, Sam Nunn, while Republican Senator Alphonse D'Amato argued for lifting the ban. As Paul Varnell wrote in a 1994 column about the "fight the Right" approach to gay activism,

> We need to remind ourselves that we have quite a number of potential and actual allies on "the Right" as varied as Barry Goldwater, Alphonse d'Amato, and Los Angeles Mayor Richard Riordan. Do we really want to "fight" these people, or do we want their numbers to increase? . . . Frankly, we might to better to "Fight the Left," since they keep treating gays as a progressive fiefdom, which makes it that much more difficult for us to persuade the center and the right to listen to us with an open mind. How can we persuade people to listen to us if they think we are fighting them?

In a 1994 speech at Yale, Rich Tafel, national director of Log Cabin Republicans, argued that the rise of the religious right as gay rights' leading enemy makes it imperative for gays to work within both parties:

> The gay movement can only move ahead when we stop running to safe cities, safe political parties, and safe "gay only" organizations. . . . The movement will only move ahead when we challenge traditionally conservative organizations, such as the Republican party, America's religious institutions, and big corporations. Challenge them not with your fist, but by standing up on the inside and staking your rightful claim. If any or all of them move in our direction on gay rights, we will have made substantial, long-range progress in our cause.
>
> Recently, when I was in San Francisco, one member of the audience said that "I feel embraced as a gay man in the Democratic party." He is right. If you merely want to be embraced in politics, then you are not prepared to be on the front lines.

Traditional notions about the American right have also been challenged by the strong pro-gay stance of the veteran conservative Barry Goldwater. In two *Washington Post* op-ed articles, Goldwater attacked the ban on gays in the military and advocated equal job opportunity. As he wrote in the latter piece:

> Some will try to paint this as a liberal or religious issue. I am a conservative Republican, but I believe in democracy and the separation of church and state. The conservative movement is founded on the simple tenet that people have the right to live life as they please, as long as they don't hurt anyone else in the process. No one has ever shown me how being gay or lesbian harms anyone.

Another voice is that of Representative Steve Gunderson of Wisconsin, the only openly gay Republican member of Congress. A leader of his party's moderate wing, Gunderson insisted in a widely quoted 1994 address that "one can be pro-family without being anti-gay" and that gay believers must overcome "the absolutism of past religious thought" by proclaiming "the love, the understanding, and the justice of our Judeo-Christian beliefs" and by supporting churches in their "struggle to reconcile these issues."

After the 1994 elections, Stephen H. Miller reflected in the *Native* on what the GOP landslide meant to gay Americans. Most gay political activists, he wrote, have "chosen to mandate gay rights through big-government interventionism rather than by, say, pursuing ties with libertarian-minded conservatives whose ideological framework stresses the exercise of personal liberty and defense of individualism—core beliefs to which arguments for gay equality could have been tethered." Suggesting that left-wing gay activists' support for affirmative action and welfare-state programs has muddied the movement's goals and convinced "a large segment of the public that it is 'special rights' and not equality that we're after," Miller noted that

> at a time when the public is rightly appalled by the fraying social fabric—the seeming disappearance of stable families with live-in fathers, skyrocketing rates of illegitimacy among teenage mothers, welfare as a way of life, crime, and so on—many gay activists still think support for *any* traditional "bourgeois" values amounts to a sellout to the religious right.
>
> With the gay movement ceding these issues to the far right and linking itself to everything that is anti-normative, it's no surprise that most straights haven't taken a strong stand in support of gay rights.

Recognizing the truth of this contention, the essays in this section contemplate the present and proper relation of gay individuals and the gay rights movement to the Republican party, to conservative ideas, and to the "religious right."

CAROLYN LOCHHEAD

A graduate of the University of California at Berkeley, Carolyn Lochhead studied journalism at Columbia University and has been the Washington correspondent of the *San Francisco Chronicle* since 1991. This essay appeared in the August/September 1993 issue of *Reason,* a libertarian magazine.

THE THIRD WAY

Whether measured by the pitch of national emotion it stirs, the prominence of the magazine covers it graces, the quantity of congressional hearings it generates, the number of Hollywood B-movies it spawns, or the volume of press releases that pour out of newsroom fax machines, the debate over lesbian and gay rights clearly has come of age.

Just as clearly, it was the election of Bill Clinton, the first president to openly embrace homosexual rights, and the consequent debate over lifting the ban on gays in the military that propelled the movement out of the gay ghettos of New York City and San Francisco to the center of national discussion in Washington and in living rooms, coffee shops, and workplaces across the country. Somewhat unexpectedly, the movement thus finds itself at a watershed. Its sudden prominence has forced gay and lesbian leaders to articulate their aims, even as they grope for a political strategy to achieve them.

The classic civil rights approach adopted by blacks seems to predominate for now. While many want to distance the movement from the radical left, with rare exceptions the leaders of gay and lesbian groups hew to a left-liberal political plank, demanding a new civil rights bill that would add homosexuals to the panoply of groups granted legal status as protected classes.

Surprisingly, however, a quite different path is also emerging and appears to be gaining popularity among the gay intellectual and political elite, offering the possibility that this civil rights movement could veer off on an unexpected course. The values of this new politics are far more traditional, even conservative, and yet its demands are also much more radical. It enjoys a distinctly American moral appeal that disarms opponents, even as its radicalism inspires a fierce, instinctive opposition.

Its primary political and legal aim is to end discrimination by the state; those who embrace it fully would leave private discrimination legally unaddressed. Its linchpin is government sanction of same-sex marriage. On the social front, the primary goal of the new politics is to gain social acceptance—not, as the gay left would do, to subvert straight culture and superimpose its own. And its method is not an act of Congress, but the deeply personal acts of thousands of individuals who emerge from the closet and declare their homosexuality.

"It is clear to me," says Tim McFeeley, executive director of the Human Rights Campaign Fund, the largest and perhaps most influential gay and lesbian organization in the country, "that regulation, to the point of preventing any two people from loving each other or entering into a public commitment that declares and publicizes two people's commitment and love for each other, is really central in terms of the government's control over our lives."

Marriage, many gay leaders now insist, is the most obvious and profound form of state discrimination against gays and lesbians. An entire body of law hinges on the marriage contract, they argue, and with it an entire body of rights that constitute the essence of the legal bias against homosexuals—from property rights to hospital-visitation privileges—as well as a deeply felt social validation. They also acknowledge that marriage is their most radical demand, considered by many, McFeeley says, to be "terrible, dangerous, countercultural."

This new politics (its leading theoretician is Andrew Sullivan, editor of the *New Republic*) has grown out of an odd confluence of accident, historical experience, and the unique nature of the homosexual taboo.

In an unplanned turn of events, just as the gay and lesbian movement achieved political momentum, the debate over the military ban suddenly switched public attention from social prejudice against Greenwich Village drag queens and leather dykes to blatant government discrimination, including classic witch hunts, against the most patriotic and socially conservative members of American society.

The movement also is reaching prominence at a time when historical experience is illuminating the pitfalls of the traditional civil rights focus on oppression and victimization. Across the board, from the radical left to conservatives, gay and lesbian leaders shun affirmative action, saying that it is not a goal and is not under discussion.

In this connection, movement leaders have been stung by the effectiveness of the conservative charge that gays and lesbians are demanding "special rights." This charge was at the core of the Colorado initiative that bars protections for homosexuals. No two words raise more hackles among movement leaders.

Alan Klein, a cofounder of Queer Nation, calls the phrase a "crafty campaign by the religious right to scare people, a scare tactic that says blacks or Latinos or gays and lesbians are looking for something more than they're entitled to. That is crazy and a misstatement. All that these groups and the gay and lesbian civil rights movement want are the same rights that everyone else has."

The problem, of course, is that the charge rings true. A federal civil rights law would, by definition, add gays and lesbians to the list of protected classes. "It is in fact true that antidiscrimination laws are special privileges," says a prominent Washington libertarian who is gay but not out publicly. "In every case, if you're talking about the private sector, these are special rights."

Jonathan Rauch, author of *Kindly Inquisitors: The New Attacks on Free Thought,* adds, "What the right has figured out is that if you can frame someone as a special pleader, a special interest in America, that person is rightly in trouble." It is the very potency of the "special rights" charge that has forced a subtle shift in political strategy—at least at the rhetorical level—away from the victim model that other groups have embraced.

Most important, however, is the recognition that while discrimination against lesbians and gays shares many characteristics with discrimination against blacks, there are profound differences as well. Lesbians and gays face a unique brand of prejudice that makes the traditional civil rights course ill-suited to their cause and in many ways unworkable. Unlike blacks or women, lesbians and gays can disguise themselves—or, in the language of Jim Crow, can "pass"—and thereby avoid discrimination. As a result, the closet remains a huge barrier both to gaining social acceptance and to adopting affirmative action.

This is because discrimination is not targeted at gays and lesbians per se but at gays and lesbians who are openly so. Unknown numbers of lesbians and gays have achieved economic success and reached the apex of their callings. Nor do bias and its potential economic consequences accumulate through generations against homosexuals as a group, as they have for blacks.

So whereas legal protections for other minorities have led irresistibly toward government-imposed quotas, it's not likely that legal protections for gays and lesbians will move in a similar direction. For one thing, numerical targets for gays and lesbians would require that they declare their sexual orientation, like it or not. Moreover, as Rauch argues, the victim model simply does not fit very well. "It's not true at the economic or the cultural level," he says. "Who enjoys more cultural influence in Hollywood today, gay people or fundamentalist Christians?"

At the same time, the closet nourishes and sustains the social taboo. "This is a very important distinction," McFeeley says. "It really comes down to the heart of whether or not we're going to be successful in the strategy of getting civil rights legislation for gay and lesbian people. And that's because the closet and the invisibility offer something that people see as a solution." It is the essence, he argues, of Georgia Sen. Sam Nunn's proposed "don't ask, don't tell" compromise on the military ban.

Indeed, movement leaders argue that the closet lies at the heart of the gay rights movement, as a matter of public policy and as a matter of its very moral legitimacy. Discrimination against gays and lesbians manifests itself less in a lack of economic opportunity than in the deep sense of shame, fear, and self-loathing that homosexuals so often feel, especially when they are young. It operates in quiet and debilitating ways, says Torie Orborn, executive director of the National Gay and Lesbian Task Force, one of the largest gay rights groups.

"It's in the teenage suicide rate," Osborn says. "It's in the number of people who are in the closet who are afraid to tell their families or their colleagues that their lover is of the same gender. It functions, in essence, to restrict our lives, our liberty, and our pursuit of happiness in a way that cuts across class and race boundaries. The closet is the most potent example of the feeling of being ashamed or embarrassed or fearful just about who you are."

Greater social tolerance and freedom are goals that every gay and lesbian seems to share. Betty Willis, a Washington lobbyist who is coming out publicly by allowing her name to be used, echoes many when she says her wish is "simply to live a normal life like everyone else, and to not have to hide, to not have to live underground, to not be afraid."

For this reason, says McFeeley, the closet is not a viable option. "It's so simple," he says. "We keep tiptoeing around this, not just the politicians but everybody, including gay people in their relations with their parents. They never confront the real issue, which is, 'Why do you have to be out?'"

The answer, he says, is, "I am a human being, and the essence of being human is loving someone else. Denying that or disguising that or hiding that love is very, very injurious to human beings. It is in fact a self-rejection of who you are." Love, celebrated in literature, in art, in commerce, and in daily life, "is something that is so natural that non-gay people don't even have to think about it. Open any magazine, you see it in the ads, men and women being together, being happy, being loving, being thoughtful, being romantic, having fun, sharing life, having kids—all those images, they're constant. But if you grow up gay, you have a sense that you're not allowed to do that. And this is what the closet is all about."

The rhetoric of politics does not admit such talk, McFeeley concedes. "This is the talk of therapy," he says. "This is not the kind of talk you usually engage in in public policy debates about taxes or aid to Bosnia. But the public policy issues [such as] should gays be in the military—you can't resolve that issue without talking about these touchy-feely subjects about people loving. We don't have any systematic language to use in discussing love as a factor in public policy debates. We're uncomfortable talking about these things not only with strangers. We have problems talking about these things with our families."

The peculiar nature of discrimination against gays and lesbians also contributes to what many feel is a confusion between the political objective of changing social attitudes and the personal objective of self-acceptance. Those who want to build social tolerance insist that radical sexual politics is self-defeating. They argue that the celebratory demonstrations of drag queens and "dykes on bikes" at gay-pride parades may be therapeutic for the participants, but smack of self-indulgence and what Rick Sincere, co-founder of Gays and Lesbians for Individual Liberty, calls "a sociology of the left that rejects hierarchy, that rejects prioritizing, that rejects value-based decision making."

April's March on Washington revealed a division between the radical gay left, which views sexual defiance and rejection of social norms as a political end, and the moderate view that the aim is not to overturn mainstream culture but to join it. Gay leaders like to smooth over differences between the ascendant mainstream organizations such as the Human Rights Campaign Fund and such activist groups as Queer Nation and ACT UP—what some call the "suits versus the queers" divide. Although organizers of the March on Washington emphasized a mainstream image, a raft of speakers made crude jokes about religious groups and public figures. One comedienne said she was pleased that "we finally have a First Lady we can fuck."

While its role may be receding, the gay left still strongly influences the movement's overall agenda, especially its powerful tendency toward political correctness. Its radicalism and politics of rejection also have clear parallels in other civil rights movements: the Black Panthers, the feminist bra burners, and the century-old debates over whether to seek integration or separation.

Denny Lee, a member of ACT UP New York, believes that acceptance alone is unacceptable. "It's not merely tolerance that we're looking for," Lee says. "It's something much more profound than that, and something much more important too." Social institutions, he says, "need to be redefined to encompass wider groups. And I think that's what the gay rights movement is doing, namely, we're trying to change the culture."

Osborn of the National Gay and Lesbian Task Force carefully allows "room for a variety of tactics." But she is "not sure what the goal is" of the "in-your-face cultural guerrilla theater. It seems to be a kind of self-expression more than anything else."

Rauch argues that rejection of social norms is "a statement about radicalism, not a statement about homosexuality." The movement, he contends, will have to address these fundamental differences in aim and strategy. "Just below the surface there's a tension between bourgeois homosexuals like me, who buy into the standard notion of American life and want to be a part of it," he says, "and the radical homosexuals who see their sexuality as implicitly rejecting bourgeois American values. It's not yet clear whether this is a movement about social liberation and egalitarianism or whether this is merely a movement about integrating homosexuals into the standard model of American life."

Rauch sees a risk that the radical agenda "isolates us. And we can't win that fight." The religious right is "not wrong about everything," he contends. "The values of stability and family, hard work and education and thrift and honesty, are bedrock values for society" and should be embraced by the gay and lesbian movement. This is why, he argues, gay and lesbian marriage is such a fundamental aim. "In the long term, I think in America hate and superstition lose when they're directly, openly confronted," he contends. "That one we win. But if we come off as anti-family, we will lose. . . . It's unwinnable. And it shouldn't be won."

The more radical groups, however, charge that mainstream gays are engaging in their own form of intolerance and hypocrisy by ostracizing drag queens and other fringe elements. "The fear is that we become hypocritical as a movement if we exclude our own members," Lee says.

Rick Sincere of Gays and Lesbians for Individual Liberty concedes the point but counters that the left too often views the gay movement as part of a larger aim to "overturn Western civilization" and insists "that they want to have sex when they want it and how they want it, no matter who it offends." Similarly, Rauch says that tolerance does not mean "that you abolish criticism and disagreement about what is good taste and what isn't."

The far right, Sincere argues, exploits the radical image with videos that show only "the drag queens and the leather queens and the people simulating fellatio in the street. The average American in rural Kentucky who has never met a gay person before is going to think this is what gay people do all the time." It's as though, he says, "you took somebody from another planet and set them down in New Orleans in the middle of February and showed them Mardi Gras and said this is what heterosexual Americans do 365 days a year. They have no context in which to judge that, and they're going to believe it."

Again, many argue, the closet is the problem, and opening it is the key to combating what Pat Buchanan calls the "visceral recoil" straights feel toward lesbians and gays. When the black civil rights movement began, notes the Washington libertarian, "all blacks were visible, and they all in some way represented their race. And they may have resented that. They may have said, 'Listen, I didn't ask to be an ambassador of the black race. I want to live my life and not worry about what other people think.' But like it or not, you could see them all, and in some sense you judged the black community by all the blacks you knew as well as the ones you saw on television."

The lesbians and gays most likely to be seen demonstrating on television are those who are most alienated from the mainstream, he argues, while those most able to counter that image are also most likely to be closeted and invisible. Hilary Rosen, a recording industry lobbyist, board member of the Human Rights Campaign Fund, and a liberal Democrat, maintains that those gays and lesbians who are most offended by the images put out by the radical left are precisely those who must come out. "If I have an obligation as a Democrat to be active and out and vocal," she says, "I can't think of anybody who has more of an obligation than a gay Republican."

The Washington libertarian, aware of his self-contradiction, argues that the more people who come out, "the more people there are who are going to know a gay person and like or love that person and realize that these people are not some figment of Pat Buchanan's fevered imagination, but their next-door neighbor, their son, their boss, their secretary. And that changes the way people think."

He recalls attending a gathering of some 200 gay and lesbian Republicans in suburban Washington, "all well dressed, well coiffed." Their biggest concern was that every time gay people were on television, "they were prancing in the Castro Street parade wearing jockstraps," he says. But at the end of the cocktail hour, when asked for volunteers for a new gay organization's board of directors, nobody, including him, raised a hand.

ANDREW SULLIVAN

Andrew Sullivan has been editor of the *New Republic* since 1991. Born and raised in Great Britain, he holds a B.A. in modern history and modern languages from Oxford University and a Ph.D. in political science from Harvard University. The following essay, which appeared in the *New Republic* on 10 May 1993, essentially outlines the argument of Sullivan's 1995 book *Virtually Normal*.

THE POLITICS OF HOMOSEXUALITY

Over the last four years I have been sent letters from strangers caught in doomed, desperate marriages because of repressed homosexuality and witnessed several thousand virtually naked, muscle-bound men dance for hours in the middle of New York City, in the middle of the day. I have lain down on top of a dying friend to restrain his hundred-pound body as it violently shook with the death-throes of AIDS and listened to soldiers equate the existence of homosexuals in the military with the dissolution of the meaning of the United States. I have openly discussed my sexuality on a television talk show and sat on the porch of an apartment building in downtown D.C. with an arm around a male friend and watched as a dozen cars in a half hour slowed to hurl abuse. I have seen mass advertising explicitly cater to an openly gay audience and watched my own father break down and weep at the declaration of his son's sexuality.

These different experiences of homosexuality are not new, of course. But that they can now be experienced within one life (and that you are now reading about them) *is* new. The cultural categories and social departments into which we once successfully consigned sexuality—departments that helped us avoid the anger and honesty with which we are now confronted—have begun to collapse. Where once there were patterns of discreet and discrete behavior to follow, there is now only an unnerving confusion of roles and identities. Where once there was only the unmentionable, there are now only the unavoidable: gays, "queers," homosexuals, closet cases, bisexuals, the "out" and the "in," paraded for every heterosexual to see. As the straight world has been confronted with this, it has found itself reaching for a response: embarrassment, tolerance, fear, violence, oversensitivity, recognition. When Sam Nunn conducts hearings, he knows there is no common discourse in which he can now speak, that even the words he uses will betray worlds of conflicting experience and anxieties. Yet speak he must. In place of the silence that once encased the lives of homosexuals, there is now a loud argument. And there is no easy going back.

This fracturing of discourse is more than a cultural problem; it is a political problem. Without at least some common ground, no effective compromise to the homosexual question will be possible. Matters may be resolved, as they have been in the case of abortion, by a stand-off in the forces of cultural war. But unless we begin to discuss this subject with a degree of restraint and reason, the visceral unpleasantness that exploded earlier this year will dog the question of homosexuality for a long time to come, intensifying the anxieties that politics is supposed to relieve.

There are as many politics of homosexuality as there are words for it, and not all of them contain reason. And it is harder perhaps in this passionate area than in any other to separate a wish from an argument, a desire from a denial. Nevertheless, without such an effort, no true politics of sexuality can emerge. And besides, there are some discernible patterns, some sketches of political theory that have begun to emerge with clarity. I will discuss here only four, but four that encompass a reasonable span of possible arguments. Each has a separate analysis of sexuality and a distinct solution to the problem of gay–straight relations. Perhaps no person belongs in any single category; and they are by no means exclusive of one another. What follows is a brief description of each: why each is riven by internal and external conflict; and why none, finally, works.

I.

The first I'll call, for the sake of argument, the conservative politics of sexuality. Its view of homosexuality is as dark as it is popular as it is unfashionable. It informs much of the opposition to allowing openly gay men and women to serve in the military and can be heard in living rooms, churches, bars, and computer bulletin boards across America. It is found in most of the families in which homosexuals grow up and critically frames many homosexuals' view of their own identity. Its fundamental assertion is that homosexuality as such does not properly exist. Homosexual behavior is aberrant activity, either on the part of heterosexuals intent on subverting traditional society or by people who are prey to psychological, emotional, or sexual dysfunction.

For adherents to the conservative politics of sexuality, therefore, the homosexual question concerns everyone. It cannot be dismissed merely as an affliction of the individual but is rather one that afflicts society at large. Since society depends on the rearing of a healthy future generation, the existence of homosexuals is a grave problem. People who would otherwise be living productive and socially beneficial lives are diverted by homosexuality into unhappiness and sterility, and they may seek, in their bleak attempts at solace, to persuade others to join them. Two gerundives cling to this view of homosexuals: practicing and proselytizing. And both are habitually uttered with a mixture of pity and disgust.

The politics that springs out of this view of homosexuality has two essential parts: with the depraved, it must punish; with the sick, it must cure. There are, of course, degrees to which these two activities can be promoted. The recent practice in modern liberal democracies of imprisoning homosexuals or subjecting them to psychological or physiological "cures" is a good deal less repressive than the camps for homosexuals in Castro's Cuba, the spasmodic attempt at annihilation in Nazi Germany, or the brutality of modern Islamic states. And the sporadic entrapment of gay men in public restrooms or parks is a good deal less repressive than the systematic hunting down and discharging of homosexuals that we require of our armed forces. But the differences are matters of degree rather than of kind, and the essential characteristic of the conservative politics of homosexuality is that it pursues the logic of repression. Not for conservatives the hypocrisy of those who tolerate homosexuality in private and abhor it in public. They seek rather to grapple with the issue directly and to sustain the carapace of public condemnation and legal sanction that can keep the dark presence of homosexuality at bay.

This is not a distant politics. In twenty-four states sodomy is still illegal, and the constitutionality of these statutes was recently upheld by the Supreme Court. Much of the Republican party supports this politics with varying degrees of sympathy for the victims of the affliction. The Houston convention was replete with jokes by speaker Patrick Buchanan that implicitly affirmed this view. Banners held aloft by delegates asserted "Family Rights For Ever, Gay Rights Never," implying a direct trade-off between tolerating homosexuals and maintaining the traditional family.

In its crudest and most politically dismissible forms, this politics invokes biblical revelation to make its civic claims. But in its subtler form, it draws strength from the natural law tradition, which, for all its failings, is a resilient pillar of Western thought. Following a Thomist argument, conservatives argue that the natural function of sexuality is clearly procreative; all expressions of it outside procreation destroy human beings' potential for full and healthy development. Homosexuality—far from being natural—is clearly a perversion of, or turning away from, the legitimate and healthy growth of the human person.

Perhaps the least helpful element in the current debate is the assertion that this politics is simply bigotry. It isn't. Many bigots may, of course, support it, and by bigots I mean those whose "visceral recoil" from homosexuals (to quote Buchanan) expresses itself in thuggery and name-calling. But there are some who don't support anti-gay violence and who sincerely believe discouragement of homosexuality by law and "curing" homosexuals is in the best interest of everybody.

Nevertheless, this politics suffers from an increasingly acute internal contradiction and an irresistible external development. It is damaged, first, by the growing evidence that homosexuality does in fact exist as an identifiable and involuntary characteristic of some people, and that these people do not as a matter of course suffer from moral or psychological dysfunction; that it is, in other words, as close to "natural" as any human condition can be. New data about the possible genetic origins of homosexuality are only one part of this development. By far the most important element is the testimony of countless homosexuals. The number who say their orientation is a choice make up only a tiny minority, and the candor of those who say it isn't is overwhelming. To be sure, it is in the interests of gay people to affirm their lack of choice over the matter; but the consensus among homosexuals, the resilience of lesbian and gay minorities in the face of deep social disapproval and even a plague, suggests that homosexuality, whatever one would like to think, simply is not often chosen. A fundamental claim of natural law is that its truths are self-evident: across continents and centuries, homosexuality is a self-evident fact of life.

How large this population is does not matter. One percent or 10 percent: as long as a small but persistent part of the population is involuntarily gay, then the entire conservative politics of homosexuality rests on an unstable footing. It becomes simply a politics of denial or repression. Faced with a sizable and inextinguishable part of society, it can only pretend that it does not exist, or needn't be addressed, or can somehow be dismissed. This politics is less coherent than even the politics that opposed civil rights for blacks thirty years ago, because at least that had some answer to the question of the role of blacks in society, however subordinate. Today's conservatives have no role for homosexuals; they want them somehow to disappear, an option that was once illusory and is now impossible.

Some conservatives and conservative institutions have recognized this. They've even begun to use the term *homosexual,* implicitly accepting the existence of a constitutive characteristic. Some have avoided it by the innovative term *homosexualist,* but most cannot do so without a wry grin on their faces. The more serious opponents of equality for homosexuals finesse the problem by restricting their objections to "radical homosexuals," but the distinction doesn't help. They are still forced to confront the problem of *un*radical homosexuals, people whose sexuality is, presumably, constitutive. To make matters worse, the Roman Catholic Church—the firmest religious proponent of the conservative politics of homosexuality—has explicitly conceded the point. It declared in 1975 that homosexuality is indeed involuntary for many. In the recent Universal Catechism, the church goes even further. Homosexuality is described as a "condition" of a "not negligible" number of people who "do not choose" their sexuality and deserve to be treated with "respect, compassion and sensitivity." More critically, because of homosexuality's involuntary nature, it cannot of itself be morally culpable (although homosexual *acts* still are). The doctrine is thus no longer "hate the sin but love the sinner"; it's "hate the sin but accept the condition," a position unique in Catholic theology, and one that has already begun to creak under the strain of its own tortuousness.

But the loss of intellectual solidity isn't the only problem for the conservative politics of homosexuality. In a liberal polity, it has lost a good deal of its political coherence as well. When many people in a liberal society insist upon their validity as citizens and human beings, repression becomes a harder and harder task. It offends against fundamental notions of decency and civility to treat them as simple criminals or patients. To hunt them down, imprison them for private acts, subject government workers to surveillance and dismissal for reasons related to their deepest sense of personal identity becomes a policy not simply cruel but politically impossible in a civil order. For American society to return to the social norms around the question of homosexuality of a generation ago would require a renewed act of repression that not even many zealots could contemplate. What generations of inherited shame could not do, what AIDS could not accomplish, what the most decisive swing toward conservatism in the 1980s could not muster, must somehow be accomplished in the next few years. It simply cannot be done.

So even Patrick Buchanan is reduced to joke-telling; senators to professions of ignorance; military leaders to rationalizations of sheer discomfort. For those whose politics are a mere extension of religious faith, such impossibilism is part of the attraction (and spiritually, if not politically, defensible). But for conservatives who seek to act as citizens in a secular, civil order, the dilemma is terminal. An unremittingly hostile stance toward homosexuals runs the risk of sectarianism. At some point, not reached yet but fast approaching, their politics could become so estranged from the society in which it operates that it could cease to operate as a politics altogether.

II.

The second politics of homosexuality shares with the first a conviction that homosexuality as an inherent and natural condition does not exist. Homosexuality, in this politics, is a cultural construction, a binary social conceit (along with heterosexuality) forced upon the sexually amorphous (all of us). This politics attempts to resist this oppressive construct, subverting it and subverting the society that allows it to fester. Where the first politics takes as its starting point the Thomist faith in nature, the second springs from the Nietzschean desire to surpass all natural necessities, to attack the construct of "nature" itself. Thus the pursuit of a homosexual existence is but one strategy of many to enlarge the possibility for human liberation.

Call this the radical politics of homosexuality. For the radicals, like the conservatives, homosexuality is definitely a choice: the choice to be a "queer," the choice to subvert oppressive institutions, the choice to be an activist. And it is a politics that, insofar as it finds its way from academic discourse into gay activism (and it does so fitfully), exercises a peculiar fascination for the adherents of the first politics. At times, indeed, both seem to exist in a bond of mutual contempt and admiration. That both prefer to use the word *queer*—the one in private, the other in irony—is only one of many resemblances. They both react with disdain to those studies that seem to reflect a genetic source for homosexuality. And they both favor, to some extent or other, the process of outing, because for both it is the flushing out of deviant behavior; for conservatives, of the morally impure, for radicals, of the politically incorrect. For conservatives, radical "queers" provide a frisson of cultural apocalypse and a steady stream of funding dollars. For radicals, the religious right can be tapped as an unreflective and easy justification for virtually any political impulse whatsoever.

Insofar as this radical politics is synonymous with a subcultural experience, it has stretched the limits of homosexual identity and expanded the cultural space in which some homosexuals can live. In the late 1980s the tactics of groups like ACT UP and Queer Nation did not merely shock and anger, but took the logic of shame-abandonment to a thrilling conclusion. To exist within their sudden energy was to be caught in a liberating rite of passage, which, when it did not transgress into political puritanism, exploded many of the cozy assumptions of closeted homosexual and liberal heterosexual alike.

This politics is as open-ended as the conservative politics is closed-minded. It seeks an end to all restrictions on homosexuality, but also the subversion of heterosexual norms as taught in schools or the media. By virtue of its intellectual origins, it affirms a close connection with every other minority group, whose cultural subversion of white, heterosexual, male norms is just as vital. It sees its crusades—now for an AIDS czar, now against the Catholic Church's abortion stance, now for the Rainbow Curriculum, now against the military ban—as a unified whole of protest, glorifying in its indiscriminateness as in its universality.

But like the conservative politics of homosexuality, which also provides a protective ghetto of liberation for its disciples, the radical politics of homosexuality now finds itself in an acute state of crisis. Its problem is twofold: its conception of homosexuality is so amorphous and indistinguishable from other minority concerns that it is doomed to be ultimately unfocused: and its relationship with the views of most homosexuals—let alone heterosexuals—is so tenuous that at moments of truth (like the military ban) it strains to have a viable politics at all.

The trouble with gay radicalism, in short, is the problem with subversive politics as a whole. It tends to subvert itself. ACT UP, for example, an AIDS group that began in the late 1980s as an activist group dedicated to finding a cure and better treatment for people with AIDS, soon found itself awash in a cacophony of internal division. Its belief that sexuality was only one of many oppressive constructions meant that it was constantly tempted to broaden its reach, to solve a whole range of gender and ethnic grievances. Similarly, each organizing committee in each state of this weekend's march on Washington was required to have a 50 percent "minority" composition—even *Utah.* Although this universalist temptation was not always given in to, it exercised an enervating and dissipating effect on gay radicalism's political punch.

More important, the notion of sexuality as cultural subversion distanced it from the vast majority of gay people who not only accept the natural origin of their sexual orientation, but wish to be integrated into society as it is. For most gay people—the closet cases and barflies, the construction workers and investment bankers, the computer programmers and parents—a "queer" identity is precisely what they want to avoid. In this way, the radical politics of homosexuality, like the conservative politics of homosexuality, is caught in a political trap. The more it purifies its own belief about sexuality, the less able it is to engage the broader world as a whole. The more it acts upon its convictions, the less able it is to engage in politics at all.

For the "queer" fundamentalists, like the religious fundamentalists, this is no problem. Politics for both groups is essentially an exercise in theater and rhetoric, in which dialogue with one's opponent is an admission of defeat. It is no accident that ACT UP was founded by a playwright, since its politics was essentially theatrical: a fantastic display of rhetorical pique and visual brilliance. It became a national media hit, but eventually its lines became familiar and the audience's attention wavered. New shows have taken its place and will continue to do so—but they will always be constrained by their essential nature, which is performance, not persuasion.

The limits of this strategy can be seen in the politics of the military ban. Logically, there is no reason for radicals to support the ending of the ban: it means acceptance of presumably one of the most repressive institutions in American society. And, to be sure, no radical arguments have been made to end the ban. But in the last few months, "queers" have been appearing on television proclaiming that gay people are just like anybody else and defending the right of gay midwestern Republicans to serve their country. In the pinch, "queer" politics was forced to abandon its theoretical essence if it was to advance its purported aims: the advancement of gay equality. The military ban illustrated the dilemma perfectly. As soon as radicalism was required actually to engage America, its politics disintegrated.

Similarly, "queer" radicalism's doctrine of cultural subversion and separatism has the effect of alienating those very gay Americans most in need of support and help: the young and teenagers. Separatism is even less of an option for gays than for any other minority, since each generation is literally connected umbilically to the majority. The young are permanently in the hands of the other. By erecting a politics on a doctrine of separation and difference from the majority, "queer" politics ironically broke off dialogue with the heterosexual families whose cooperation is needed in every generation if gay children are to be accorded a modicum of dignity and hope.

There's an argument, of course, that radicalism's politics is essentially instrumental; that by stretching the limits of what is acceptable, it opens up space for more moderate types to negotiate; that without ACT UP and Queer Nation, no progress would have been made at all. But this both insults the theoretical integrity of the radical position (they surely do not see themselves as mere adjuncts to liberals) and underestimates the scope of the gay revolution that has been quietly taking place in America. Far more subversive than media-grabbing demonstrations on the evening news has been the slow effect of individual, private Americans becoming more open about their sexuality. The emergence of role models, the development of professional organizations and student groups, the growing influence of openly gay people in the media, and the extraordinary impact of AIDS on families and friends have dwarfed radicalism's impact on the national consciousness. Likewise, the greatest public debate about homosexuality yet—the military debate—took place not because radicals besieged the Pentagon, but because of the ordinary and once-anonymous Americans within the military who simply refused to acquiesce in their own humiliation any longer. Their courage was illustrated not in taking to the streets in rage but in facing their families and colleagues with integrity.

And this presents the deepest problem for radicalism. As the closet slowly collapses, as gay people enter the mainstream, as suburban homosexuals and Republican homosexuals emerge blinking into the daylight, as the gay ghettos of the inner cities are diluted by the gay enclaves of the suburbs, the whole notion of a separate and homogeneous "queer" identity will become harder to defend. Far from redefining gay identity, "queer" radicalism may actually have to define itself in opposition to it. This is implicit in the punitive practice of "outing" and in the increasingly anti-gay politics of some "queer" radicals. But if "queer" politics is to survive, it will either have to be proved right about America's inherent hostility to gay people or become more insistent in its separatism. It will have to intensify its hatred of straights or its contempt for gays. Either path is likely to be as culturally creative as it is politically sterile.

III.

Between these two cultural poles, an appealing alternative presents itself. You can hear it in the tone if not the substance of civilized columnists and embarrassed legislators, who are united most strongly by the desire that this awkward subject simply go away. It is the moderate politics of homosexuality. Unlike the conservatives and radicals, the moderates do believe that a small number of people are inherently homosexual, but they also believe that another group is susceptible to persuasion in that direction and should be dissuaded. These people do not want persecution of homosexuals, but they do not want overt approval either. They are most antsy when it comes to questions of the education of children but feel acute discomfort in supporting the likes of Patrick Buchanan and Pat Robertson.

Thus their politics has all the nuance and all the disingenuousness of classically conservative politics. They are not intolerant, but they oppose the presence of openly gay teachers in school; they have gay friends but hope their child isn't homosexual; they are in favor of ending the military ban but would seek to do so either by reimposing the closet (ending discrimination in return for gay people never mentioning their sexuality) or by finding some other kind of solution, such as simply ending the witch hunts. If they support sodomy laws (*pour décourager les autres*), they prefer to see them unenforced. In either case, they do not regard the matter as very important. They are ambivalent about domestic partnership legislation but are offended by gay marriage. Above all, they prefer that the subject of homosexuality be discussed with delicacy and restraint, and they are only likely to complain to their gay friends if the latter insist upon "bringing the subject up" too often.

This position too has a certain coherence. It insists that politics is a matter of custom as well as principle and that, in the words of Nunn, caution on the matter of sexuality is not so much a matter of prejudice as of prudence. It places a premium on discouraging the sexually ambivalent from resolving their ambiguity freely in the direction of homosexuality, because, society being as it is, such a life is more onerous than a heterosexual one. It sometimes exchanges this argument for the more honest one: that it wishes to promote procreation and the healthy rearing of the next generation and so wishes to create a cultural climate that promotes heterosexuality.

But this politics too has become somewhat unstable, if not as unstable as the first two. And this instability stems from an internal problem and a related external one. Being privately tolerant and publicly disapproving exacts something of a psychological cost on those who maintain it. In theory, it is not the same as hypocrisy: in practice, it comes perilously close. As the question of homosexuality refuses to disappear from public debate, explicit positions have to be taken. What once could be shrouded in discretion now has to be argued in public. For those who privately do not believe that homosexuality is inherently evil or always chosen, it has become increasingly difficult to pretend otherwise in public. Silence is an option—and numberless politicians are now availing themselves of it—but increasingly a decision will have to be made. Are you in favor of or against allowing openly gay women and men to continue serving their country? Do you favor or oppose gay marriage? Do you support the idea of gay civil rights laws? Once these questions are asked, the gentle ambiguity of the moderates must be flushed out; they have to be forced either into the conservative camp or into formulating a new politics that does not depend on a code of discourse that is fast becoming defunct.

They cannot even rely upon their gay friends anymore. What ultimately sustained this politics was the complicity of the gay elites in it: their willingness to stay silent when a gay joke was made in their presence, their deference to the euphemisms—roommate, friend, companion—that denoted their lovers, husbands, and wives, their support of the heterosexual assumptions of polite society. Now that complicity, if not vanished, has come under strain. There are fewer and fewer J. Edgar Hoovers and Roy Cohns, and the thousands of discreet gay executives and journalists, businessmen and politicians who long deferred to their sexual betters in matters of etiquette. AIDS rendered their balancing act finally absurd. Many people—gay and straight—were forced to have the public courage of their private convictions. They had to confront the fact that their delicacy was a way of disguising shame; that their silence was a means of hiding from themselves their intolerance. This is not an easy process; indeed, it can be a terrifying one for both gay and straight people alike. But there comes a point after which omissions become commissions; and that point, if not here yet, is coming. When it arrives, the moderate politics of homosexuality will be essentially over.

IV.

The politics that is the most durable in our current attempt to deal with the homosexual question is the contemporary liberal politics of homosexuality. Like the moderates, the liberals accept that homosexuality exists, that it is involuntary for a proportion of society, that for a few more it is an option and that it need not be discouraged. Viewing the issue primarily through the prism of the civil rights movement, the liberals seek to extend to homosexuals the same protections they have granted to other minorities. The prime instrument for this is the regulation of private activities by heterosexuals, primarily in employment and housing, to guarantee nondiscrimination against homosexuals.

Sometimes this strategy is echoed in the rhetoric of Edward Kennedy, who, in the hearings on the military gay ban, linked the gay rights agenda with the work of such disparate characters as John Kennedy, Cesar Chavez and Martin Luther King, Jr. In other places, it is reflected in the fact that sexual orientation is simply added to the end of a list of minority conditions in formulaic civil rights legislation. And this strategy makes a certain sense. Homosexuals are clearly subject to private discrimination in the same way as many other minorities, and linking the causes helps defuse some of the trauma that the subject of homosexuality raises. Liberalism properly restricts itself to law—not culture—in addressing social problems; and by describing all homosexuals as a monolithic minority, it is able to avoid the complexities of the gay world as a whole, just as blanket civil rights legislation draws a veil over the varieties of black America by casting the question entirely in terms of non-black attitudes.

But this strategy is based on two assumptions: that sexuality is equivalent to race in terms of discrimination, and that the full equality of homosexuals can be accomplished by designating gay people as victims. Both are extremely dubious. And the consequence of these errors is to mistarget the good that liberals are trying to do.

Consider the first. Two truths (at least) profoundly alter the way the process of discrimination takes place against homosexuals and against racial minorities and distinguish the history of racial discrimination in this country from the history of homophobia. Race is always visible; sexuality can be hidden. Race is in no way behavioral; sexuality, though distinct from sexual activity, is profoundly linked to a settled pattern of behavior.

For lesbians and gay men, the option of self-concealment has always existed and still exists, an option that means that in a profound way, discrimination against them is linked to their own involvement, even acquiescence. Unlike blacks three decades ago, gay men and lesbians suffer no discernible communal economic deprivation and already operate at the highest levels of society: in boardrooms, governments, the media, the military, the law, and industry. They may have advanced so far because they have not disclosed their sexuality, but their sexuality as such has not been an immediate cause for their disadvantage. In many cases their sexuality is known, but it is disclosed at such a carefully calibrated level that it never actually works against them. At lower levels of society, the same pattern continues. As in the military, gay people are not uniformly discriminated against; *openly* gay people are.

Moreover, unlike blacks or other racial minorities, gay people are not subject to inherited patterns of discrimination. When generation after generation is discriminated against, a cumulative effect of deprivation may take place, where the gradual immiseration of a particular ethnic group may intensify with the years. A child born into a family subject to decades of accumulated poverty is clearly affected by a past history of discrimination in terms of his or her race. But homosexuality occurs randomly anew with every generation. No sociological pattern can be deduced from it. Each generation gets a completely fresh start in terms of the socioeconomic conditions inherited from the family unit.

This is not to say that the psychological toll of homosexuality is less problematic than that of race, but that it is different: in some ways better, in others worse. Because the stigma is geared toward behavior, the level of shame and collapse of self-esteem may be more intractable. To reach puberty and find oneself falling in love with members of one's own sex is to experience a mixture of self-discovery and self-disgust that never leaves a human consciousness. If the stigma is attached not simply to an obviously random characteristic, such as skin pigmentation, but to the deepest desires of the human heart, then it can eat away at a person's sense of his own dignity with peculiar ferocity. When a young person confronts her sexuality, she is also completely alone. A young heterosexual black or Latino girl invariably has an existing network of people like her to interpret, support, and explain the emotions she feels when confronting racial prejudice for the first time. But a gay child generally has no one. The very people she would most naturally turn to—the family—may be the very people she is most ashamed in front of.

The stigma attached to sexuality is also different than that attached to race because it attacks the very heart of what makes a human being human: her ability to love and be loved. Even the most vicious persecution of racial minorities allowed, in many cases, for the integrity of the marital bond or the emotional core of a human being. When it did not, when Nazism split husbands from wives, children from parents, when apartheid or slavery broke up familial bonds, it was clear that a particularly noxious form of repression was taking place. But the stigma attached to homosexuality *begins* with such a repression. It forbids, at a child's earliest stage of development, the possibility of the highest form of human happiness. It starts with emotional terror and ends with mild social disapproval. It's no accident that later in life, when many gay people learn to reconnect the bonds of love and sex, they seek to do so in private, even protected from the knowledge of their family.

This unique combination of superficial privilege, acquiescence in repression, and psychological pain is a human mix no politics can easily tackle. But it is the mix liberalism must address if it is to reach its goal of using politics to ease human suffering. The internal inconsistency of this politics is that by relying on the regulation of private activity, it misses this its essential target—and may even make matters worse. In theory, a human rights statute sounds like an ideal solution, a way for straights to express their concern and homosexuals to legitimate their identity. But in practice, it misses the point. It might grant workers a greater sense of security were they to come out in the office; and it might, by the publicity it generates, allow for greater tolerance and approval of homosexuality generally. But the real terror of coming out is deeper than economic security, and is not resolved by it; it is related to emotional and interpersonal dignity. However effective or comprehensive antidiscrimination laws are, they cannot reach far enough to tackle this issue; it is one that can only be addressed person by person, life by life, heart by heart.

For these reasons, such legislation rarely touches the people most in need of it: those who live in communities where disapproval of homosexuality is so intense that the real obstacles to advancement remain impervious to legal remedy. And even in major urban areas, it can be largely irrelevant. (On average some 1 to 2 percent of antidiscrimination cases have to do with sexual orientation; in Wisconsin, which has had such a law in force for more than a decade and is the largest case study, the figure is 1.1 percent.) As with other civil rights legislation, those least in need of it may take fullest advantage: the most litigious and articulate homosexuals, who would likely brave the harsh winds of homophobia in any case.

Antidiscrimination laws scratch the privileged surface while avoiding the problematic depths. Like too many drugs for AIDS, they treat the symptoms of the homosexual problem without being anything like a cure. They may buy some time, and it is a cruel doctor who, in the face of human need, would refuse them. But they have about as much chance of tackling the deep roots of the gay–straight relationship as AZT has of curing AIDS. They want to substitute for the traumatic and difficult act of coming out the more formal and procedural act of legislation. But law cannot do the work of life. Even culture cannot do the work of life. Only life can do the work of life.

As the experience in Colorado and elsewhere shows, this strategy of using law to change private behavior also gives a fatal opening to the conservative politics of homosexuality. Civil rights laws essentially dictate the behavior of heterosexuals, in curtailing their ability to discriminate. They can, with justification, be portrayed as being an infringement of individual liberties. If the purpose of the liberal politics is to ensure the equality of homosexuals and their integration into society, it has thus achieved something quite peculiar. It has provided fuel for those who want to argue that homosexuals are actually seeking the infringement of heterosexuals' rights and the imposition of their values onto others. Much of this is propaganda, of course, and is fueled by fear and bigotry. But it works because it contains a germ of truth. Before most homosexuals have even come out of the closet, they are demanding concessions from the majority, including a clear curtailment of economic and social liberties, in order to ensure protections few of them will even avail themselves of. It is no wonder there is opposition, or that it seems to be growing. Nine states now have propositions to respond to what they see as the "special rights" onslaught.

In the process, the liberal politics of homosexuality has also reframed the position of gays in relation to straights. It has defined them in a permanent supplicant status, seeing gay freedom as dependent on straight enlightenment, achievable only by changing the behavior of heterosexuals. The valuable political insight of radicalism is that this is a fatal step. It could enshrine forever the notion that gay people are a vulnerable group in need of protection. By legislating homosexuals as victims, it sets up a psychological dynamic of supplication that too often only perpetuates cycles of inadequacy and self-doubt. Like blacks before them, gay people may grasp at what seems to be an escape from the prison of self-hatred, only to find it is another prison of patronized victimology. By seeking salvation in the hands of others, they may actually entrench in law and in their minds the notion that their equality is dependent on the goodwill of their betters. It isn't. This may have made a good deal of sense in the case of American blacks, with a clear and overwhelming history of accumulated discrimination and a social ghetto that seemed impossible to breach. But for gay people—already prosperous, independent, and on the brink of real integration—that lesson should surely now be learned. To place our self-esteem in the benevolent hands of contemporary liberalism is more than a mistake. It is a historic error.

V.

If there were no alternative to today's liberal politics of homosexuality, it should perhaps be embraced by default. But there is an alternative politics that is imaginable, which once too was called liberal. It begins with the view that for a small minority of people, homosexuality is an involuntary condition that can neither be denied nor permanently repressed. It adheres to an understanding that there is a limit to what politics can achieve in such an area, and trains its focus not on the behavior of private heterosexual citizens but on the actions of the public and allegedly neutral state. While it eschews the use of law to legislate culture, it strongly believes that law can affect culture indirectly. Its goal would be full civil equality for those who, through no fault of their own, happen to be homosexual; and would not deny homosexuals, as the other four politics do, their existence, integrity, dignity, or distinctness. It would attempt neither to patronize nor to exclude.

This liberal politics affirms a simple and limited criterion: that all *public* (as opposed to private) discrimination against homosexuals be ended and that every right and responsibility that heterosexuals enjoy by virtue of the state be extended to those who grow up different. And that is all. No cures or re-educations; no wrenching civil litigation; no political imposition of tolerance; merely a political attempt to enshrine formal civil equality, in the hope that eventually the private sphere will reflect this public civility. For these reasons, it is the only politics that actually tackles the core *political* problem of homosexuality and perhaps the only one that fully respects liberalism's public–private distinction. For these reasons, it has also the least chance of being adopted by gays and straights alike.

But is it impossible? By sheer circumstance, this politics has just been given its biggest boost since the beginning of the debate over the homosexual question. The military ban is by far the most egregious example of proactive government discrimination in this country. By conceding, as the military has done, the excellent service that many gay and lesbian soldiers have given to their country, the military has helped shatter a thousand stereotypes about their nature and competence. By focusing on the mere admission of homosexuality, the ban has purified the debate into a matter of the public enforcement of homophobia. Unlike anti-discrimination law, the campaign against the ban does not ask any private citizens to hire or fire anyone of whom they do not approve; it merely asks public servants to behave the same way with avowed homosexuals as with closeted ones.

Because of its timing, because of the way in which it has intersected with the coming of age of gay politics, the military debate has a chance of transforming the issue for good. Its real political power—and the real source of the resistance to it—comes from its symbolism. The acceptance of gay people at the heart of the state, at the core of the notion of patriotism, is anathema to those who wish to consign homosexuals to the margins of society. It offends conservatives by the simplicity of its demands, and radicals by the traditionalism of the gay people involved; it dismays moderates, who are forced publicly to discuss this issue for the first time; and it disorients liberals, who find it hard to fit the cause simply into the rubric of minority politics. For instead of seeking access, as other minorities have done, gays in the military are simply demanding recognition. They start not from the premise of suppliance, but of success, of proven ability and prowess in battle, of exemplary conduct and ability. This is a new kind of minority politics. It is less a matter of complaint than of pride; less about subversion than about the desire to contribute equally.

The military ban also forces our society to deal with the real issues at stake in dealing with homosexuals. The country has been forced to discuss sleeping arrangements, fears of sexual intimidation, the fraught emotional relations between gays and straights, the violent reaction to homosexuality among many young males, the hypocrisy involved in much condemnation of gays, and the possible psychological and emotional syndromes that make homosexuals allegedly unfit for service. Like a family engaged in the first, angry steps toward dealing with a gay member, the country has been forced to debate a subject honestly—even calmly—in a way it never has before. This is a clear and enormous gain. Whatever the result of this process, it cannot be undone.

But the critical measure necessary for full gay equality is something deeper and more emotional perhaps than even the military. It is equal access to marriage. As with the military, this is a question of formal public discrimination. If the military ban deals with the heart of what it is to be a citizen, the marriage ban deals with the core of what it is to be a member of civil society. Marriage is not simply a private contract; it is a social and public recognition of a private commitment. As such it is the highest public recognition of our personal integrity. Denying it to gay people is the most public affront possible to their civil equality.

This issue may be the hardest for many heterosexuals to accept. Even those tolerant of homosexuals may find this institution so wedded to the notion of heterosexual commitment that to extend it would be to undo its very essence. And there may be religious reasons for resisting this that require far greater discussion than I can give them here. But civilly and emotionally, the case is compelling. The heterosexuality of marriage is civilly intrinsic only if it is understood to be inherently procreative; and that definition has long been abandoned in civil society. In contemporary America, marriage has become a way in which the state recognizes an emotional and economic commitment of two people to each other for life. No law requires children to consummate it. And within that definition, there is no civil way it can logically be denied homosexuals, except as a pure gesture of public disapproval. (I leave aside here the thorny issue of adoption rights, which I support in full. They are not the same as the right to marriage and can be legislated, or not, separately.)

In the same way, emotionally, marriage is characterized by a kind of commitment that is rare even among heterosexuals. Extending it to homosexuals need not dilute the special nature of that commitment, unless it is understood that gay people, by their very nature, are incapable of it. History and experience suggest the opposite. It is not necessary to prove that gay people are more or less able to form long-term relationships than straights for it to be clear that, at least, *some* are. Giving these people a right to affirm their commitment doesn't reduce the incentive for heterosexuals to do the same, and even provides a social incentive for lesbians and gay men to adopt socially beneficial relationships.

But for gay people, it would mean far more than simple civil equality. The vast majority of us—gay and straight—are brought up to understand that the apex of emotional life is found in the marital bond. It may not be something we achieve, or even ultimately desire, but its very existence premises the core of our emotional development. It is the architectonic institution that frames our emotional life. The marriages of others are a moment for celebration and self-affirmation; they are the way in which our families and friends reinforce us as human beings. Our parents consider our emotional lives to be more important than our professional ones, because they care about us at our core, not at our periphery. And it is not hard to see why the marriage of an offspring is often regarded as the high point of any parent's life.

Gay people always know this essential affirmation will be denied them. Thus their relationships are given no anchor, no endpoint, no way of integrating them fully into the network of family and friends that makes someone a full member of civil society. Even when those relationships become essentially the same—or even stronger—than straight relationships, they are never accorded the dignity of actual equality. Husbands remain "friends"; wives remain "partners." The very language sends a powerful signal of fault, a silent assumption of internal disorder or insufficiency. The euphemisms—and the brave attempt to pretend that gay people don't need marriage—do not successfully conceal the true emotional cost and psychological damage that this signal exacts. No true progress in the potential happiness of gay teenagers or in the stability of gay adults or in the full integration of gay and straight life is possible, or even imaginable, without it.

These two measures—simple, direct, requiring no change in heterosexual behavior and no sacrifice from heterosexuals—represent a politics that tackles the heart of homophobia while leaving homophobes their freedom. It allows homosexuals to define their own future and their own identity and does not place it in the hands of the other. It makes a clear, public statement of equality, while leaving all the inequalities of emotion and passion to the private sphere, where they belong. It does not legislate private tolerance, it declares public equality. It banishes the paradigm of victimology and replaces it with one of integrity. It requires one further step, of course, which is to say the continuing effort for honesty on the part of homosexuals themselves. This is not easily summed up in the crude phrase "coming out"; but it finds expression in the myriad ways in which gay men and lesbians talk, engage, explain, confront, and seek out the other. Politics cannot substitute for this; heterosexuals cannot provide it. And while it is not in some sense fair that homosexuals have to initiate the dialogue, it is a fact of life. Silence, if it does not equal death, equals the living equivalent.

It is not the least of the ironies of this politics that its objectives are in some sense not political at all. The family is prior to the liberal state; the military is coincident with it. Heterosexuals would not conceive of such rights as things to be won, but as things that predate modern political discussion. But it says something about the unique status of homosexuals in our society that we now have to be political in order to be prepolitical. Our battle is not for political victory but for personal integrity. Just as many of us had to leave our families in order to join them again, so now as citizens, we have to embrace politics, if only ultimately to be free of it. Our lives may have begun in simplicity, but they have not ended there. Our dream, perhaps, is that they might.

PAUL VARNELL

The following column appeared in the *Windy City Times* on 27 August 1992.

BARRY GOLDWATER VS. PAT BUCHANAN

XENOPHON: I am perplexed, Socrates.

SOCRATES: You, my excellent man, who have an opinion on everything?

X: There is Pat Buchanan at the Republican convention attacking "homosexual rights," and yet here is this Associated Press news story that says Barry Goldwater, a conservative if there ever was one, has endorsed a gay civil rights bill in his hometown of Phoenix, Arizona. How can that be?

S: Did Goldwater say why? Sometimes what people say gives us a clue about what they mean.

X: Let's see. Yes, right here Goldwater says, "Under our Constitution we literally have the right to do anything we may want to do, as long as the performing of those acts do not cause damage or hurt to anyone else." And then he goes on to say, "I can't see any way in the world that being gay can cause damage to somebody else."

S: Sounds reasonable to me. What's the problem?

X: But he's a conservative!

S: It's even more interesting than you think. Did you see that Sen. Goldwater said that the Republican platform shouldn't oppose a woman's right to choose abortion?

X: What? Is the old man becoming a liberal?

S: Hmmm. The Constitution? Individual choice? Personal liberty? Sounds pretty conservative to me.

S: No it doesn't. Conservatives are hostile to all kinds of social change and want to squash minorities like gays. Look at Buchanan and Robertson. Wake up!

S: Keep in mind now, it was Barry Goldwater who said Rev. Jerry Falwell should be "kicked in the ass." No doubt he feels the same way about Pat Robertson.

X: It doesn't make much sense to me.

S: Goldwater has never had much patience with would-be theocrats or anyone who wanted to organize society any one way. I think one key to understanding Goldwater is to keep in mind that in 1964 he was for ending the military draft because he said it was a kind of involuntary servitude. That certainly struck a resonant chord with a lot of young people—like the young Harvey Milk.

X: I had forgotten that Harvey Milk was a Goldwater supporter. I remember that image in *The Mayor of Castro Street* of Milk getting up early every morning to distribute Goldwater literature in the New York subways. What a long route he traveled to becoming a gay activist, huh?

S: Maybe not so long after all. You haven't been paying attention. Goldwater comes out for gay rights because we should be able to do what we want, he endorses personal choice, he opposes servitude to government programs. Doesn't that sound like the mature Harvey Milk?

X: Well, maybe a little.

S: And Goldwater talked about individual freedom, personal self-esteem, confidence in your own self. He said that his basic philosophy opposed "everyone who would debase the dignity of the individual."

X: I confess I can see how that kind of language could inspire people with the courage of their convictions. Looked at as you suggest, Goldwater's language and arguments could be virtually a guide to coming out and being militant: don't be ashamed of yourself, dare to take risks, assert your own dignity.

S: Even demand an end to repressive legislation and demand "the equal protection of the laws" that the Constitution guarantees.

X: But now see here. I will not let you carry on this charade any longer. Goldwater can't have meant all that stuff to apply to gays. Look at Buchanan and Robertson and William Bennett, even President Bush. Their homophobia, their attacks on gay rights, undermines everything you say. You're just a cheap sophist like all the others.

S: What makes you think Goldwater and Buchanan have much in common?

X: They are both conservatives, you old fool!

S: Ah, you excellent man, you are letting your language do your thinking for you. That is always a danger. Perhaps the word *conservative* has changed meaning; or maybe there is more than one kind, yes? Goldwater talked about freedom, the individual, self-reliance, the government as the enemy. And Buchanan?

X: Well, Buchanan talks of religious morality, the danger gays present just by our existence, and the government as guarantor of morality. It is almost as if they were in opposite political parties.

S: In a sense beyond the mere political, they are. For Goldwater, America stands for people's freedom to do whatever they want, to live your life by your own lights, to conduct experiments in different ways of living, to try new things, to experiment with new values, even.

X: That's nothing like Buchanan. Buchanan, as a conservative Catholic, is basically saying that he already knows how we should live our lives, that we should follow the dictates of established religious authority, and that governments should make sure that happens. So is what you are saying that Goldwater is for freedom and Buchanan is for moral values?

S: Not quite. Goldwater is for moral values, too—but for him the moral values reside exactly in the dignity of the individual and the freedom of choice. The experimentation and choice-making both have moral value: they have value for the individual living out his moral autonomy, and they have value for us because we can watch and adopt for ourselves new things that seem good to us.

X: You think that applies to gays as well?

S: You said earlier you doubted that Goldwater meant his general principles to apply to gays. But, you see, he didn't mean them *not* to either. When a thoughtful person expresses a general principle, it is because he is convinced of its general truth such that he can use it to guide him in evaluating surprising new things that come along—like gay issues. As Goldwater did.

X: Well, none of this sounds much like the current Republican party. There are fundamentalists bashing gays and there is Bush capitulating all over the place. I read in the *New York Review of Books* that Bush was once a co-sponsor of the Equal Rights Amendment, for abortion rights, and was such a big proponent of family planning that one of his House colleagues called him "rubbers." Now he can't even say the word *condom*. Do you think he can win this way?

S: A lot of people seemed to think Buchanan's speech was mean-spirited and vengeful. One recent Gallup poll said that fully 50 percent of voters believed that Clinton's well-publicized positions on gays has "been about right." Only 27 percent said they thought he had gone too far. It will be interesting to see how long the fundamentalist-conservative Republicans keep trying to fight their losing battle against gays.

PAUL VARNELL

The following column appeared in the *Windy City Times* on 21 April 1994.

WHY MORE GAY CONSERVATIVES?

For perfectly understandable reasons, gay activism began on the political and social left and has, until recently, had its center of gravity there. In broad and simplified strokes:

1. Gay communities first coalesced and began their political efforts in the major U.S. cities, almost all of which were controlled by Democratic party machines. So it was the Democrats who were first lobbied by gays and befriended them as a constituency (i.e., an identifiable voter group).
2. Democrats are much more comfortable with the sort of "civil rights" language gays used to articulate their goals. Democrats are more comfortable, too, with the sort of intrusive government mechanisms needed to guarantee those rights.
3. Democrats and (non-communist) leftists generally have held up "equality" as their preeminent social goal: certainly equality of status, often equality of condition. Such a commitment—however merely verbal—seemed to provide an obvious conceptual basis on which to make demands on behalf of gays.

4. Some (many?) of the activists in the immediate post-Stonewall period had already been involved in the antiwar effort, primarily an exercise of the left. They simply transferred over to the new movement, bringing their ideology as well as their energy.

It all could have been different. It would be a fascinating exercise in alternative history to imagine how a gay movement might have eventually begun on the right. Or to imagine how little different conditions need have been for one not to have risen on the left. It is sufficient for the moment to understand how contingent was the creation of the gay movement in the way it was. It is only after the fact that history gives the illusion of being inevitable.

But now we are suddenly confronted with a significant increment in gay openness and assertiveness on the political right.

- Log Cabin Republicans under Rich Tafel opened a Washington office and promptly began working within the party to neutralize homophobes.
- Longtime conservative gray eminence Marvin Liebman founded the National Coalition for Understanding to promote acceptance of gays in the language and concepts of moderate conservatism.
- Controversial conservative journalist David Brock chose to interpret a public charge of "misogyny" as an "outing" and promptly came out in a *Washington Post* interview. Yet he is being retained as a chief writer by the sophomorically homophobic *American Spectator.*
- Moderate Republican Wisconsin Rep. Steve Gunderson delivered a ringing endorsement of gays in the military on the House floor, referring to his recent experience of being "outed," announced for reelection, and then addressed a Baltimore dinner of the Human Rights Campaign Fund where he talked about "Rob and I."
- In the wake of Bruce Bawer's important *A Place at the Table,*

there are more books in process by gay conservative authors. Some of them are "coming-out books"; others are analyses of gay-related issues. I am told there is work in progress that suggests the identity of (though apparently without naming) many of the gays in Republican and conservative circles.

No doubt, since such activity on the (moderate) right follows activism on the left, it has been influenced by it. But we may assume from its sudden growth now that it also has its own objective conditions and its own dynamic. The task is to figure out what those are.

Here are some hypotheses, not an exhaustive list, to consider as part of the explanation.

1. *International communism vaporized.* It is important to keep in mind that many gays in conservative and Republican circles shared the view in those circles that communism was the main threat to American liberties. So thinking, many were unwilling to make any major public claims on behalf of their sexuality (so long as it could be conducted unobtrusively with relative freedom) because they did not want to cause dissension in the organizations they were working with, taint them in public opinion, or—frankly—jeopardize their own ability to contribute. The point was not to make waves while there was real work to be done.

   I have talked to many gay leftists who delayed a public coming out for analogous reasons related to their own issues.
2. *Disestablishment.* For the first time in a dozen years and—except for the feeble Carter interregnum—for the first time since Stonewall, the Republican party was swept from power. That means that there was far less benefit in paying silent obeisance to party orthodoxy, trying to avoid offending the sensibility of party leaders, no lure to stay near power by staying in the closet. There is little possibility of patronage or promotion to

positions of influence. And there exists no longer the rationale (or rationalization) of staying in the closet in order to be able to fight conservative homophobes from "the inside."

3. *Houston.* The Republican Party orthodoxy, at least its agenda of social conservatism, was seriously harmed by "Houston"—the 1992 Republican National Convention, where the bared teeth, narrowness, and ignobility of the social conservative agenda were clearly revealed in speeches by Pat Buchanan, Pat Robertson, etc. Harmed—"delegitimized," we might say—even "desacralized."

   Many conservative gays realized, "If that is where the party is going, I want nothing to do with it," and many more were angered enough—anger being a great solvent of fear and decorum—to actively oppose that agenda on their own behalf. The subsequent electoral defeat gratifyingly confirmed to them, too, the political reasonableness of their position.

4. *The world has "objectively" changed.* It is far easier now to come out than it was ten or twenty years ago. The social climate is more comfortable, major institutions more receptive. In many circles, though, it remained not so much bad or wrong to be gay, but somehow simply tasteless, or a breach of social etiquette, to bring up one's homosexuality, much less insist on it. "They know, but we don't talk about it," is the frequent claim by many conservative gays.

   But now with "gay" constantly in the air—literature, theater, discussion of gays in the military—occasions for "mentioning" it, even making a (low-key) issue of it, have been multiplied. Many people who were sort of "in" found to their surprise that they are a little more "out." And once that trajectory has begun, it will not automatically stop at any particular place.

PAUL VARNELL

The following column appeared in the *Windy City Times* on 11 August 1994.

GETTING A GRIP ON REALITY

Last May, Colorado for Family Values hosted a conference for like-minded members of the Religious Right to counter the gains made by the gay rights movement. Though the conference was held clandestinely, someone eventually leaked tapes of the proceedings, and useful articles describing the conference have now been published by civil liberties watchdogs Michael Shaver and Skipp Porteous.

Briefly, the bad news is that these people seem to hate and fear us. The good news is that they seem to be a bunch of raving loonies, without a clear grasp of what to do or what they are up against.

I put it this way because while these people can do local damage and we need to monitor them carefully, at the same time it is important not to overestimate their significance or power.

Gay activists often exaggerate the threat posed by our opponents. (Anti-gay groups do the same, of course.) But the proper response is always a proportionate response, one that does not drain too much of our time and energy from our chief tasks of promoting tolerance and empathy for gays and lesbians.

Consider the types of people who attended the conference. Some were from tiny local groups such as Warriors Not Wimps for Jesus, Mothers Against Bad Government, and the Chinese Family Alliance. If the organizers had to dig this deep, they were clearly having trouble finding forty people interested in attending. Even people from better-known organizations such as Concerned Women for America and the American Family Association were actually from state affiliates rather than the national organizations—and few of those at that.

Of the eleven speakers, five were local people, from Colorado for Family Values or the Colorado-based Focus on the Family. Best-known among the remainder were garrulous homophobe Paul Cameron, who even former Rep. William Dannemeyer said was "obsessed with homosexuality"; Judith Reisman, who has flamboyantly attacked sex researcher Alfred C. Kinsey; and Peter LaBarbera, who publishes a nifty, hostile little newsletter on everything we all do.

Clearly, major players in the mainstream conservative movement stayed away in droves. Even leaders of the Religious Right itself seem to have avoided the conference out of apprehension or disdain. When one moderate Democrat saw the list of attendees he commented, "These are not even people on the fringe. They are on the fringe of the fringe." The only seeming exception was Howard Phillips of the Conservative Caucus. Once a leader of the New Right, Phillips has lost most of his power and influence in recent years and no longer has any political significance.

The tactical recommendations that came out of the "brainstorming" sessions ranged from the obvious to the bizarre. Many were remarkable chiefly for what they suggested no one on the Religious Right was doing—things *we* have been doing for years. The group proposed, for instance, to compile lists of gay activists and gay elected officials, to monitor where major corporations put their advertising revenue, to make lists of pro- and anti-gay politicians and media personalities, to record successes and failures of anti-gay efforts, and to watch (or "track"—it sounds more assertive) the scientific literature on homosexuality.

They also agreed to mount a "media blitzkrieg" against Kinsey, apparently believing they can undo the sexual revolution by delegitimizing Kinsey. Though this was clearly a sop to Reisman, the group nevertheless apparently had so few good ideas on how to go about attacking and undermining gay advances at the cultural and intellectual levels that they were willing to accept even implausible and ineffective schemes such as this.

One major problem for these people is that they really do not seem to have a clue about us. They disagree among themselves about how many of us there are, whether a few hundred thousand (Reisman) or a few million (Cameron). They disagree on whether we are wealthy and upscale (Reisman) or mostly "waiters and busboys and bums and hobos and jailbirds and so forth" (Cameron). They think there is a causal relationship between homosexuality and pornography, and that organized crime provides most of our political lobbying money.

Almost touchingly, they all seem to agree, as one speaker put it, that homosexuality "destroy[s] the souls and the lives of those who embrace it." And somehow they fail to realize that the ordinary lives of millions of happy, productive gays and lesbians daily undermine those perceptions in the minds of most people.

They really do not understand why we have made the political, social, and cultural progress we have. Lacking an explanatory model for our progress—or indeed for the last thirty years of social change—they floundered around for a way to reverse it. Bizarrely, they seem to think that promoting "family values" will by itself persuade people (including gays) to come to regard homosexuality "as a sad pathology."

Finally though, there are some lessons in all this for us as well.

- One speaker, John Eldredge of Focus on the Family, freely acknowledged that the basic American values of individualism and autonomy "tilt the field" against their efforts and in favor of ours. He is right, of course. That suggests we would be wise to help promote just those values in the culture. And it means that the collectivist and communitarian rhetoric coming out of certain segments of the gay community is actually counterproductive and harmful to our progress.
- Since they regard a major task as winning over the churches, they greatly fear gay evangelicals such as Mel White and progay ones such as Peggy Campolo. As Eldredge affirmed, "That sort of thing is extraordinarily damaging to our movement." That means that regardless of our views on religion, at least at a political level we would be prudent to support White and people like him and help him lure out of the closet as many other gay evangelicals as possible: He and they can speak persuasively to people whom the rest of us can never reach.
- They seem to realize that somehow we are, if not in the mainstream, at least closer to it than they are. "Even Christian legal groups won't touch this issue," complained a man from the National Legal Foundation. That suggests that what would work best for us is an approach that emphasizes sharing our common humanity rather than attacking the mainstream and portraying ourselves as an aggrieved, victimized, and petulant minority. It is, after all, the homophobes who are the sad, isolated, troubled little clot of obscurantists.

PAUL VARNELL

The following column appeared in the *Windy City Times* on 20 April 1995.

WHAT HOMOPHOBES THINK

If we want to find out what activist conservatives think about gays, there is no better place to begin than a symposium titled "Sex and God in American Politics: What Conservatives Really Think," published in *Policy Review* (Summer 1984), the quarterly magazine of the Heritage Foundation.

The magazine asked "thirteen leading conservatives" for their thoughts on topics such as abortion, divorce, child abuse, school prayer, and unwed motherhood. And one of the questions was, "What explains the sudden prevalence of overt homosexuality?"

Among the participants were Sen. Orrin Hatch, Rep. Jack Kemp, columnist M. Stanton Evans, Rev. Jerry Falwell, Conservative Caucus director Howard Phillips, Midge Decter (Mrs. Norman Podhoretz), Irving Kristol, and Phyllis Schlafly.

Conceptually, these people were all over the map. Thus homosexuality is a "tendency," "a choice," "learned" (i.e., not a simple choice), a "tendency" although acting on the tendency is a choice, or "not inherited" and therefore a choice (an obvious false dichotomy), while some people are "encouraged by the social environment to be homosexual."

Homosexuality is "one of the ultimate acts of rebellion against God," "against nature," "contrary to human nature," an "act of self-centeredness and selfishness," a "deviant lifestyle," a "means of escaping from girls and women," and "a handy escape from . . . fatherhood."

Finally, it is "a sign of civilizational decadence" (i.e., a result or effect), it "produces a social evil" (i.e., a cause), it is "symptomatic of serious social ills" (a result), and is "existential" and "self-destructive" (causal).

The lesson here seems to be that there is no unified conservative position about gays except that homosexuality is a bad thing. They do not seem to be particularly well informed, and one gets the impression that they have not thought much about the issue and prefer not to think about it.

The point becomes even clearer when they try to say what they object to about gays. Most of them insist that they are little concerned with private behavior. Evans is "not in favor of the government policing what people do in their bedroom." Schlafly says, "Really, no one cares about someone's private sexual practices." Paul Weyrich says he does not want to impose "any cruel and unusual punishment."

Even here doubts creep in. Weyrich believes that gay sexual relationships "should remain illegal" (i.e., there should be a punishment that is not cruel or unusual). And Schlafly compares homosexuality to prostitution, saying that "no one can stop you if you want to be a prostitute or patronize a prostitute." But as Schlafly must know, prostitution is illegal: the police do (try to) stop you, and some people are now in jail for engaging in it. To say "no one objects" but that it is all right for the law to object is not a coherent position.

However, what most of them object to is anything other than

our absolute secrecy. "Homosexuals should stay in the closet." "It is the responsibility of homosexuals to keep their sexual life as private as possible." Gays have only the "right to conduct their own private lifestyles." "As long as they mind their own business, society will mind its own business."

And that brings us to the very center of most of the conservative objections to homosexuality—our increasing openness and comfort with our lives.

And the reason for that? Immediately after Kristol says that gays should keep their sex life private he adds, "No society . . . is going to accept homosexuality as equal to heterosexuality." But if Kristol really believes that, we have to ask why he says it is our responsibility (to whom? to society?) to keep our sexual lives private? What could be the harm? So one suspects that Kristol is far from confident about society's unwillingness to accept homosexuality.

The others seem to agree. "There should be a social stigma attached to homosexuality." "Homosexuals should stay in the closet. They certainly should not be role models." If homosexuality becomes acceptable, "then all sorts of people will come forth who otherwise would not have been willing to admit the practice."

It is troubling that gays want "public recognition of homosexuality as an acceptable way of life." "Homosexuals are trying to . . . force the rest of us to respect their lifestyle." "The state does have an obligation to protect us from . . . proselytizing."

In fact, Kristol is willing to gut the Constitution to block our openness. "I don't think the advocacy of homosexuality really falls under the First Amendment."

It is important to see how easily these people pass from openness by gays and lesbians, to the acceptability of homosexuality, to more people coming out, to our being (however inadvertently) role models, to proselytizing, to recruitment. What looks at first like a continuum is really just one thing: coming out or being out amounts to recruitment of those who never had a homosexual thought before.

This conflation of concepts is caught nicely in such broad terms as "flaunting his lifestyle," or even "public homosexuality." What could public homosexuality be? It cannot be actual copulation in the streets, although that is hinted at, since that is already illegal for everyone. Is it saying one is gay? Talking of one's lover? Two men holding hands or kissing? Advocating our civil rights? Gay demonstrations?

It is in this conceptual miasma that the military's current claim that merely saying one is gay amounts to homosexual conduct finds its natural home.

Surely there is some intentionality here. By using ambiguous and undefined terms that allow a wide range of possible interpretations, homophobes can elicit the broadest possible range of support and the strongest possible emotional response; but if pressed they need only defend the most temperate of the possible interpretations.

It is one thing when rapscallions and common rabble-rousers use vague and slippery language. We expect it of them. But when presumed intellectuals (in a serious policy journal) use the same style, we may suspect that their concepts are no clearer and their arguments are no better than those of the lowest bigot.

As Irving Kristol bluntly says, "I do not like homosexuality." And Paul Weyrich admits: "What I read of these people's practices, in their own publications, is absolutely sickening. It is vile."

Well, thank you for sharing.

BRUCE BAWER

This was my *Advocate* column for 24 January 1995.

APOCALYPSE? NO

For gay Americans the year that marked the twenty-fifth anniversary of the Stonewall riots has been an important one. Gays came out of the closet in (I suspect) record numbers, and gay activism took big steps toward the center. It was also, alas, the year of Newt Gingrich, whose party's mammoth victory at the polls has been placed in useful historical context by a December 5 *New Republic* article: Since 1968, notes Michael Lind, traditional liberalism—"the liberalism of the New Deal and the original, colorblind civil rights revolution"—has been eclipsed by a progressive ideology dedicated to "patronizing liberal tokenism" and "bribery by means of proliferating entitlements." For a quarter century this progressivism has ruled the Democratic party and gradually driven white middle-class Democrats to the GOP.

This history is especially relevant to gays, because the gay rights movement has, since Stonewall, been a creature of that progressive left and has remained tethered to it even though our voting patterns suggest that gays are, on average, politically moderate. (A *New York Times*/CBS News poll indicated that in the November election gays, lesbians, and bisexuals voted 60% Democratic, 40% Republican. I'm routinely labeled a "gay conservative," yet as a New York Democrat who voted the straight Liberal Party line, I'm clearly left of center for gay America.) The GOP win, Lind argues persuasively, marked the progressive left's demise and created "the best opportunity in a quarter century" for the resurgence of traditional liberalism.

There's a vital truth here for the gay rights movement—namely, that we need urgently to put behind us an ideology that quixotically rejects and ridicules everything the average American believes in (God, country, capitalism), that touts diversity while condemning any breach of the party line as right-wing heresy, and that sees the Republican party as an implacable foe and middle Americans as unchangeable bigots. Let's remember that voters did not deliver an anti-gay mandate: The initiatives in Oregon and Idaho both failed, while all three openly gay congressmen won reelection (including newly out Steve Gunderson, a Republican who represents a rural Wisconsin district).

Let's acknowledge too that *Republican* and *homophobe* aren't synonyms. Bigots—and gay rights supporters—can be found in all parties. In the Connecticut U.S. Senate race, the liberal (and Orthodox Jewish) incumbent, Joseph Lieberman, opposed school-counseling programs for gay teens, while the conservative Republican he defeated, Gerald Labriola, supported them because he's a pediatrician who knows what gay teens suffer. Is Labriola a closet liberal? No; he's a conservative who recognizes that according equal rights and respect to gay people is a matter not of Right and Left but of right and wrong.

That's something most straight Americans can come to recognize—provided, of course, someone explains it to them. Indeed, what the November election results underscore for us is that the only way to achieve secure, lasting change for gays in America is to look primarily not to legislators but to their constituents.

There's little hope of making Gingrich pro-gay, but we can all do more in 1995 and beyond to help the voters—in whose hands political power ultimately rests—to understand that homosexuality is not a "counterculture" phenomenon, that there's no connection between homosexuality and the real social problems (such as violent crime and teen pregnancy) with which they're legitimately concerned, and that a thoughtful devotion to moral principles and "family values" compels not rejection but acceptance of gays.

Perhaps the chief lesson of 1994, then, is that gay activism shouldn't focus too narrowly on effecting changes that can be swept away with a single election or constitutional amendment. For a generation we've let ourselves be swayed by the illusion that if we win over enough legislators—or a president—we can achieve equal rights even if most Americans oppose us. Not for long, we can't. Some, to be sure, maintain that middle-American homophobia is intractable. But I've been astonished to discover how little many straight people know about homosexuality and how dramatically (and quickly) some people's views can be changed if they're talked to reasonably, patiently, and respectfully.

That's the good news here: We *can* eradicate the fear and hate that politicians such as Gingrich have cynically exploited. In his recent remark that it's "absurd" to consider a gay couple a family, Gingrich himself unintentionally summed up what should be our chief task in the years ahead: to work at the level of home and workplace, church and school board, neighborhood and city hall to bring together in the minds of straight Americans the institution they claim to cherish above all (namely, the family) and the phenomenon that many of them most passionately despise (homosexuality). If we can do that, everything else will follow, and the more we succeed in replacing ignorance with understanding and prejudice with acceptance, the less reason we'll have to feel threatened as gay people by transfers of congressional power from one party to the other.

JOHN W. BERRESFORD

John W. Berresford is an attorney in Washington, D.C., and specializes in the application of antitrust law to telecommunications. He hold degrees in Russian and law, and he has published extensively in those fields as well as in legal history, future interests, and oil and gas law reform in the former Soviet Union. The following article, which appeared in the *Washington Post*'s Sunday "Outlook" section on June 11, 1995, is his first foray into gay issues.

A GAY RIGHT AGENDA

I am gay and have been in the gay rights movement since I came out in 1981. I am also a conservative, a libertarian.

Sad to say, the gay rights movement has always been seen as being on the political left, as one more whining interest group claiming entitlement to all sorts of special treatment from the government. Or we are seen as having a simply fabulous time cavorting at Gay Pride parades and throwing condoms at Catholic services. Whether as crybabies or as Dionysian celebrants, we always appear outside the mainstream.

I cringe at both images. Most gay men and women do not go around demanding government favors or living a hedonistic "gay lifestyle." But just enough of us act out these images, or tolerate them, that they become real in the public mind. Middle America feels uncomfortable about this, at the very least. Our right-wing enemies love it, because it gives them someone to hate and someone to use as a foil for attracting mainstream support to their own causes. By accepting, and in some cases cultivating, these images, we lose friends and help our enemies.

As a conservative, I wish such images would evaporate. If there was ever a time when they made sense, on grounds of either truthfulness or usefulness, it ended when the Republicans took control of Congress. The waiting line for government benefits now leads nowhere, and public frolics now gain nothing but disapproval.

What can government give gays? Merely the form, not the substance, of what we need and want. What we are really after is not merely legal rights but acceptance into the mainstream of American life—and acceptance is granted or withheld by the mainstream majority at its pleasure. If we want to be accepted, we must be welcomed. Lord knows it's easier to change the votes of a few legislators than the hearts and minds of millions of our fellow citizens. But politicians are weathervanes; they are not the wind.

So we should end some of our present practices:

- We should loudly reject all "compensatory" agendas: hiring quotas, affirmative action, and group reparations—all of which I've heard advocated for "when we get our rights." The people who benefit most from such programs are the bureaucrats who administer them and the members of the "victim" groups with the best political connections.
- We should stop pressing for "domestic partners" legislation. It creates a special class of rights for a small class of people. The real beneficiaries would be the lawyers who would litigate the

differences and similarities between domestic partnership and marriage.

- We should not hate Jesse Helms, Pat Robertson and their allies. Leave the hating to them. They will eventually destroy themselves, as Joe McCarthy and other haters did.
- We should stop feeling sorry for ourselves. We may be victims, but frankly no one cares. This country's wellsprings of liberal guilt began running dry about twenty years ago, and by now they are flat empty.
- Finally, we should stop seeing AIDS as anybody else's problem. The sad fact is that every gay man who got AIDS by sex got it from another gay man, and by doing something he chose to do. People with AIDS deserve sympathy, but it is the sympathy one extends to a chain smoker who comes down with lung cancer. It is not the same kind of sympathy one feels for someone who was struck by lightning or run down by a drunk driver.

But that's enough on the negative side. What positive actions can we take?

- For starters, each of us should come out whenever it is reasonably safe. The best way to explode the myths about us is for each of us to become known as just another human being with the same needs, goals, and drives as other human beings—except in a single respect that poses no threat to anyone else.
- Our legislative goal should be for civil rights legislation with disclaimers of any quotas, guidelines, reparations, or government-imposed and group-based remedies. It should emphasize private lawsuits for damages rather than enforcement by a bureaucracy.
- In the legislatures, we should also lobby for the right to marry. Domestic-partners legislation makes us an officially sanctioned class of oddities and freaks. By seeking marriage, we demon-

strate our wish to be part of the great American middle-class way of life.

- Among ourselves, we must be willing to talk about morals, to impose them on ourselves, and to do so conspicuously. As long as our primary image is one of gleeful promiscuity—an image promoted not only by our enemies but also by our own magazines and our own bars—we will be ostracized. Until we start imposing honesty, fidelity, and emotion on our lives—in other words, until we are willing to talk about moral standards—we will make little real progress in social acceptance.

In a curious way, AIDS itself may be helping us find social acceptance. This terrible disease has brought to a screeching halt—at least in my generation of gay men—the manic boozing, drugging, and screwing of the '70s and '80s. It has forced us to attend more to friendships, stability, and the consequences of our actions. It has opened us to human suffering; one friend told me that caring for someone with AIDS was the first unselfish thing he had done in his adult life. AIDS has enabled us to show, to ourselves and to the mainstream, that we too are capable of great suffering, compassion, work, and sacrifice. By our work with each other, we have shown mainstream society what we have to offer it, and how much it loses and wastes by excluding us.

The common theme of all this is simply facing the facts, working to bring out the best in ourselves and offering something admirable to the mainstream. All these views put me in odd company politically. But if you had to agree about everything with everyone else in an organization before you could join it, we'd have 260 million political parties in this country. Conservatives are the people I happen to agree with most of the time. At least they are attempting to deal with the moral issues of our time (such as welfare dependency and violence) on a moral plane, and not as something for which the only remedy is another government program and more spending.

After I come out to them, I find that most conservatives are perfectly tolerant (and not as cloyingly condescending as my liberal straight friends). The Helmses and Robertsons are in the minority. And it eventually dawns on the conservatives that if they want to keep the support of gays like me, they had better keep at least a distance between themselves and the haters.

Finally, moving in conservative circles permits me to ask my conservative friends where this country would be without those great gays—Whittaker Chambers, J. Edgar Hoover, Walt Whitman, and Cardinal Spellman. It's a polite way to remind them that we have been in their midst and doing good deeds from the beginning.

My liberal friends tend to employ three styles of attack on my views. The first is ad hominem: How can you talk about morality when we all know that once you did this or that randy deed? My answer is that (a) the fact that your first response is to attack the messenger (me) shows that you can't repel the message; and (b) I had my adolescence like everyone else, and it's over.

My liberal friends' second attack is some variation on "Do you mean that you're against all attempts to right the wrongs that have been done to us?" My answer is that I am as much in favor of basic civil rights for gays as they are. Where we differ is in the need for group-based remedies and in perceiving ourselves as victims whose main recourse should be coercion by the government.

The third attack from my liberal friends is usually some form of "Well, you have a good point, but. . . ." At that, I know I've made some progress.

I have a feeling there are many more conservative gays than there seem to be. The time is ripe for us to leave the plantation of liberal government and start acting like what we are—a group of adults who want to live lives as normal and as healthy as everyone else in the mainstream. If we do, I think we will be on the path to my dream—an America in which being gay is no more remarkable than being left-handed.

SECTION III

BEYOND OPPRESSION

Where do gay people stand in relation to the society in which they live? Where can gay people reasonably aspire to go in that society, and how should they try to get there? What do we need to think about—and do—in order to effect meaningful change in the lives of gay people in society? What, indeed, will *constitute* meaningful change?

The queer establishment has traditionally offered a monolithic set of answers to these questions: gay people, by definition, stand on the outside of mainstream society; instead of reasonable aspirations, they have utopian dreams; in place of lucidly articulated thoughts about change, they have a prefabricated set of subversive, mix-and-match slogans about oppression and victimhood.

In recent years, however, more and more writers on gay politics have refused to accept an alienated role, to embrace utopian dreams, or to echo mind-numbing slogans. Instead, they have done serious, original thinking about society with a mind to discovering practical solutions to the problem of prejudice. They have probed into previously uncharted territory and posed previously unasked questions.

The essays in this section are representative of this new direction. They reflect, among other things, a lively concern with defining terms, with clarifying long-standing confusions, with understanding the hard realities behind such oft-bandied-about words as *prejudice* and *oppression, victimhood* and *rights, tolerance* and *acceptance.* Through decades of mechanical and sloganeering use, these and other terms have not only been reduced to the level of clichés but have, indeed, made it harder to think and talk in a useful, productive way about the place of gay men and lesbians in society. Putting slogans aside, the authors of these essays want to know how people in Western society today really relate to one another, how the barriers of ideology and bigotry can be surmounted, and how sensible, workable political strategies can realistically be forged.

A Paul Varnell column not included here typifies these essays' pragmatic approach. Entitled "How to Create Tolerance," the column suggests that gay activists "be required to offer for each of their efforts . . . a *psychological impact statement*" that explains "what they expect the psychological impact of any action will be—how it will promote tolerance, understanding, and empathy among the people who are its main targets, as well as among onlookers and those who see it on television." Of special interest to both Varnell and Jonathan Rauch are hate-crime laws and speech codes, which queer-establishment leaders have traditionally upheld and which these two writers deplore.

JONATHAN RAUCH

Rauch is the author of *Kindly Inquisitors: The New Attacks on Free Thought,* in which he writes as an openly gay advocate of free speech, and of *Demosclerosis: The Silent Killer of American Government.* His essays have appeared in the *National Journal,* the *New Republic,* the *Atlantic Monthly, Harper's,* the *New York Times,* and the *Wall Street Journal.* A native of Phoenix, Arizona, he spent most of 1995 as a visiting correspondent for the *Economist* in London. The following essay appeared in the *New Republic* on 7 October 1991.

THOUGHT CRIMES

Mayor David Dinkins marched with the gay contingent this year in New York's St. Patrick's Day parade. Michael Burke, a thirty-year-old resident of New Jersey, threw a can of beer at him. Burke missed, thus avoiding a felonious assault charge. Instead he was charged with reckless endangerment and disorderly conduct. Because the crime was deemed bias-related, and because it was Burke's first offense, the prosecutors recommended, and the defendant and the judge accepted, what's known as an alternative sentence: forty hours of community service in the New York Mayor's Office for the Lesbian and Gay Community.

Burke might have gone to jail, surely an appropriate sentence for a man who tried to brain a public official. He might have done community service at a head-trauma clinic, where he could see the consequences of violent acts like his own. Instead he was sent to work with gays. This penalty makes sense only as a corrective for his repugnant attitude toward homosexuals.

Hardly anyone seems to share my dismay. The *New York Times* article about the sentence carried the approving headline: "Beer-Flinger Sent to a Fitting Cooler." At the Sentencing Project in Washington, assistant director Marc Mauer says that such sentences may help prevent violent acts in the future. "I think we do have a responsibility, purely from a crime-control point of view, to confront the causes of his action." Matt Foreman, the executive director of the Gay and Lesbian Anti-Violence Project in New York, said he was thrilled with the sentence.

Should prejudice, which often leads to injustice, be punished? Should hate, which often leads to violence, be a crime? More and more well-meaning Americans are now saying yes to both questions. It's the wrong answer. I say this despite being a member of the class that Burke allegedly sought to denigrate. The minority-led march toward attitude activism and prejudice policing is dangerous and counterproductive.

To see why, consider separately the two component issues in the beer-can incident. One, a man hurled a dangerous object at a public official. Two, he did this because ostensibly—he denied it—he was prejudiced against homosexuals. Obviously the act of violence deserves punishment. The hard question is: What do you do about the prejudice that lay behind the act?

One option is the by-now-familiar inculcation of tolerance—racial, sexual, cultural—being pursued in universities around the country. Everyone has heard the stories. A University of Michigan student who makes a tasteless joke is required to attend gay-sensitivity sessions and publish a piece of self-criticism called "Learned My Lesson." The University of Maine posts messages on the inside of bathroom stall doors: "Sexual harassment is not defined by the intentions of the accused . . . [but] by the effect on the victim." People for the American Way, a liberal group originally founded to counter the thought-policing influence of right-wing fundamentalists, recently issued a report urging universities to combat prejudice even "when there have been few, if any, overt expressions of intolerance on campus."

The campus efforts to stamp out prejudice have been failing egregiously and noisily, just as they should. Universities' business is to test prejudices in debate, not to regulate them. But short of hard-core political correctness is a compromise approach, one that is much harder to object to. This is the hate-crimes approach. It says that prejudice by itself should not be punished, but prejudice together with violence should be.

There's something to be said for hate-crimes laws. The argument is that crimes such as cross burnings are a threat directed against a whole class, and a vulnerable class at that. Clearly, throwing a swastika-emblazoned rock through a synagogue window is not the same as throwing any old rock through any old window. More and more state legislatures agree. At least two-thirds of them, according to the Anti-Defamation League, have adopted statutes against hate crimes. For instance, Michigan's law specifies up to two years in prison and up to $5,000 in fines for "ethnic intimidation," in which a person assaults, vandalizes, or threatens "with specific intent to intimidate or harass another person because of that person's race, color, religion, gender, or national origin."

The trouble is that in practice such laws come close to criminalizing prejudice. Ohio passed an "ethnic intimidation" law, which deems crimes more serious if committed "by reason of the race, color, religion, or national origin of another person or group of persons." This verges on making what a defendant says or believes about race a part of the crime—and, as a state appellate court pointed out in overturning the law, it "vests virtual complete discretion in the hands of the state to determine whether a suspect committed the alleged acts based on . . . race, color, religion, or national origin." A St. Paul, Minnesota, ordinance (also under challenge) goes a step further: the law makes it a misdemeanor to place "on public or private property a symbol, object, appellation, characterization, or graffiti, including but not limited to a burning cross or Nazi swastika, which one knows or has reasonable grounds to know arouses anger, alarm, or resentment in others on the basis of race, color, creed, or religion." This seems to say that it's a hate crime to upset someone. In Florida a black man has been charged under the state's hate-crime law for calling a white policeman a "cracker."

Why shouldn't the law be used to combat destructive attitudes? For instance, why shouldn't a violent racist be sentenced to work for the NAACP, where he can confront the humanity of the people he hates? Why shouldn't a swastika-scrawler be sentenced to study the Holocaust?

First, because forced reeducation rarely works. A lot of governments have tried it, and the results are to be seen in the rubble of communism.

Second, because the biggest problem in America today—for minorities and non-minorities alike—is not racism, prejudice, homophobia, or what have you. It's also not drugs, medical underinsurance, or even poverty. It's violence. Young black men face more risk in the streets of Chicago's South Side and Los Angeles's Watts than American soldiers faced in Vietnam. Hate-crimes activists argue that bias-motivated crime deserves special handling because it is especially harmful to society. But they have a hard time explaining why this is so. Why is it more terrorizing or socially destabilizing to stab someone because he's Jewish, for instance, than to stab someone for his sneakers? The former signals that Jews are in danger; the latter signals that everyone is in danger. And there's an insidious cost to coming down especially hard on violence that's linked to bias, drugs, or other secondary ills. Necessarily, if you say that assault motivated by bias is especially objectionable, you also say that assault not motivated by bias is less objectionable. Tying the fight against violence to other political agendas clutters and compromises what needs to be a clarion message: violence is intolerable, period.

Third, and most important, because the goal itself is misguided. The ADL, in a 1988 report, said, "Importantly, laws which more severely punish violent manifestations of anti-Semitism and bigotry demonstrate the country's resolve to work toward the elimination of prejudice." For private groups such as the ADL and the NAACP, as well as for parents and preachers, "elimination of prejudice" is indeed a worthy goal. But different groups will have different ideas of what constitutes "prejudice." (Is secular humanism prejudice against Christians? Is Afrocentrism prejudice against whites?) That is why eliminating prejudice is exactly what "the country"—meaning its governmental authorities—must *not* resolve to do. Not only is wiping out bias and hate impossible in principle, in practice "eliminating prejudice" through force of law means eliminating all but one prejudice—that of whoever is most politically powerful.

Personally, being both Jewish and gay, I do not expect everybody to like me. I expect some people to hate me. I fully intend to hate those people back. I will criticize and excoriate them. But I will not hurt them, and I insist that they not hurt me. I want unequivocal, no-buts protection from violence and vandalism. But that's enough. I do not want policemen and judges inspecting opinions.

I think it's ironic and a little sad that gays, of all people, would endorse a criminal sentence that has overtones of forced reeducation. Homosexuals know a thing or two about being sent for therapy or reeducation to have their attitudes straightened out. Jews, too, know something about courts that decide whose belief is "hateful." As on campus, so in the courtroom: the best protection for minorities is not prejudice police but public criticism—genuine intellectual pluralism, in which bigots, too, have their say. Minorities above all should be worrying about Michael Burke's sentence.

JONATHAN RAUCH

The following essay appeared in the *New Republic* on 10 May 1993.

BEYOND OPPRESSION

At 10:30 on a weeknight in the spring of 1991, Glenn Cashmore was walking to his car on San Diego's University Avenue. He had just left the Soho coffee house in Hillcrest, a heavily gay neighborhood. He turned down Fourth Street and paused to look at the display in an optician's window. Someone shouted, "Hey, faggot!" He felt pain in his shoulder and turned in time to see a white Nissan speeding away. Someone had shot him, luckily only with a pellet gun. The pellet tore through the shirt and penetrated the skin. He went home and treated the wound with peroxide.

Later that year, on the night of December 13, a seventeen-year-old named John Wear and two other boys were headed to the Soho on University Avenue when a pair of young men set upon them, calling them "faggots." One boy escaped, another's face was gashed, and Wear (who, his family said, was not gay) was stabbed. Cashmore went to the hospital to see him but, on arriving, was met with the news that Wear was dead.

This is life—not all of life, but an aspect of life—for gay people in today's America. Homosexuals are objects of scorn for teenagers and of sympathy or moral fear or hatred for adults. They grow up in confusion and bewilderment as children, then often pass into denial as young adults and sometimes remain frightened even into old age. They are persecuted by the military, are denied the sanctuary of publicly recognized marriage, occasionally are prosecuted outright for making love. If closeted, they live with fear of revelation; if open, they must daily negotiate a hundred delicate tactical issues. (Should I bring it up? Tell my boss? My coworkers? Wear a wedding band? Display my lover's picture?)

There is also AIDS and the stigma attached to it, though AIDS is not uniquely a problem of gay people. And there is the violence. One of my high-school friends—an honors student at Brophy Prep, a prestigious Catholic high school in Phoenix—used to boast about his late-night exploits with a baseball bat at the "fag Denny's." I'm sure he was lying, but imagine the horror of being spoken to, and about, in that way.

If you ask gay people in America today whether homosexuals are oppressed, I think most would say yes. If you ask why, they would point to the sorts of facts that I just mentioned. The facts are not blinkable. Yet the oppression diagnosis is, for the most part, wrong.

Not wrong in the sense that life for American homosexuals is hunky-dory. It is not. But life is not terrible for most gay people, either, and it is becoming less terrible every year. The experience of gayness and the social status of homosexuals have changed rapidly in the last twenty years, largely owing to the courage of thousands who decided that they had had enough abuse and who demanded better. With change has come the time for a reassessment.

The standard political model sees homosexuals as an oppressed minority who must fight for their liberation through political action.

But that model's usefulness is drawing to a close. It is ceasing to serve the interests of ordinary gay people, who ought to begin disengaging from it, even drop it. Otherwise, they will misread their position and lose their way, as too many minority groups have done already.

"Oppression" has become every minority's word for practically everything, a one-size-fits-all political designation used by anyone who feels unequal, aggrieved, or even uncomfortable. I propose a start toward restoring meaning to the notion of oppression by insisting on *objective* evidence. A sense of grievance or discomfort, however real, is not enough.

By now, human beings know a thing or two about oppression. Though it may, indeed, take many forms and work in different ways, there are objective signs you can look for. My own list would emphasize five main items. First, direct legal or governmental discrimination. Second, denial of political franchise—specifically, denial of the right to vote, organize, speak, or lobby. Third—and here we move beyond the strictly political—the systematic denial of education. Fourth, impoverishment relative to the non-oppressed population. And, fifth, a pattern of human rights violations, without recourse.

Any one or two of those five signposts may appear for reasons other than oppression. There are a lot of reasons why a people may be poor, for instance. But where you see a minority that is legally barred from businesses and neighborhoods and jobs, that cannot vote, that is poor and poorly educated and that lives in physical fear, you are looking at, for instance, the blacks of South Africa, or blacks of the American South until the 1960s; the Jews and homosexuals of Nazi Germany and Vichy France; the untouchable castes of India, the Kurds of Iraq, the women of Saudi Arabia, the women of America one hundred years ago; for that matter, the entire population of the former Soviet Union and many Arab and African and Asian countries.

And gay people in America today? Criterion one—direct legal or governmental discrimination—is resoundingly met. Homosexual relations are illegal in twenty-three states, at least seven of which specifically single out acts between persons of the same sex. Gay marriage is not legally recognized anywhere. And the government hounds gay people from the military, not for what they do but for what they are.

Criterion two—denial of political franchise—is resoundingly not met. Not only do gay people vote, they are turning themselves into a constituency to be reckoned with and fought for. Otherwise, the Patrick Buchanans of the world would have sounded contemptuous of gay people at the Republican convention last year, rather than panicked by them. If gay votes didn't count, Bill Clinton would not have stuck his neck out on the military issue during the primary season (one of the bravest things any living politician has done).

Criterion three—denial of education—is also resoundingly not met. Overlooked Opinions Inc., a Chicago market-research company, has built a diverse national base of 35,000 gay men and lesbians, two-thirds of whom are either not out of the closet or are only marginally out, and has then randomly sampled them in surveys. It found that homosexuals had an average of 15.7 years of education, as against 12.7 years for the population as a whole. Obviously, the findings may be skewed if college-educated gay people are likelier to take part in surveys (though Overlooked Opinions said that results didn't follow degree of closetedness). Still, any claim that gay people are denied education appears ludicrous.

Criterion four—relative impoverishment—is also not met. In Overlooked Opinions' sample, gay men had an average household income of $51,624 and lesbians $42,755, compared with the national average of $36,800. Again, yuppie homosexuals may be more likely to answer survey questions than blue-collar ones.

But, again, to call homosexuals an impoverished class would be silly.

Criterion five—human rights violations without recourse—is also, in the end, not met, though here it's worth taking a moment to see why it is not. The number of gay bashings has probably increased in recent years (though it's hard to know, what with reporting vagaries), and, of course, many gay-bashers either aren't caught or aren't jailed. What too many gay people forget, though, is that these are problems that homosexuals have in common with non-gay Americans. Though many gay-bashers go free, so do many murderers. In the District of Columbia last year, the police identified suspects in fewer than half of all murders, to say nothing of assault cases.

And the fact is that anti-gay violence is just one part of a much broader pattern. Probably not coincidentally, the killing of John Wear happened in the context of a year, 1991, that broke San Diego's all-time homicide record (1992 was the runner-up). Since 1965 the homicide rate in America has doubled, and the violent crime arrest rate for juveniles has more than tripled; people now kill you to get your car, they kill you to get your shoes or your potato chips, they kill you because they can do it. A particularly ghastly fact is that homicide due to gunshot is now the second leading cause of death in high-school-age kids, after car crashes. No surprise, then, that gay people are afraid. So is everyone else.

Chances are, indeed, that gay people's social class makes them safer, on average, than other urban minorities. Certainly their problem is small compared with what blacks face in inner-city Los Angeles or Chicago, where young black males are likelier to be killed than a U.S. soldier was in a tour of duty in Vietnam.

If any problem unites gay people with non-gay people, it is crime. If any issue does not call for special-interest pleading, this is it. Minority advocates, including gay ones, have blundered insensitively by trying to carve out hate-crime statutes and other special-interest crime laws instead of focusing on tougher measures against violence of all kinds. In trying to sensitize people to crimes aimed specifically at minorities, they are inadvertently desensitizing them to the vastly greater threat of crime against everyone. They contribute to the routinization of murder, which has now reached the point where news of a black girl spray-painted white makes the front pages, but news of a black girl murdered runs in a roundup on page D6 ("Oh, another killing"). Yes, gay-bashing is a problem. But, no, it isn't oppression. It is, rather, an obscenely ordinary feature of the American experience.

Of course, homosexuals face unhappiness, discrimination, and hatred. But for everyone with a horror story to tell, there are others like an academic I know, a tenured professor who is married to his lover of fourteen years in every way but legally, who owns a split-level condo in Los Angeles, drives a Miata, and enjoys prestige and success and love that would be the envy of millions of straight Americans. These things did not fall in his lap. He fought personal and professional battles, was passed over for jobs, and left the closet when that was much riskier than it is today. Asked if he is oppressed, he says, "You're damn straight." But a mark of oppression is that most of its victims are not allowed to succeed; they are allowed only to fail. And this man is no mere token. He is one of a growing multitude of openly gay people who have overcome the past and, in doing so, changed the present.

"I'm a gay person, so I don't live in a free country," one highly successful gay writer said recently, "and I don't think most straight people really sit down and realize that for gay people this is basically a totalitarian society in which we're barely tolerated." The reason straight people don't realize this is because it obviously isn't true. As more and more homosexuals come out of hiding, the reality of gay economic and political and educational achievement becomes more evident. And as that happens, gay people who insist they are oppressed will increasingly, and not always unfairly, come off as yuppie whiners, "victims" with $50,000 incomes and vacations in Europe. They may feel they are oppressed, but they will have a harder and harder time convincing the public.

They will distort their politics, too, twisting it into strained and impotent shapes. Scouring for oppressions with which to identify, activists are driven further and further afield. They grab fistfuls of random political demands and stuff them in their pockets. The original platform for April's March on Washington called for, among other things, enforced bilingual education, "an end to genocide of all the indigenous peoples and their cultures," defense budget cuts, universal health care, a national needle exchange program, free substance-abuse treatment on demand, safe and affordable abortion, more money for breast cancer "and other cancers particular to women," "unrestricted, safe and affordable alternative insemination," health care for the "differently-abled and physically challenged" and "an end to poverty." Here was the oppression-entitlement mentality gone haywire.

Worst of all, oppression politics distorts the face of gay America itself. It encourages people to forget that homosexuality isn't hell. As the AIDS crisis has so movingly shown, gay people have built the kind of community that evaporated for many non-gay Americans decades ago. You don't see straight volunteers queuing up to change cancer patients' bedpans and deliver their groceries. Gay people—and unmarried people generally—are at a disadvantage in the top echelons of corporate America, but, on the other hand, they have achieved dazzlingly in culture and business and much else. They lead lives of richness and competence and infinite variety, lives that are not miserable or squashed.

The insistence that gay people are oppressed is most damaging, in the end, because it implies that to be gay is to suffer. It affirms what so many straight people, even sympathetic ones, believe in their hearts: that homosexuals are pitiable. That alone is reason to junk the oppression model, preferably sooner instead of later.

If the oppression model is failing, what is the right model? Not that of an oppressed people seeking redemption through political action; rather, that of an ostracized people seeking redemption through personal action. What do you do about misguided ostracism? The most important thing is what Glenn Cashmore did. After John Wear's murder, he came out of the closet. He wrote an article in the *Los Angeles Times* denouncing his own years of silence. He stepped into the circle of people who are what used to be called known homosexuals.

This makes a difference. The *New York Times* conducted a poll on homosexuals this year and found that people who had a gay family member or close friend "were much more tolerant and accepting." Whereas oppression politics fails because it denies reality, positive personal example works because it demonstrates reality. "We're here, we're queer, get used to it," Queer Nation's chant, is not only a brilliant slogan. It is a strategy. It is, in some ways, *the* strategy. To move away from oppression politics is not to sit quietly. It is often to hold hands in public or take a lover to the company Christmas party, sometimes to stage kiss-ins, always to be unashamed. It is to make of honesty a kind of activism.

Gay Americans should emulate Jewish Americans, who have it about right. Jews recognize that to many Americans we will always seem different (and we are, in some ways, different). We grow up being fed "their" culture in school, in daily life, even in the calendar. It never stops. For a full month of every year, every radio program and shop window reminds you that this is, culturally, a Christian nation (no, not Judeo-Christian). Jews could resent this, but most of us choose not to, because, by way of compensation, we think hard, we work hard, we are cohesive, and we are interesting. We recognize that minorities will always face special burdens of adjustment, but we also understand that with those burdens come rewards of community and spirit and struggle. We recognize that there will always be a minority of Americans who hate us, but we also understand that, so long as we stay watchful, this hateful minority is more pathetic than threatening. We watch it; we fight it when it lashes out; but we do not organize our personal and political lives around it.

Gay people's main weapons are ones we already possess. In America, our main enemies are superstition and hate. Superstition is extinguished by public criticism and by the power of moral example. Political activists always underestimate the power of criticism and moral example to change people's minds, and they always overestimate the power of law and force. As for hate, the way to fight it is with love. And that we have in abundance.

PAUL VARNELL

This column appeared in the *Windy City Times* on 3 November 1994.

THE NICENESS SOLUTION

Sometimes when I have been walking out to my favorite tavern(s) of an evening. I have been yelled at by a group of boys in a passing car.

"Hey, homo," they yell. Or, sometimes, "Faggot!"

It is disconcerting, even irritating, as they intend it to be irritating. And, of course, depending on one's mood, it can be felt as vaguely threatening.

So it is hard not to sympathize with the motives of the good citizens of Raritan, New Jersey, whose city council recently passed 5-0 a law banning rude behavior, including rude speech.

The new law states that anyone found "behaving in a disorderly way . . . by using profane, vulgar, or indecent language, by making insulting remarks or comments to others" can be fined as much as $500 and jailed for up to ninety days.

Raritan mayor Anthony De Cicco explained the purpose of the law: "All we, the town fathers, are looking for is to maintain civility and the quality of our lives."

The idea of enforcing civility is hardly new, of course. Courtesy codes of various sorts have been tried on several college campuses in recent years. But the earliest example I know of is the one that Michel de Montaigne encountered at the health spa in Plombière during his travels in 1580.

That code read in part, "Be it known that in order to secure the repose and tranquility of sundry ladies and other notable personages assembling from various religions and countries at these baths.

"All persons, of whatever quality [i.e., social level], condition, region, and province they may be, are forbidden to provoke one another by insulting language tending to pick a quarrel, to bear arms . . . to give the lie . . . on pain of being severely punished as disturbers of the peace."

And the code gave special attention to the women of 1580: "All persons are forbidden to use toward the ladies, gentlewomen, or other women and girls who are at the said baths, any lascivious or shameless language."

According to Montaigne's journal, the people of Plombière, whom he describes as "good people, free, sensible, and considerate" each year renew these laws on a tablet in front of the largest bathhouse—in both German and French, since the spa drew patrons from both countries.

There is something deeply touching about these efforts to make people act nice toward one another: it is generous and humane of us to realize that hostile speech can be felt as demeaning to another person's humanity, that it can be psychologically as well as socially harmful. (Although the Plombière bottom line seems to be that rude speech can cause fights.)

But as we keep learning, attempts to force people to behave better generally do not work well, tend to be greatly abused, and equally generally have far greater costs in the long run than benefits.

What Churchill famously said about democracy being the worst form of government except for all the rest could also be said about speech limitations—that "no limits" is the worst except for all the others—and for about the same reasons.

But there are several serious objections to speech limitations besides the obvious fact that they will be struck down by courts on First Amendment grounds.

For one thing, they assume a much clearer line than actually exists between (a) mere information and discussion of issues, and (b) rude, insulting, or hostile remarks or comments to others. One man's information can be another man's defamation. Anti-gay religious groups say they are only attacking "homosexuality," not us as people. But to us (as well as heterosexuals) our sexuality is a constitutive element of who we feel we are as people, and the "disagreement" or argument feels like a personal attack.

In the same way, if I disagree with someone's religious beliefs and argue that the beliefs (e.g., reincarnation, virgin birth, the efficacy of animal sacrifice) are wrong (unscientific, self-contradictory, morally vile, or whatever), a devout person may take offense and claim that their religious beliefs are a constitutive element of their personal identity, of who they are and how they relate to the cosmos. So that when I say their beliefs are false, I am attacking them as a person.

A second problem with speech or niceness codes is that they suffer from a reversal of cause and effect. Whether on a college campus or in society at large, tolerance, understanding, and respect are, to a high degree, the *result* of education and the discussion process, not the precondition or starting point.

No one is born and few grow up with a genuine respect and appreciation for the way others are. Rather it is experience in the world, in the rough and tumble of vigorous and uninhibited discussion, that most people learn how different other people can be and how many interesting and plausible reasons those others can offer for why their way is good or valid. In fact, the whole point of a good old-fashioned liberal education was precisely to try to achieve just such a broad and humane appreciation for the remarkably varied way people have lived and the kinds of greatness of their achievements.

A third problem with niceness codes is that they assume everyone is exquisitely sensitive to disagreement, rudeness, or being disliked, whether the response takes the form of "He criticized my report, and I am just devastated emotionally" or "The dude looked at me wrong, so I wasted him with my AK-47."

"I fall upon the thorns of life, I bleed," said Shelley's Sensitive Plant. But we do not even try to orient a family to such sensitivities. Rather than preserve and foster such infirmity, our response should be: Grow a skin. Grow up, for goodness sake. Why are you overreacting? Why are you letting other people's speech get to you? Ignore it. Laugh at it.

A final objection to speech codes is that they embody the notion of government *in loco parentis*—in the place of parents, as the ultimate "nanny," treating "its" citizens as if they were children to be trained and shaped or puppies to be housebroken. The doctrine is as popular on the left, where it is embodied in the utopian dream of creating the "new Socialist man," as it is on the right, where it is embodied in the title of columnist George Will's book *Statecraft As Soulcraft*.

Ultimately, niceness codes express an exasperation with the inevitable tensions among the people and groups that exist in any large and diverse society. They reflect a primitive longing for uniform and placid citizens none of whom wants anything very much, nor who disagree very strongly about anything only because nothing is very important to them.

Sensibly, Raritan Police Chief Joseph Sferro said he would not enforce the new ordinance.

MEL DAHL

Dahl is a Boston attorney and writer. After he was involuntarily discharged from the U.S. Navy for being gay, he went to law school and then sued that military branch over its anti-gay policy; he is the only military plaintiff to have represented himself before the U.S. Court of Appeals on this issue. He now practices domestic relations and general litigation law in Boston. The author of a syndicated column carried by approximately twenty gay publications nationally and of the legal advice column for *Bear* magazine, Dahl conducts seminars on the legal rights of gay people and is a recipient of the 1993 Liberty Award from the Lambda Legal Defense and Education Fund. The following essay appeared in *Bay Windows,* a gay newspaper published in Boston, on 10 March 1994.

NO 'SPECIAL RIGHTS' FOR ANYBODY

Whenever I hear that about "no special rights for gays," I'd like to know just what special rights they are talking about. But let's let that pass for the moment.

On the other hand, let's not. Because defining our terms may enable us to find the creative solution that we need.

As anyone who has been gay for more than ten minutes is aware, the notion that gay people have, or want, special rights is ludicrous. Just a cursory glance at our legal system compels the conclusion that it is heterosexuals who have a whole plethora of special rights: the right to legal recognition for their relationships, the right to serve in the military without lying about who they are, the right to raise their own children without fear that somebody will take their children because of who they are, the right to not have employers and landlords poke around in their private business. Gay people have none of these rights in most places, and in many places still have the legal status of criminal.

In fact, the worst example of this inequality is in the area of relationships: when straight people marry, they automatically get a long list of rights that include the right to be consulted and informed about their partner's policies, the right to inherit if the partner should die without a will, the right to be considered a social unit, the right to death benefits and social security benefits, etc. Not only do gay people not get these things automatically as a matter of right, some of them are not available at all and others only by jumping through lots of legal hoops.

Thus, the idea that gay people somehow seek special rights is more than ludicrous: it is an utterly breathtaking example of hypocrisy.

There is a solution, and it has been staring me in the face for so long that I'm dumbstruck that I have missed it for so long. It will shut our opponents' mouths and remove their foundation from beneath them. It will be the end of probably three-quarters of their blather. And it may even work.

What we have done to this point is seek passage of laws adding sexual orientation to the list of categories protected by anti-discrimination laws. (Except for domestic partnership laws in some places, we haven't even started the task of equalizing governmental recognition of our relationships.) The problem with this approach is that middle America has always been suspicious that all of these civil rights laws are simply special rights for people who fit the categories on the list. And in fact, most people do support equality but when they see a list of groups protected from discrimination—by race, sex, or sexual orientation—it is easy for heterosexual white males, still the most powerful voting bloc, to view it as a quota system that gives special treatment to minorities.

In fact, I suspect that professional racists could probably argue with equal plausibility that laws which protect blacks from discrimination are "special rights" rather than equal rights.

The solution? Forget all about amending existing civil rights laws. Don't even bother with them; they are a waste of time. Instead, let us concentrate on passing a law that says the following: "Before the law, heterosexuals and homosexuals are equal. Neither heterosexuals nor homosexuals shall be entitled to special rights or treatment because of their sexual orientation. The law shall treat them both the same."

First, that would be the end of right-wing raving about special rights. How could any fundamentalist, who has insisted up until now that all he opposes are special rights, possibly oppose such a law without admitting to being a hypocrite?

Second, in one fell swoop we would have pure equality before the law. The state would have to recognize our relationships; it would have to stay out of our private affairs, and the law would probably cover employment and housing discrimination, although that would require some litigation. Thus we quickly and relatively painlessly obtain the entire "homosexual agenda" rather than doing it piecemeal.

Third, it would appeal to the masses of fair-minded people who really do not oppose equality; they have simply been sold a bill of goods that special rights is what we are after. For quite some time now the only way the right wing has been able to win popular elections against us is by claiming we are after special rights; most people don't have a problem with equal treatment.

We even have a ready-made campaign slogan: "No special rights for heterosexuals."

One of our major premises, after all, is that the law should not be treating anybody more favorably than anyone else. As a gay person, I don't seek special rights before the law; I would be perfectly happy with equality.

In fact, what the gay liberation movement seeks is not to be treated more favorably than straight people, but that straight people not be treated more favorably than us.

We do not seek to be considered superior to heterosexuals and lord it over them. Nor are we willing to have them be considered superior to us. What we seek—and are increasingly unwilling to forgo—is equal footing.

After all, I am more than willing to give up any bid for special rights if straight people will do the same.

STEPHEN H. CHAPMAN

Chapman, a heterosexual columnist for the *Chicago Tribune*, has routinely sought to disentangle legitimate conservative concerns and values from anti-gay prejudice. This column appeared on 27 November 1994.

IF THE VOTERS ARE ANGRY, HOW COME THEY'RE SO TOLERANT?

Peter Jennings's post-mortem on the election was that the "voters had a temper tantrum." *Time* magazine said Newt Gingrich has merely exploited "the politics of anger." Maybe these experts were too angry themselves to see the obvious. They have overlooked abundant evidence that behind the results was a rational and benign impulse to live and let live.

Everyone tells us that the American people were in a nasty mood on November 8th—everyone except the American people. A post-election survey by Republican pollster Frank Luntz asked, "Do you consider yourself an 'angry voter'?" Twenty-five percent of respondents said yes, 71 percent no. Not to belabor the point, but a 71-to-25 margin is a victory for the calm, not the angry.

It is no secret by now that Americans strongly prefer to send a smaller share of each paycheck to Washington and keep more for their own humble uses, even if it means relying less on the eager generosity of Uncle Sam. Democrats were heavily weighed down by Bill Clinton's tax increases and reputation for big spending. They also suffered for his health care plan, which most people feared would not only cost money but install bureaucrats in the operating room.

If distrust of government is conservative, then color Americans conservative. But anyone who thinks this is the same as intolerant, conformist, or narrow-minded—a mistake made not only by many liberals but by some conservatives—is missing the point. In one state after another, voters demonstrated a broad faith in tolerance and a respect for individual choice. When they say they want the government out of their lives, they mean bedrooms as well as bank accounts.

Sentiments about homosexuality, which mortally offends true believers on the right, provide a gauge. Voters not only in liberal Oregon but in Idaho (which last voted Democratic in a presidential election in 1964) rejected anti-gay ballot measures.

The election also brought to 216 the number of out-of-the-closet gays holding various offices around the country. The head of the Gay and Lesbian Victory Fund said that this year, "It was far more hazardous to be an openly Democratic candidate than openly gay and lesbian."

This is in step with a national trend, writes Paul Varnell in Chicago's gay *Windy City Times,* noting that in recent years, opposition to letting gays teach in public schools and serve in the military has declined sharply. A majority now favors both.

Efforts to curb abortion, pornography, and suicide also failed at the ballot box, which may not be quite what the religious right had in mind. Oregonians and Coloradans turned down amendments to their state constitutions that would have unleashed the vice squad on videos and magazines baring too much flesh. Wyomingites took the position that individual freedom includes the right to abortion.

At the other end of the life span, a referendum in Oregon—must have been a long ballot in Oregon this year—made it the first state to let doctors give lethal drugs to patients with fatal diseases who want to hasten the inevitable.

As a lifelong contrarian, I am automatically leery of anyone who suggests that my opinion on anything enjoys popular favor. So it is somewhat reassuring that on abortion and euthanasia, in my view, supporters are misapplying the principle of individual liberty. But I can't deny that they are upholding the right principle. At the heart of those votes is not disdain for life, but reluctance to let the government interfere with a crucial decision.

The same impulse sealed the doom of any number of congressional candidates who had voted for gun control—which proponents advertise as a blow to criminals but which skeptics see as an obstacle only to the law-abiding. One reason for the GOP sweep, especially in the South, was that 69 percent of gun owners voted Republican. Among the victims were such important figures as House Speaker Tom Foley, Oklahoma Rep. Mike Synar, and House Judiciary Committee chairman Jack Brooks.

An electorate that repudiates gun control while accepting homosexuality, that wants something "conservative" like lower taxes but also something "liberal" like the right to suicide, may seem badly confused to those imprisoned in traditional ideological straitjackets. It should not be surprising, though, in a country whose founding document celebrated every person's right to life, liberty, and the pursuit of happiness.

Nor is it inconsistent with a desire to scale back the size, cost, and authority of the government. The message of the election is that Americans want Washington to wield less control over their lives and are ready to accept the responsibilities that go with taking more control themselves. A citizenry accustomed to the comforts and constraints of the nanny state has resolved to try adulthood.

SECTION IV

GAY CULTURE, GAY IDENTITY

In the eyes of the queer establishment, gay people share not only a sexual orientation but a culture, a community, a common identity; they belong to a tribe. For a gay person to criticize the icons of what is called "gay culture," to question the received values of what is known as the "gay community," or to reject the idea that being gay makes one a member of a club with a monolithic set of social and cultural allegiances is to invite attacks from the gay-left establishment.

That establishment's rules are clear: creators and creations that it has recognized as icons of "lesbigay culture" (for example, Tony Kushner, Paul Monette, and Sarah Schulman, but not Edward Albee, James Merrill, or Elizabeth Bishop) are to be applauded; the established view of the "gay community" as an entity defined by its most extreme elements is to be honored; the tribe's official heroes and values are to be regarded as sacrosanct, inviolable, beyond criticism. The gay-left establishment may not have done a good job of teaching straight America about gays, but it has done a highly effective job of instructing many gay people as to how they should and shouldn't think about who they are.

Yet in the last couple of years even longtime spokespeople for "gay culture" and "the gay community" have spoken up against the defining ideas that they once heartily espoused. Early in 1994, gay-establishment writers called me "sex-negative" for noting that many young gay men become promiscuous because they are encouraged by gay culture and the gay community "to believe that that's what one does, what one *must* do." Only a few months later Michelangelo Signorile, author of *Queer in America,* issued a bracing critique of gay culture for teaching young gay men that "sex . . . is the be-all and end-all of being gay," that "it is something they should have as often as possible, even for the wrong reasons."

In the 1980s gay writers, such as the late Randy Shilts, who dared to suggest that bathhouses be closed to prevent the spread of AIDS were depicted in the gay-left press as right-wing, sex-negative traitors to the community. In the mid-1990s, though, Signorile and the columnist Gabriel Rotello, both solid members of the gay-left establishment (and the fathers of the "outing" controversy, on which Andrew Sullivan and David Link comment in the pieces that open this section) mounted a full-scale attack on gay bathhouses with which some of the libertarians represented in the present book would probably disagree.

Among the issues relating to gay culture and identity are those involving groups of people that gay-left activists have brought under the "queer" umbrella. Paul Varnell, in a 1994 column entitled "Gay, Bi, Trans, Drag, Etc.," noted the recent proliferation of "add-ons to the gay liberation movement":

> First, the words *and lesbian* were added on the ground that lesbians had a separate identity and deserved nominal visibility—though that was achieved at some cost to the visibility of women who thought of themselves as "gay."
>
> Then *and bisexual* was added because bisexuals, though sort of gay, were really not quite just "gay."
>
> Last year the National March on Washington made clamorous "de-

> mands" on behalf of "lesbian, gay, bisexual, and transgender" people, *transgender* apparently referring to both transsexual and transvestite.

Varnell acknowledges that "these are all fine people and deserve all kinds of freedom," but asks "how close these various people's concerns are to our own. . . . Are these people in any reasonable sense 'gay' or 'gay and lesbian'? Are their issues ours? Do they experience discrimination because of their sexual orientation?" His answer: No. Most male transvestites, he notes, are heterosexual; so are most transsexuals. To tie these phenomena to homosexuality is to reinforce the fallacious notion, on the part of many straight people, that gay men are men who want to be women or to dress up as women.

What of bisexuals? In a 1995 article for the *New York Native,* I addressed the sudden widespread interest in bisexuality, giving particular attention to the popular notion among queer academics and writers that sexual orientation is fluid—that, deep down, we're all bisexual. I argued that this notion (which is, of course, philosophically related to the fluidity of the term *queer*) is deeply problematic.

> It can be morally compelling for a gay person to tell a straight person, "This is the way I am made to love!" It is less morally compelling for a self-identified bi to say, "Well, this is what I feel like doing this week." P-FLAG [Parents and Friends of Lesbians and Gays, an organization] struggles to help gay kids' parents to say, "I accept my child because this is what he (or she) is." If trend-happy academics and journalists can convince such parents that we're all essentially bisexual, then what happens to that kind of parental understanding? "You're not gay," one imagines a concerned parent telling a kid. "You're bi. You're just as capable of finding fulfillment with the opposite sex as with the same sex. So cut out this gay stuff pronto!"

The bottom line, I concluded, was that "in order to educate straight Americans about the nature of sexual orientation, we need clarity, truth, integrity. We don't need modish academic fetishization of ambiguity—or insipid mass-media glamorizing of people who can't face who they really are."

After a long silence, in short, queer-establishment constructions of gay culture, gay community, and gay identity are being shaken up all over.

ANDREW SULLIVAN

This piece appeared as a "Washington Diarist" item in the *New Republic* on 9 September 1991.

SLEEPING WITH THE ENEMY

In all the recent brouhaha over the "outing" of alleged homosexuals, one fallacy has remained virtually unchallenged. It's the notion of a simple "closet" and the crude assertion that one is either in it or out of it. I know of no one to whom this applies. Most homosexuals and lesbians whose sexualities are developed beyond adolescence are neither "in" nor "out." They hover tentatively somewhere in between. And most outings are not essentially about dragging someone out of anything. They are crude assertions about invariably complex people that have very little to do with the nature of someone's sexuality, and all to do with who controls the disclosure of it. Properly understood, outing is not a resolution of something, a final act. It's when the intricate steering of self-disclosure, with which every homosexual is intimately familiar, is suddenly seized by someone else, when one's ability to describe oneself, one's freedom to say who one is, is peremptorily taken away.

Most gay lives, by virtue of the culture we live in, know dozens of such moments of powerlessness. I remember in my early twenties being casually asked in the back seat of a car by an open-minded acquaintance, "Are you gay?" and not being able to answer yes or no. The question was as benign as it comes, but the effect was temporarily terrifying. The panic, for most homosexuals, periodically returns: when the subject crops up, and the throat becomes intolerably dry; when the insult is hurled across the street, and shame mysteriously returns. What's worse is that one is complicit in such moments: without a sense of embarrassment, there would be no loss of power, no handing over of control. But the trauma is real nonetheless. It is the sense of asphyxiation you feel when someone defines you without your consent.

This element of uncontrol, of course, is not exclusive to homosexuals. The racial slur has a similar effect. It demeans a person because it defines him against his own particular self-image. The word *nigger* stings because it hammers an intricate human achievement into a communal blur. It erases dignity because it denies individuality. But with homosexuals, this expression of contempt can find a way of sounding legitimate. Because homosexuality is largely invisible, the act of control can often be disguised as an act of revelation. Declaring someone gay can come in the guise of news; it can be sanctified with the mantle of fact. And what, after all, can be wrong with a fact? And who can oppose it, except those who are themselves "homophobic," who choose the hypocrisy generated by shame over the liberation afforded by fact?

In the world of intimacy, however, there are few such facts. Human sexuality is too mysterious and too fluid to be reduced to such simplicities. Honesty can destroy relationships; candor in the affairs of the heart is almost always a means to assert some sort of control. And there is little moral difference between a straight person forcing one to hide one's identity and a gay person forcing one to declare it. But the most disturbing element of the outing craze is not simply that it is initiated by gay people—whose lives, one might think, would be testimony to the cruelty of others' control—but that it is done in the name of political conformity. All the targets have been gay people at odds with the agenda of fringe activists. All have been justified as ways of exposing "hypocrisy" but have, in fact, been ways of enforcing control. A recent outing, for example, was of a congressman who had a 100 percent legislative rating from a leading gay group but still failed to please one particular activist. In New York a politician felt obliged to declare that he was HIV-positive after a mounting whispering campaign to that effect. In another case a man was outed for whom there was no proof of his hostility to homosexuals, and some evidence that he may have been doing good, but who was employed by an institution that is anathema to the outers—the Pentagon—and so was fair game. No crimes were cited, except an imputation of cowardice. Regardless of his own motives, the taint of collaboration (he is a civilian in the Defense Department) was enough. In one last-resort defense of the outing, a leading gay activist actually said: "[His] silence in the last couple of years has hurt us. And I think his silence now is hurting us." His *silence?*

There are times and places, to be sure, when silence is indeed a culpable act, and the way in which the Pentagon treats gay and lesbian soldiers in its ranks is a disgrace—brutal in its bigotry, callous in its effect, as this magazine has repeatedly pointed out. But the sacrifice of another gay man, deemed "guilty" before proved "innocent," as an indirect means to undermine the policy requires an ethic of a peculiarly twisted kind. One is reminded of Orwell's remark about the morality of those "always somewhere else when the trigger is pulled." One is also reminded of all those other political movements around the world in which silence is invariably an unacceptable form of conduct. They demand an active, even eager, participation in a particular politics, a mouthing of certain words, a performance of certain actions. Inaction is the same as treachery; weak souls in the ranks are treated with greater viciousness than any putative enemy. But they have rarely been sympathetic to a liberal society. And they have never been tolerant of homosexuals.

Not so long ago I thought this was an exaggeration about some fringe elements in the gay movement. Whatever the differences among gay men and lesbians, there was always a sense that everyone was essentially on the same side. Now I'm not so sure. It's not so much that, within the gay world, there are now those who have assumed the rhetoric of the historic enemy. Nor even that, in the heat of battle, some have taken to desecrating others' religious beliefs and practices, embracing the very forms of intolerance that homosexuals, of all people, have historically shrunk from. It is that they have attacked the central protection of gay people themselves. They have assailed the ability to choose who one is and how one is presented, to control the moment of self-disclosure and its content. They have declared that the bonds of common sympathy must be sacrificed to ideology, that the complexities of love and loyalty and disclosure can be resolved by the uniformity that is the classical objective of terror. The gleam in the eyes of the outers, I have come reluctantly to understand, is not the excess of youth or the passion of the radical. It is the gleam of the authoritarian.

DAVID LINK

Link, a writer in Los Angeles whose essays have appeared in *Reason,* the *Los Angeles Times, Frontiers,* and *California Lawyer,* has also published a law-review article on the rights of same-sex couples and has contributed to the collection *Positively Gay.* In addition to writing, he practices appellate law in southern California. This essay appears for the first time in *Beyond Queer.*

WHY OUTING DOESN'T WORK

To out or not to out—that was the question that preoccupied lesbians and gay men during the early 1990s. The conundrum made national headlines for a brief time, but the media had other conflicts to exploit, other groups to kibitz. In early 1995 outing flared up again briefly as *Rolling Stone*'s Jann Wenner and the Church of England's Bishop David Hope found their sexual orientation in the news. But the headlines were getting smaller.

Now that the initial storm over outing has died down, it may be time to take a closer look at the controversy and how it fits in the developing history of gay rights. Even though outing remains a controversial subject for the media, and for lesbians and gay men both in and out of the closet, its juice seems to be gone. In large part, this is due to some fundamental misunderstandings about what outing is, and many misplaced hopes about what it could accomplish.

Any discussion of outing begins with Michelangelo Signorile. It isn't necessary to agree with Larry Kramer's dust-jacket hyperbole for Signorile's *Queer in America* ("I consider *Queer in America* to be one of the most important books of the twentieth century") to recognize Signorile as an articulate and thoughtful writer about homosexuality. He is unambiguous in his condemnation of the closet, and in his book he details the extraordinary effort we go to in this culture to believe—sometimes against all the evidence—that a lesbian or gay man is really heterosexual at heart. He provides critical analysis both of heterosexuals who continue to insist on the maintenance of the fiction of the closet, and of lesbians and gay men who submit to and offer their assistance in the fabrication.

But Signorile is most well known for going a step further, defending the outing of closeted lesbians and gay men in certain situations. Signorile is the person most associated with outing, and his defense of it—the most complete offered by anyone—is both thoughtful and, as far as it goes, logical. But somewhere along the line his argument disintegrates. The main reason is that outing fails to take into account the complexity of human identity, and specifically the part that character plays in the decision to acknowledge being homosexual. Outing relies on a false assumption, or at least an arguable one: that it is possible to know objectively who is homosexual. At some point, objective factors such as sexual behavior are not sufficient to make a final determination of a person's sexual orientation; at least part of the latter involves a person's own judgment about how his or her sexual activity, public and private relationships, and romantic attractions fit together within an integrated identity. In short, sexual orientation is not like a birthmark, something capable of clear, external verification. Rather, it is part of a person's subjective self-perception. By definition, that is something that cannot be assigned without consent.

Signorile begins the argument in favor of outing by demolishing the false and conveniently used argument about privacy. It is this long-needed liquidation of one of the foulest red herrings in the discussion about homosexuality that provides the foundation for his thesis. He argues that a person's sexual orientation is not and never has been private—if that person's sexual orientation happens to be heterosexual. Every time the media reports on whom a person is dating, married to, divorcing, or lusting after, they reveal at the very least important evidence of their subject's sexual orientation. When the subject is heterosexual, though, we do not give this "outing" a second thought.

Different rules, however, apply to lesbians and gay men. Their sexual orientation is believed to be a matter of privacy. It is supposed to be indelicate to reveal a person's homosexuality (by revealing, for example, whom they are dating). Signorile points out the primary reason for this different treatment: the confused distinction between sexual orientation and sexual activity. Sexual orientation, when it manifests itself in relationships people wish to acknowledge, is something most heterosexuals take pride in making public. In contrast, sexual activity is (and, for those of us who still believe a little in modesty or decorum, should be) private.

The distinction between sexual orientation and sexual activity is generally respected when heterosexuality is on the table, but it breaks down when the subject is homosexuality. It is important to examine how that breakdown occurs.

It is not clear whether the case of *Bowers v. Hardwick* is the reason that so many people have accepted the notion that heterosexuals enjoy a right to privacy in their sexual lives while lesbians and gay men do not, or whether *Hardwick* simply articulated a distinction that most people were already vaguely aware of. In either case, though, *Hardwick* is the landmark where discussion about the question of sexual privacy went off the track.

Up until *Hardwick,* it was a more or less accepted principle of constitutional law that American citizens enjoyed the right of privacy in their bedrooms. While some Supreme Court justices—such as Byron White, who authored the five-member majority opinion in *Hardwick*—had grave reservations about its existence, a majority had always been able to coalesce around the right when it came up in an unambiguously heterosexual context. The first cases dealt with the rights of parents to raise their children as they saw fit and to marry whom they chose. But soon enough the cases moved explicitly into the arena of sexual behavior: the right to procreate; the right of a married couple to use birth control; the right of unmarried couples to use birth control; and, finally (and more obliquely), the right of a woman to decide what to do once she'd had sex and become pregnant. In addition, the Court had ruled that such privacy was important enough as a matter of constitutional law that, whatever control government may have over obscenity, police could not arrest someone merely for possessing obscene movies at home.

Hardwick would logically have come within these dual protections: the right to make private decisions about intimate sexual matters, and the right to privacy in your own home. Michael Hardwick, having sex with an unnamed male partner in his bedroom, suddenly found Georgia police standing at the door, gaping at him. While Hardwick was initially arrested for violating Georgia's sodomy law, the prosecutor (as is so often the case) decided not to press charges. But Hardwick and others felt it was time to challenge the validity of the law, hoping to make clear that private, consensual sodomy between adults fell within the Constitution's already articulated rights.

It almost worked. Five Supreme Court justices were initially prepared to strike down Georgia's law. The case looked an awful lot like the previous sexual privacy cases, and it came squarely within the protection for privacy of the home. But *Hardwick* involved a factual difference from previous cases dealing with sexual activity in the home: the relative gender of the people having sex. This presumably should have been irrelevant, since the sodomy law in Georgia applied regardless of whether it was practiced by heterosexual or homosexual Georgians. Lawrence Tribe, who argued Hardwick's case, never once in his opening brief mentioned the gender of Hardwick's partner. The state of Georgia, though, made this fact appear to be relevant.

Some time after the Court's initial vote was taken, Justice Lewis Powell switched his vote, and Byron White was assigned to write the newly formed majority's opinion upholding Georgia's law. One of the long-time opponents of any constitutional right to privacy was now given the opportunity to deny it, and the tortured opinion makes some of the most unconvincing distinctions in Supreme Court jurisprudence. Consistently and repeatedly referring not to sodomy but to homosexual sodomy, Justice White found that the right to privacy did not extend to Hardwick because what he was doing in his bedroom did not relate to the right to family, marriage, or procreation that White claimed had been the real issue in prior privacy cases. And to White, the privacy of the home simply did not matter at all.

It is not necessary to reiterate here the many criticisms of *Hardwick,* which remains one of the most disparaged decisions in modern Court history; Powell himself has since repudiated his vote-switch. But one criticism is directly relevant to a discussion of outing: The Court's reference to procreation is clearly specious. With one exception, the cases about procreation were in fact about the right *not* to procreate—which is exactly the net effect of sodomy. What the cases involving private sexual activity were about was the decision whether to engage in procreative or non-procreative sexual activity, with the Court taking the view that the state should not be making such a decision for consenting adults. If a couple wanted to engage in procreative sex, that was fine, but the state could not mandate it; if the couple wanted to engage in nonprocreative sex by, say, using birth control, that too should be their decision.

The Court's focus on homosexual acts then becomes the only rational way to distinguish *Hardwick* from the previous privacy cases. An alternate reading, that the state can proscribe all sodomy, would require a rule of constitutional law that sexual privacy depends on what body parts come into contact, a theory even *Hardwick*'s most generous supporters do not take seriously. As a practical matter for police enforcement, then, heterosexuals (whether married or unmarried) can claim a right to privacy in making decisions about how to conduct their sexual lives, while lesbians and gay men cannot. Apparently the Constitution absolutely protects a couple's right to decide what consensual, adult and private sexual activity they prefer, even if the activity is nonprocreative, unless that couple is homosexual. But this obviously makes a hash of the concept of privacy. A mixed threesome, for example, would provide enough questions about who is entitled to what level of constitutional privacy, and why, for any number of law school exams.

More important here, the way *Hardwick* finessed the privacy issue provides one reason closeted lesbians and gay men retreat to privacy arguments when their sexual orientation is brought up. For heterosexuals, there is a clear and defined fence between sexual orientation and sexual behavior. Because that boundary is clear, we can learn that a heterosexual is heterosexual without confusing that fact with what specific sexual behavior they engage in.

For lesbians and gay men, though, there is no such boundary, constitutional or otherwise. When we learn they are homosexual, we feel we have the right to conjecture about their private sexual lives. This is epitomized in the now-infamous military regulations concerning homosexuality, which proscribe not only persons who engage in homosexual conduct but those who show "a propensity" to engage in such conduct. This is an indirect authorization to speculate—to conflate a person's homosexual orientation into their presumed sexual conduct, find them guilty of probably engaging in such conduct, since they have a propensity to, and remove them for the possibility of a violation, rather than an actual violation. Privacy completely disappears in this scheme, and public identity is the same thing as sex. Yet the military does not worry about anyone's propensity to engage in heterosexual conduct.

This tacit permission to violate the distinction between sexual orientation and sexual conduct when we discuss homosexuality has led wild-eyed senators to recite in gruesome detail and for the record what sexual acts gay men (it is seldom lesbians) are believed to engage in. A similar recital of the sexual acts those presumptively heterosexual senators could engage in (an illustrative and suitably scary list could be drawn from the writings of the Marquis de Sade or Henry Miller, among many others, and would of course include sodomy) is left unpronounced as a matter of propriety, a respect for the genuinely private lives of those senators.

Signorile is exactly right to focus on the fact that when he outs someone as lesbian or gay, he has said nothing about their sexual behavior, violated no right of privacy, and treated them exactly the way we treat heterosexuals. He is also right to suggest that lesbians and gay men ought to be able to insist on this line between sexual orientation and sexual behavior.

Privacy is not the reason that outing ultimately doesn't accomplish much. Something far more important is. It can be found in gossip columnist Liz Smith's sincere but circuitous defense against those who wanted to out her:

> I don't want to make statements about my mythical sex life. Millions of people don't want to be defined by their sexuality. I'd like to be defined by my

> work, my life. These people you see soul-kissing in the Gay [Pride] parade, they want to be defined by their sexuality, and they are. But what happens when their libido dies down? What will they be defined by then? I'm a divorced woman. I spent my adult, mature life married for ten years. Let people speculate. I'll lead my life the way I choose to.

One of the issues that get too easily buried in the debate about outing is the question of identity, of self-definition. In this respect, you have to sympathize with Smith. She wants people to know her as a writer. She wants her sex life to be "mythical."

In one sense, this is naive. Sexual orientation is a natural part of anyone's identity, a part that is regularly acknowledged when it is heterosexual. What Smith is struggling with is the public perception of the part sexual orientation plays in the lives of lesbians and gay men. Particularly now, this perception is largely formed by the antics of the young and more libidinous. Smith makes a point that heterosexuals in her age range might sympathize with: anyone over a certain age would probably suffer if her or his sex life were regularly compared to those of people who are twenty.

But there is a difference. For lesbians and gay men, sexuality is presumed to be paramount, irrespective of age, in a way it is not for heterosexuals. With the barrier of privacy removed, homosexual sexual orientation equals sexual activity, and it is hard in the public imagination to envision lesbians and gay men apart from their sexuality. Thus, to know Liz Smith is a lesbian is to have public permission to begin picturing her sexual activities, a picture Smith is probably not alone in wanting people to avoid. If she were known as unambiguously heterosexual, her sex life would be presumed to be her own business.

By the same token, it is hard for lesbians and gay men themselves to keep the issues of sexual orientation and sex distinct. The "soul-kissers" that Smith is concerned about are making a political point. But why on earth is kissing politics? When heterosexuals soul-kiss in public places, they're making a statement about their relationship, if anything, not about society. Lesbians and gay men resent heterosexuals' relentless interest in them, resent having the most ordinary affectionate conduct turned into a proxy for sex. But simply by acting the way heterosexuals act, they are charged with "flaunting" their sexual orientation.

This denies to lesbians and gay men something heterosexuals take for granted—the ability to determine how much importance sexuality will have within an individual's identity. That is a task stereotypes accomplish for lesbians and gay men. Signorile's book decimates this bigotry indirectly with example after example of lesbians and gay men whose identities traverse the entire spectrum of human experience, who have given vastly different positions to the part their own sexuality plays in their identities: Anne-Imelda Radice, Richard Rouilard, Barney Frank, Robert Mapplethorpe, Marvin Liebman, Donna Minkowitz, Frank Kameny. While all of them are homosexual, they are homosexual (and, specifically, sexual) in very different ways.

But the point isn't fully made until it is viewed the way heterosexuals get to view it. Some heterosexuals are, you could say, more heterosexual than others. To popular television characters like Sam Malone on "Cheers" and Rue McClanahan's Blanche Devereaux on "Golden Girls," their sexual orientation was everything. They were popular precisely because they were so unashamedly libidinous. Other characters on the same shows—Norm and Cliff on "Cheers," Rose on "Golden Girls"—are also heterosexual, but their sexuality is sometimes all but invisible relative to other parts of their characters.

That is the position Smith wants to give her sexuality. In a neutral world (where sexual orientation is a difference distinct from identity), it would not be necessary to say someone is more or less heterosexual, more or less homosexual; it would suffice to say someone was more or less sexual. Sexuality would be assumed to be part of their identity, but not an identity in itself. But this is not a neutral world, and to say someone is homosexual is to get a fix on what we believe *is* their identity. Heterosexuals must exhibit some extreme sexual behavior in order for their sexuality to become equally prominent within their identity. What Liz Smith insists on is that even in the non-neutral world, a person's own assessment of her identity still means something, even if privacy does not.

And that is the reason outing does not work. Smith is the perfect example to illustrate why.

When the question of a person's sexual orientation (almost always homosexual) arises, we immediately begin looking at the evidence. How does Signorile support his claim that Smith is lesbian? According to his book, "It is well known that Liz had been involved with another woman for many years. It wasn't something Liz tried to hide in her social circles, but she never mentioned it in interviews, and certainly never in her own column."

It is not hard to move from Smith's lengthy involvement with another woman to a claim that they are having sex. No third party has apparently been in Smith's bedroom to witness such activity, but sometimes it strains credibility to assume otherwise. This is, of course, just the kind of evidence the military would look for to prove a "propensity" to engage in homosexuality activity. A long-term relationship with someone of the same sex is not definitive evidence of sexual activity between them, but it will do as long as you know clearly enough what you're trying to prove. And as Smith well knows, what everyone here is trying to prove is sexual activity.

But the focus on sexual activity goes only so far; even military regulations are pragmatic enough about that. Military personnel who engage in homosexual activity have the option under military rules of saying they were drunk or experimenting and are not really homosexual—a provision known as "queen for a day." Such an assertion allows people to remain in the armed forces in good standing because they didn't mean to be perceived as homosexual, they just got their rocks off. If homosexual activity is some kind of a mistake and can be separated from the person's identity, then even the military can tolerate it.

It is in this context that outing was doomed to fail. Only an open acknowledgment of homosexuality is or should be enough to amount to authentic homosexuality, because, unlike heterosexuality, homosexuality, as it exists right now, is still viewed as an identity by default. That default identity, usually referred to as a "homosexual lifestyle," demands some response; once it has been brought up, it cannot simply be ignored. Stereotypes still corrupt the notion of identity for lesbians and gay men, and those stereotypes cannot be left unanswered. Whenever an individual is said to be homosexual, that individual is expected to make some response to the specters of promiscuity, gender rejection, child molestation, and subversiveness. This is true regardless of the individual's actual sexual orientation.

It is hard to acknowledge being homosexual because it is not easy to answer such charges about who you are. Like Smith, people who deny being homosexual or evade the question generally try to put the focus on more integral parts of their identity—integral, that is, to *them*. Whether gay or straight, they do not view sexuality as paramount in their self-perception, and they feel they have to defend their identity from the allegation of sexual saturation.

When a person refuses to come out and say she or he is homosexual, what they effectively do is deny their "accusers" a day in court. This reduces outers to mere gossip-mongers. Smith, the gossip columnist, knows better than most that gossip depends largely on what people are eager to believe, and much of society has a deep craving to conclude that people are really heterosexual. This is especially true of the respected, highly placed people outers most want to expose. For example, the military will generally accept a mere denial of homosexuality even if there is clear evidence of homosexual conduct, because the military is not alone in *wanting* to believe its soldiers are heterosexual. That's why the "tell" part of "don't ask, don't tell" is so critical. Telling is open defiance; if people are just quiet about their homosexuality, we can continue believing the fiction of heterosexuality. It worked with Liberace, for heaven's sake, it can certainly work with Keith Meinhold if he'd just play along.

Smith understands how this mechanism works. If the target of an outing chooses simply to ignore the issue, the outer has little credibility with a public unwilling to believe the truth of such rumors. While it is fun for a while to toy with the idea of what is seen as a transgression by a public figure, the bottom line is that usually the charges just don't stick. That is why the strategy of evasion is nearly always successful. It is not that people disbelieve the offered evidence so much as that people want even more to believe in heterosexuality. In that sense, the perception of heterosexuality is a kind of religion, an act of faith that evidence to the contrary will not upset unless the target of the outing acknowledges her or his own heresy.

Anything less than self-acknowledgment falls short of authentic homosexuality because nothing else takes identity into account. It feels wrong for something as personal as one's identity to be forced onto the unwilling. And as long as homosexuality is viewed as a kind of identity in and of itself, allegations of homosexuality from others (whether a homophobic military tribunal or a zealous outer) will lack the most critical evidence of truth—acceptance of that identity by the person in question. What any sexual activity means within a person's identity must remain up to the individual who participated in it.

The way outing fails is also illustrated in the case of former Defense Department spokesman (and now NBC news correspondent) Pete Williams. Williams's sexual orientation was at the eye of the outing storm. Signorile says he had numerous reports of Williams's attendance at gay bars, as well as firsthand accounts from people who had been with Williams sexually, even someone who had had a short affair with Williams.

But Williams refused to confirm that he was gay. When directly asked—first by Signorile, then later at a press conference—Williams retreated to his job description. He told Signorile that the Defense Department doesn't "pay me to speak about my personal opinions, and they don't pay me to speak about my personal life. I'm not going to talk about myself. It just wouldn't be appropriate." This was the line he reiterated at a press conference: "As a government spokesperson, I stand here and I talk about government policy. I am not paid to discuss my personal opinions about that policy or talk about my personal life, and I don't intend to."

Williams was, from Signorile's point of view, stepping around the truth. From Williams's point of view, he was trying to defend his conception of his own identity against a competing version. And his identity, or at least his public identity, clearly did not include homosexuality—or heterosexuality, for that matter. Williams was not willing to talk about sex at all. He refused to give meaning to his (in Liz Smith's phrase) "mythical" sexual activities.

Irrespective of the reasons, Williams had made a decision not only about his sexuality, but about his identity in public. If he had to be known at all, he wanted to be known not as a sexual person, but as a worker bee. He presented himself as the adult equivalent of the student who studies too hard. Whether that student just enjoys studying more than any other activity, or is trying to avoid human relationships that are viewed for whatever reason as troublesome, their self-perception as devotedly studious has to be taken at face value. Anything else would be mere hypothesis.

The struggle to out Williams, then, could not be (and to this day has not been) won. Signorile saw a hypocritical gay man stuck in the closet, working for an institution that takes homophobia in dead earnest. Williams, in contrast, saw himself in much more modest terms. He was no champion of anything, not even of himself. While he and Signorile differed as to what part sexuality would play in his identity, something bigger was on the line as well. Signorile demanded a public identity of Williams; Williams wanted as little public identity as possible.

This insistence on privacy made Williams resistant to outing. By ducking the issue, Williams wanted to make himself irrelevant. This was not because the sexual orientation of the spokesman for the Defense Department is unimportant. Rather, by retreating into privacy as a refuge, Williams made it clear that although the battle over gay rights was going on in his own backyard—the Defense Department—he was, like Achilles, removing himself from the war for personal reasons.

I do not know whether Williams engaged in same-sex sexual activity, or whether any of the reports Signorile claims to have are true. But even if everything reported to Signorile is 100 percent correct, that would not make Williams any more gay than Liz Smith's ten-year marriage makes her straight. Sexual orientation is of no consequence to these people; it does not resonate in them. They have chosen to view their sexual activities as independent of their identities, and nothing anyone else does can change the position they have adopted for their sex lives.

The factor that makes homosexuality a public issue, perhaps more than any other, is relationships. It's easy enough to avoid making a public commitment to your sexual orientation when you haven't made a public commitment to another person. Some commitedly single people can minimize the importance of their sexuality (Supreme Court Justice David Souter, for example, or David Letterman, or Attorney General Janet Reno), and it makes no difference because for them the presumption of heterosexuality holds fast.

But when you make a commitment to another person, that other person's gender will generally be reasonably obvious, and the sexual orientation of both parties becomes public. It is possible to conceal the relationship, of course, but as time goes on, hiding behind the fiction of heterosexuality becomes infinitely harder and more degrading to both parties. At that point, being private about homosexuality becomes a more public act than being public about it. Closets do not occur in nature; they have to be manufactured and maintained, sometimes on an hourly basis. What message do you put on the phone machine? Whom do you take to the company picnic? How do you explain bedroom arrangements? What do you tell your secretary? Your mother? Real life becomes a constant and conscious fiction, and it gets very wearing.

In this situation, there are only two options for lesbians and gay men: embrace homosexuality, with all of its perceived faults, and try to disprove the stereotypes; or retreat entirely from the discussion, reinforcing the stereotypes by default. Every time lesbians and gay men retreat into privacy they give their blessing to the status quo, making the insane battle over statistics that much more important. Those of us who are making the public arguments have to rely on speculation as to how many people want or need the rights we are claiming, because we seem to be claiming them for people who either don't exist or don't much care.

The alternative, of course, is for many, a hard one. Claiming your own homosexuality in a world that resists acknowledging it means having to swim against the current, having to demonstrate the most ordinary facts about yourself, sometimes almost daily. In the politically charged world of sexual orientation it means, as Pete Williams and Liz Smith both feared, having a public identity as a sexual person whether you want one or not.

That is why it is so important for lesbians and gay men to claim their homosexuality. Only by claiming it can they assert for themselves how they view their own sexuality. Those who do not claim it enjoy the benefits of having their character assessed apart from the sexuality, but leave the stereotypes about homosexuality intact. Unlike heterosexuality, where individual character is an open field entirely apart from sexual orientation, lesbians and gay men who claim their homosexuality have to prove their individuality against that backdrop, arguing time after time that they are not the stereotype. Or, if they choose to adopt some or all of the stereotypes, they have to argue that drag, unashamed sexuality, or gender-defying mannerisms are parts of the kind of person they are. Either way it's a struggle.

By claiming their homosexuality, lesbians and gay men enter a daily campaign over their individual character. This requires a certain sureness of the self, and a willingness to accept that some people will want or need to fight over their faith in stereotypes. Not everyone is up to such conflict.

What Signorile and many of us are yearning for is people with the kind of character that makes them undistinguished heroes. Gerry Studds is an excellent example. When his homosexuality was revealed because of an affair with a page, Studds was ultimately forthright, acknowledged being gay, and—having claimed the issue—has become an articulate, witty, and honorable advocate for gay equality. But in order to respond like Gerry Studds, you have to have the character of a Gerry Studds. And that raises a question in many people's minds: how extraordinary is he?

For lesbians and gay men, character is always on the line. One of the prominent myths about homosexuality is that it is, in itself, a character flaw. Lesbians and gay men who believe that are doing no more than responding to cultural cues, the ones bigots hope and pray they'll respond to.

But character is bigger than stereotypes. True character demands action, and it does not fully exist until it has been fired in the crucible of controversy. Everything else is just talk. In this culture, the opposition to homosexuality provides an opportunity for homosexual women and men to forge their characters by rising to the dare, but not everyone takes the opportunity. People like Studds and Signorile, Larry Kramer, Urvashi Vaid, Torie Osborn, Roberta Achtenberg, and many others have risen to that challenge. From some well of the self they have refused to be pushed around, have chosen to act on what they believe. Many, many others will agree to a little pushing around, or at least can rationalize it. It is not in them to defy.

But sometimes people live up to the adversity they face, developing stronger characters than they otherwise might have. This is something Signorile knows about. He tells the story of having been kicked out of Catholic school for being gay. In public school, in order to shore up a non-homosexual identity, he joined other boys who were throwing basketballs at a more obviously gay boy. Years later, Signorile discovered the boy had developed into a fully integrated gay man, ready to go to the high school reunion and come out, something Signorile says he himself was not willing to do. Signorile expresses his admiration for the boy's bravery in facing the pain of his past honestly and squarely as an adult.

Self-acknowledgment is ultimately what coming out is all about. It is one of the reasons those who have come out are impatient with those who haven't. We want them to know that of course it will be difficult, but you'll be better for having been through it. Coming out is a kind of psychological basic training. While it is not the only sign of character that lesbians and gay men can exhibit, coming out is a touchstone, and for many a threshold.

Signorile is irritable with those who are in the closet partly because he knows that the timid can be more dangerous than the strong. He is right, but being right is the end of it. Coming out is a decision about your own identity, or it is nothing. It is the resolution that you will have to fight to give sexuality its proper place in your life, a place each person has to recognize individually. Being openly gay in the world we live in cannot be imposed, because it requires coming to terms with conflict and addressing preformulated identities. Like it or not, being openly homosexual demands taking a stand about who you are. That is something that each individual has to wrestle with at his or her core.

The people who wind up as the targets of outing become targets because of a seething frustration. Outers view them as shapeless conformists, willing to accept their sexual invisibility for the trade-offs society offers. The help that they could provide they don't, and outing them becomes a seductive option because it appears to punish them for their cowardice and accomplish a kind of public relations goal. But good public relations is not achieved by invoking spokespeople who don't believe in the product.

I think it's probably better to leave the closeted alone. People who aren't comfortable dealing with the prejudices and presumptions about homosexuality are of little or no use toward furthering gay equality, because they are willing to settle for less. Whatever their public notoriety or fame, the part of their humanity that really counts when it comes to the fight—the spirit and the fire—is lacking. They can continue to cling to the vestiges of privacy this society offers the timid, but they will never have a truly private life. The irony is sad, but it is theirs. Society's prejudices will continue to haunt them, in and out of their bedrooms. As long as they can evade the truth, and as long as society is willing to believe the lies, they will always be safe. Outing will not cause them to be seen, because they are invisible even to themselves.

DANIEL MENDELSOHN

Mendelsohn, who lives in New York City, has published essays and criticism in the *Nation,* the *Village Voice, American Theater,* and in *Out* magazine, to which he is a regular contributor; he was also the culture columnist for the now-defunct *QW.* His political satire and opinion pieces for the *New York Times* and the *Toronto Globe and Mail* have been widely reproduced in other papers, as well as in the collection *The Best American Humor.* Mendelsohn was educated at the University of Virginia and holds a doctorate in classics from Princeton, where he was a leader of the gay community for several years. He is currently at work on a book about narcissism and unhappiness in upscale gay culture, to be published by Little, Brown in 1996. The following essay appears for the first time in *Beyond Queer.*

SCENES FROM A MALL

Of all the posters, banners, and signs you saw at the big gay and lesbian March on Washington in 1993, the one that made the biggest impression on many spectators (and, to judge from its appearance the next day in the *New York Daily News,* on photo editors and some other journalists, too) was a big cardboard rectangle held up by a quintet of handsome, shirtless young men who were lounging in a window along the parade route. Unlike many of those marching below, who chanted angrily and carried placards advocating their demands for gay life and liberty *now,* these boys were pretty nonchalant. With the offhand good looks and overwrought physiques that are currently *de rigueur* for young gay men, they could have passed for the cast of some new Fox television series ("Dupont Circle 20008"). Their sign said "WE NEED HUSBANDS," and it reminded you that many gay people—men, especially, and most especially young white middle-class men, the kind you're most likely to know if, say, you're a thirtysomething writer living in a big city like New York—enjoy their lives and liberties pretty much as fully as anybody else does. (In New York, everyone gets bashed.) For gay men who fit that particular demographic bill, the problem isn't how to avoid discrimination in employment or housing, but rather how to make a life worth working for and how to find someone to live with: that is, how to succeed in what you might call the pursuit of gay happiness.

Yet if the boys and their sign appeared to shed some light on the stubbornly unspoken truth of gay life—that what so many gay men want, and yet what most eludes them, is to be "married"—they did so almost unwittingly. After all, "WE NEED HUSBANDS" didn't seem to strike those marching below as particularly poignant, or indeed even that serious. In one photograph taken of that scene, you can see the five boys waving from their perch to the marchers below; the demonstrators are waving back and laughing.

If the boys' outfits showed a lot of skin, it was their laughter that was most revealing. In gay culture, after all, the operating assumption tends to be that stratospheric cheekbones and Marky Mark-y muscles will more or less guarantee happiness: they are their own (usually successful) advertisements for husbands. And despite the political battles and health crises that have galvanized the gay community over the past few years, many gay men remain at least as preoccupied with the right gym, or the right outfits, as they are with rights of the First Amendment kind. (Being "political" is often just another fashion accessory. Or at least it's hard not to think as much when you keep hearing that ACT UP meetings are the best place to meet hot boys.) All this helps to explain the complicit laughter that greeted "WE NEED HUSBANDS." In this particular subculture, the mere suggestion that you can look like a Bruce Weber ephebe and *still* need a husband could only be taken as, well, a joke. And to tell the truth, the pretty quintet didn't look all that miserable.

You wonder whether they should have. After all, the greedy enthusiasm with which gay culture continues to celebrate physical attributes like those so abundantly displayed by the D.C. boys is probably the reason that so many of us still "need husbands." For many gay men, a profound emotional need such as the one expressed (however sardonically) in that plaintive slogan is constantly at war with an erotic impulse that takes delight in little more than surfaces—surfaces such as those that the D.C. boys themselves had clearly worked hard to perfect. It's no surprise that a lot of gay social life takes place in spots that provide plenty of reflective surfaces: mirrored gyms, or bars and clubs where you may go to "see and be seen." When it comes to desire, we gay men are all eyes. (It's as if our notoriously urgent sexual energy grew out of the same ground that yields our equally famous aesthetic sensitivities.) Whatever we say about looking for husbands, many of us spend a lot of time in places where the only thing we look at is ourselves.

Even for those fed up with the typical gay nightlife, with its great expectations and brief encounters—and just about everyone you talk to claims to be on a strict no-bar diet these days—the bar scene seems inevitable. The underlying reason for this is a paradox that stands, I think, at the heart of gay life in America, and that helps explain why gay happiness may remain even more elusive than gay liberty. Like Martina Navratilova, who in her speech on the Mall wryly parodied the media's habit of referring to her as "the *lesbian* tennis star," we all complain that we're tired of being identified exclusively as gay. Yet it's still usually the case that the only places we're likely to find each other are the ones where being gay is all that identifies us.

The best place to observe this central emotional conundrum of modern gay life was the Mall itself. During the rally, you kept hearing people say that this vast throng represented the "face of America," and it was true that what you saw there was as much of a "gorgeous mosaic" as the country itself. But looking around at all these people in broad daylight, you also realized why sexuality alone doesn't make for very effective grout. When all was said and done, the gay people from the Midwest seemed more midwestern than anything else; similarly, the ties that bound the gay Alabamians together looked pretty much as though they'd been fashioned from kudzu rather than, say, black leather. But what, you wondered, was holding the rest of us together?

More than a few of the friends I was marching with also noticed this: how, although the March was supposed to be a grand manifestation of identity politics, those other identities—the ones that seemed ultimately to be truer, deeper, more real somehow—kept getting in the way. Yet it's an observation I've never heard anyone make about gay bars, where big crowds of gay people who have little in common are routinely thrown together and expected to make not just a weekend, but a whole *life* together. If the April 1993 demonstration demonstrated anything about happiness, as opposed to just life and liberty, it was that being gay isn't in itself a valid basis for a relationship—for "finding a husband"—any more than being straight is.

Aerial photographs of the Mall on the day of the March (and you were liable to see a lot of these, since they were used to settle the fiercely debated issue of how many people actually marched) show an enormous if rather narrow rectangle about a third filled with people, most of whom are clustered to one end. It was an oddly familiar scene. As you stood there, clumped together with lots of people you didn't necessarily feel you had a whole lot in common with, you may have been reminded of some other long, narrow spaces you've spent time in. Bars, perhaps, but something else as well—the closet. Mall, bar, closet: All three spaces are constructed according to the same reductive blueprint. In all three, being gay is the only thing that matters, the only thing you are. You end up in the closet, of course, because your sexuality matters so much to *other* people that you're forced into hiding; and there's no question that that outside pressure (or, as the speakers at the March rightly called it, oppression) must end. But it's no less unpleasant or destructive of individual identity when the barriers are being built from within—especially when the only thing the people inside have in common is the outside oppression.

That's why gay identity politics is ultimately so limited, why it can't solve the problem of gay happiness. The politics will last as long as the identity (which is to say, as long as the oppression), but then what? The day that we finally do get our rights will, ironically, be the day when any gathering—whether of two or two hundred thousand—that is based on the solitary fact of a shared sexual identity will have become obsolete. Yet that day will also leave us free, or forced, to explore the full extent of our identities beyond the narrow confines of the closet. I'm talking here not only about the sunless and airless space that "they" or "society" or "the church" have built for us, but about the equally narrow ideological and social and political cupboards we've built for ourselves. To put it a bit differently, if our bars are just the flip side of our closets—crowded and badly lit, but cozy in a way—then the real test for those who claim to "need husbands" will be to see whether they will leave the former as willingly as they do the latter. You can't pursue happiness in the dark.

Light was plentiful on the day of the March itself. Early that Sunday morning, I made my way up Connecticut Avenue, en route to a rendezvous with friends near Dupont Circle. The usually well-kept streets in this tony northwest neighborhood seemed messily hung over after the predictably frenzied array of pre-March parties and dances the night before; the shuttered houses along the route I took looked puffy-eyed, resentful of the strong morning sun.

Equally resentful, perhaps, was the youth who came toward me, red-haired and red-eyed, squinting against the daylight. He couldn't have been more than nineteen or twenty, but the oversized army fatigues he had on made him look younger still, like a boy who'd gotten into his father's clothes. Or perhaps like a soldier from some improbable, New Age color guard: in one pale hand he held a flagpole bearing the rainbow-striped banner of the gay rights movement. (Necklaces of matching multicolored rings adorned the brawny necks of many marchers.) It was clear that he was just now coming from one of last night's events. The hand that wasn't carrying the banner absently held a half-drunk bottle of Heineken; on the pale skin of his own slender neck, a hickey bloomed.

But despite his paramilitary mien, this boy seemed less victorious than perplexed, less purposeful than lost. His forlorn visage haunts me. Caught in the limbo between moonlit self-indulgence and the sober realities of morning, he seems a symbol for what is perhaps the most difficult issue that faces gay men—not how or when we will secure our liberty, but what we plan to do with ourselves once we're truly free.

BRUCE BAWER

The following column appeared in the *Advocate* on 23 August 1994.

SEX-NEGATIVE ME

Among the gay press's responses to my 1993 book *A Place at the Table* was the charge by some critics that I'm "sex-negative." Frank Browning griped that I want "to have everyone put on 30 pounds, buy a Brooks Brothers suit, and wander off on the golf links, becoming [an] upper-class version of Ozzie and Harry. Those who don't want to take risks should join Mr. Bawer on the golf course. Those who want to feel alive will benefit from the exploration of our bodies and what our bodies can grant."

Golf? Ozzie and Harry? Brooks Brothers? What, I wondered, does any of this have to do with what I've written? I've never been on a golf course. Or worn a Brooks Brothers suit. And when did I join the upper class? Of course I want gay people to enjoy what their bodies can grant. I also want them to have equal rights under the law, the love and respect of their friends and families, and a meaningful life beyond their orgasms. I want gay kids to grow up knowing that, as wonderful as sex can be, gay identity amounts to more than belonging to a "culture of desire."

Browning and others mocked me for being "serious." Well, isn't discovering oneself as a gay individual in this society a serious challenge? Isn't gay rights a serious issue? Being serious about gay rights in public discourse doesn't preclude being able to have fun in one's personal life. Yet if some right-wing critics can't write about homosexuality without smirking, some gay writers seem unable to address the subject without prattling frivolously about their own sex lives and longings.

Which is a shame, because it's vitally important for us to recognize that at the heart of homophobia lies an inability to see that gays can love each other as deeply and as seriously as straights can. Explaining why he'd refused to print my review of the film *Longtime Companion,* an *American Spectator* editor told a *New York Observer* reporter, "Bawer was striking a total equivalence between a heterosexual couple in love and a homosexual couple in love. To me, that wasn't convincing." That editor isn't alone in rejecting the idea of the moral equivalence of gays and straights.

It's not only heterosexuals who draw these sex-related distinctions. "The defining thing about being gay," a gay man tells Susan Bergman in her new memoir, *Anonymity,* "is that you like to have sex a lot." Many gays agree. Yet plenty of straight men would tell you that copulation is the be-all and end-all of their lives too. To suggest that gays are more defined by their libidos is to collaborate in the widespread, dehumanizing view that gay sex is invariably mechanical, impersonal, even bestial, while straight sex is an integral part of the complex web of human feeling, connectedness, and commitment before God. That, in short, we're about lust and they're about love.

On the radio the other day, Howard Stern was interviewing a gay college student. They both agreed that when you're gay your whole life centers on sex, and it doesn't matter at all whom you're having it with. One of Stern's sidekicks commented delightedly, "Like dogs!"

Or, perhaps, like children. At the close of a recent AIDS benefit in New York City, the emcee exhorted to the audience, "Play safe!" I winced. Why? Because it irks me that gay sex is routinely described as play—as if we're children, coupling sportively behind the barn—while straight adult sex is never referred to in this way. The implication is that straight sex is grown-up and gay sex is kid stuff.

"[Bawer] is the kid in grade school who just got mad at the other kids because they didn't do what the teacher said," the late John Preston told the *Advocate* in 1993. "Bawer doesn't like sex." Preston's metaphor is illuminating: Deep down many folks (gay as well as straight) *do* see gays as kids and straights as bossy teachers out to thwart their fun. It's not sex I deplore but this systematic devaluing of gay life.

To be sure, as a friend notes, "Sex is what makes us gay." But our sexual orientation doesn't define us any more than straights are defined by their orientation. Anti-gay propagandists depict gay rights as a battlefield on which gays fight selfishly for the sake of their decadent, undisciplined sex lives while straights fight selflessly in defense of their innocent children. That's an outrageously fraudulent picture of the conflict, and we can't let it stand. We must communicate to straight America that when it comes to children, the interests of parents and gays—many of whom *are* parents—are congruent. The conflict should more properly be seen as a dialogue between, on the one hand, gays and straights of goodwill who care about families and understand homosexuality and, on the other, straights who don't understand homosexuality or don't want to or don't give a damn one way or the other.

As for sex, we must help straights see that for us, as for them, sex can be anything from casual fun to a fundamental component of a loving, committed relationship. Until we make that clear, to many of them we'll continue to look like a somewhat lower order of being whose personal lives can't possibly be morally equivalent to their own. And thereupon hang our rights.

BRUCE BAWER

The following column appeared in the *Advocate* on 18 October 1994.

CONFUSION REIGNS

While channel surfing one day a few months ago, I came across a gay public-access show on which an interviewer fired names at gay activist-journalist Michelangelo Signorile, asking him to respond with the first word that came to mind. "Bruce Bawer," the interviewer said. "Confused," Signorile replied.

The answer made me laugh—and it also made me do some thinking about confusion. There's a lot of it around. Indeed, the more I've talked to other people—both gay and straight—about homosexuality and related subjects, the more I've come to recognize how important a part confusion has played not only in the perpetuation of homophobia (which, after all, involves in many cases a confusion of homosexuality with pederasty or subversion or misogyny) but also in the conflicts that are raging in gay circles between, well, people like me and Signorile.

Certainly a lot of confusion has arisen from the fact that many of us use the same words to mean different things. Take *gay* and *homosexual*. Most of us use these words to designate a natural orientation. Some gay activists, however, use them to refer only to a natural orientation that's acted upon and openly acknowledged—you're only gay, in other words, if you're out loud and proud. Some, like Larry Kramer, have additional criteria: "Any gay who says he's conservative," Kramer has maintained, "is not a gay."

Meanwhile, a lot of straight people, as we all know, genuinely think that homosexuality is a subversive choice—that gay people choose to be gay and could, if they wished, choose to be straight. We need to correct this confusion—but the task isn't made any easier by the fact that we can't even get it clear among ourselves what we're talking about when we use the words *homosexual* and *gay*.

Nor are we clear among ourselves about the goals of the gay rights movement. Do we want social acceptance and respect, equal rights under the law, sexual liberation, increased self-esteem, Marxist utopia? All of the above? Or do we simply want to vent our anger at society, get the rage out of our system? Is the movement's role to provide gays (or, perhaps, the world generally) with a more ambitious vision of sexual pleasure or human relations than that reflected in the relationships of our parents? Or do we just want an excuse to throw condoms at priests or run naked up Fifth Avenue?

Different people have different answers to these fundamental questions. Many have never really figured out what their answer is; for some, the answer seems to vary according to mood or the weather or whoever they've listened to most recently. And some think they know what their answer is but contradict themselves. A certain gay person may say, for instance, that the proper goal of gay politics is to achieve equal respect and acceptance, but if he hears you speaking to heterosexuals about homosexuality in a way that'll help them understand and accept it, he'll accuse you of sucking up to the enemy, of caring too much about what straight people think. Or another gay person may say she wants equal rights, then engage in blatantly counterproductive forms of protest and defend her actions by saying, "Well, I felt like it" or "All gay self-expression is good." I see this kind of confusion about first principles constantly, and it's a big reason, I think, why our movement seems so terribly out of focus and so much less successful than it should be.

One corollary of this widespread confusion is an often unconscious tendency to obscure the lines dividing several closely related but decidedly different topics of discourse. Homosexuality, gay culture, the "gay community," gay sex, your or my personal life, gay politics: these are all different entities. To talk about one does not oblige you to talk about the others. This may seem a simple and obvious point, but if you listen to some gay political leaders on TV or read books by some queer-studies scholars, you're liable to find these entities hopelessly confused with one another.

A famous gay writer, in an important piece about gay politics for a major political journal, devotes several sentences to describing the physical attractions of two other gay writers with whom he disagrees. A noted queer-studies scholar, in the essay on gay literature in an influential history of the American novel, spends several paragraphs on his own childhood. This is not just run-of-the-mill inappropriateness—it's the product of a sensibility that refuses to honor the distinctions among the various entities listed above.

We've been encouraged to see such rhetorical practices as displaying a fabulous irreverence, an impertinent refusal to observe distinctions or social niceties, that's distinctively gay—and indeed there's a place for irreverence and for personal references in public discourse. But in routinely failing to observe the distinctions I've mentioned and discuss subjects in an appropriate tone, we only increase the confusion of straight people who are making a sincere effort to "get it." And that doesn't get us anywhere.

BRUCE BAWER

The following column appeared in the *Advocate* on 16 May 1995.

CANON FODDER

Gay culture. We hear—and use—the phrase all the time, but what does it mean? Well, if we're talking about gay men, it can mean camp. It can mean Streisand, "Dynasty," Madonna. Some months ago a guest *Advocate* columnist raised the question of whether the shared interest of many gay men in such cultural phenomena is innate. A straight friend of his had claimed that the gay-icon status of a Judy Garland, say, was simply the consequence of gay men taking their cues from other gay men. The writer of the piece demurred, insisting that gay boys feel strongly drawn to certain things at a very young age.

I agree. To be sure, not all gay men respond powerfully to the same stuff. I never cared for "Dynasty," for example, nor am I a big opera fan. But I do find myself watching *Mildred Pierce, Mommie Dearest,* and *Auntie Mame* virtually every time they're on TV, and I enjoy them out of all proportion to their objective merits. The same goes for the British sitcom "Absolutely Fabulous"; not till weeks after I fell for it did I discover that it was a nationwide gay favorite.

Obviously these tastes have something to do with my being a gay man. But what, exactly? For every canonical gay taste I share, there are ten I don't. In any event, I don't think such tastes are a direct consequence of my homosexuality. Would Alexander the Great have loved *Auntie Mame*? Would Richard the Lion-Hearted have become addicted to "Ab Fab"? When a ten-year-old gay kid finds himself drawn to such phenomena, I suspect, it's not because of a genetic link between sexual orientation and cultural tastes but because of some complex conjunction between his as-yet-unarticulated awareness of his own differentness and society's signals to him about emotional orientation, sexual identity, and gender roles.

There's a distinction, of course, between "Ab Fab" and gay culture as it's understood by people who give prizes for "gay books" and such. But the dividing line isn't clear. Must a "gay movie" be written and directed by gays? Does a "lesbian novel" require a lesbian author, a lesbian protagonist? This question has plagued the Lambda Literary Awards—and to my mind has underscored the difficulty inherent in the whole notion of "gay culture" as something distinct from "straight culture."

On the one hand, I can understand the desire to honor artworks that profitably ponder the meaning of gayness. On the other hand, I'm wary about the ghettoizing of gay culture. I'm also uncomfortable with the argument that gay people must "support gay culture." What can this mean? At best it's empty political rhetoric; at worst it's an insistence that we must embrace every novel, play, or movie produced by gay people whether or not we actually like it. This is totalitarianism, pure and simple.

It's also confining, for there's no part of the cultural landscape without a gay element. Even if gays constitute as much as fifteen percent of the population, the gay contribution to Western art, architecture, music, and literature far exceeds what it should be statistically. If you accept the right-wing claim that only one in a hundred people is gay, then the gay contribution is truly extraordinary. Think about it: a group comprising one percent of the population producing Erasmus, da Vinci, Michelangelo, Raphael, Caravaggio, Marlowe, Bacon, Hölderlin, Hans Christian Andersen, Tchaikovsky, Proust . . . the list goes on and on, to include three of the four major nineteenth-century American novelists, one (perhaps both) of the two great nineteenth-century American poets, and two of the three most noted mid-twentieth-century American dramatists.

The immensity of the debt that Western civilization owes to gay and lesbian genius is pretty ironic, given that homosexuality is often described as a threat to Western civilization by those strangest of allies, the culturally philistine religious right and neoconservative intellectuals. Especially ironic is the case of Allan Bloom, the late author of *The Closing of the American Mind.* That 1987 best-seller, which defended the traditional literary canon against multiculturalism, became the neocon bible, a key text in the so-called culture wars. As those wars wore on, the neocons began to mimic the rhetoric of the religious right, bizarrely linking the decline of American art, culture, and higher education to a deterioration of "family values," which in turn was blamed mostly on increasing acceptance of gays. Gays, then, were Western civilization's worst enemies—and Bloom its most ardent defender.

Yet what few readers knew was that Bloom (who died in 1992) was gay. His allies knew, but that didn't keep them from bashing gays in print. Years ago at a social occasion, a leading neocon was overheard saying to an associate, "Isn't it a shame about Allan Bloom?" He meant, of course, "Isn't it a shame that he's gay?" In fact, the real shame was that neocons saw no moral difficulty in celebrating Bloom while vilifying gays generally—and that Bloom, for his part, never publicly confronted them with the fact that Western civilization, far from being threatened by homosexuality, is to a staggeringly disproportionate degree the *creation* of gay men and women.

"Do you want to protect your children from gay influence?" I imagine him writing. "Very well. Destroy the *Mona Lisa* and *The Last Supper,* silence *Messiah* and *Swan Lake,* and burn *Moby Dick* and *The Portrait of a Lady.* Gay culture is all around you—and it belongs to everybody."

NORAH VINCENT

Norah Vincent is a writer and assistant editor at The Free Press who lives in New York City. This piece appeared in the *New Republic* on 8–15 January 1996.

BEYOND LESBIAN

"Crate and Barrel." I said, "That sounds like a lesbian store, doesn't it?"

"Sounds like what a lesbian would wear," said Susan.

Susan and I are best friends, and both lesbians. We joke this way often. We are incessant watchers, curious about other lesbians, and whether we can literally tease them out of the crowd. But aside from the teasing, there is much serious conversation between us about what it means to be a lesbian, and what the external cues are telling us it is *supposed* to mean.

So, what does it mean to be a lesbian in 1995? We're calling it "The Gay Nineties." We're given symbols: rainbow flag, pink triangle, pink ribbon. We're given behavioral cues: "Pride" and "Act Up." Dogma is irresistible, it seems, and most real thinking is replaced by the rote slogans of a cause—"The Lesbian Avengers. We Recruit." Hence the jokes, a kind of bitter relief from orthodoxy.

But, for me, there is an urgent question under the jokes, a question the so-called "lesbian community" does not ask. Who am I?

If the straight world (and even the gay male world) has defined lesbians falsely, even maliciously, then lesbians have, to some degree, acquiesced, by forgetting the *I* and playing themselves into stereotypes. Lesbians have labels for everyone, it seems: bull dyke, granola dyke, baby dyke, power dyke, butch, soft butch, femme, lipstick lesbian. It goes on and on, and these are the same labels that make it easy for straight people, and gay men, to misrepresent lesbians. If we want the truth about lesbians, labels will not lead us to it, or at least not to an answer that will make any human difference. We, as lesbians, have amassed names, symbols, and behaviors, and they are designed to tell us and the rest of the world who we are. But this is not an answer.

If the question is, "What does it mean to be a lesbian?," then the answer is semantic, and the same for everyone—a primary sexual and emotional attraction to women. Sounds laughably clinical, doesn't it? You knew the answer when you looked it up in the dictionary at age eight. Reductive as it sounds, it is the only answer that will give lesbians the equality they demand.

Only the simplicity of what the word "lesbian" means can make *being* a lesbian a neutral fact of life to which all other traits, lifestyles, professions, proclivities are incidental and beside the point. Only this literal definition will make the word "lesbian" a nonissue in public life, because being an *I* first frustrates persecution by threading lesbianism so completely through the fabric of "the norm" that it cannot be separated from it. Being a lesbian first, however, sets you apart by your own definition, making you vulnerable as an other. The "lesbian community" defines itself by one quality, and thereby argues against its own claims for living a "normal" life. By their own design, many lesbians are living a lesbian life instead.

The straight world has taken lesbians, a numerical minority, and made them, by false argument, a moral, social, and political minority; and in retreating to the entrenched haven of group-think, the "lesbian community" has colluded in this sophistry. But if I am an individual, if "lesbian" is reduced to what it is, one among many words that describe me, it ceases to so effectively define and marginalize me.

No doubt, my critics will label this a "back to the closet" argument—i.e., if you want straight rights, then act straight—but heterocloning is not my answer to the problems lesbians face, individualism is. Lesbianism may never be as innocuous as left-handedness, but angry ghettoization will merely aggravate prejudice.

Defining oneself beyond lesbianism, however, is anathema to the group. Behaviors not sanctioned by lesbian codes of conduct are suspect in the "lesbian community," because they smack of conformity to straight life, and so called patriarchal (an absurdly over-used word) notions of womanhood. Lesbianism, for many, *has* become a lifestyle, complete with its own vocabulary, food, clothing, politics, medicine, and psychology. Dissent is no laughing matter. The cause is paramount, goodspeak the *lingua franca*.

Nearly a year ago, a woman bought me a beer in a lesbian bar, and taught me quickly this cool lesson of conformity. After setting the beer in front of me, she seemed suddenly distraught. She asked me if my jacket was made of leather. I said it wasn't. She then looked down at my shoes and asked if they were made of leather. I said they were. She asked me about my belt, and I agreed. It was also leather. She then took back my beer, saying that she couldn't buy a beer for someone who was wearing animal hide. She then pinned to my shirt a button bearing a save-the-animals slogan whose precise wording I've forgotten. She then approached the woman next to me and gave her the beer instead. (The satisfying coda to the story is that the woman next to me returned the beer, saying that she couldn't accept it in good conscience, since her parents were furriers.)

I had failed the lesbian test, and approval was rescinded, because in the "lesbian community," political loyalty is a badge of courage and a mandate for inclusion. The veterans of everything from butch/femme in the 1950s to radical feminism in the 1970s are its esteemed matriarchs, older, seasoned women, disrespectful of the young and uninitiated. While in the gay male culture, youth and beauty are apotheosized (granted, to an extreme), in the "lesbian community" they are often resented and denigrated. How many times have these "older" women said to me, "Yeah, well God knows where you were in the seventies," or leaked into the conversation a degrading reference to youth and its assumed concomitants, social and political ignorance?

Recently, I attended a fundraising event for a lesbian foundation. They were giving a staged reading of a new lesbian screenplay. The story, touted as a lesbian *Big Chill,* took place at a house in the Berkshires where a group of old friends were gathering to celebrate the birth of a child to one of the couples. The script was filled with lesbian cliches. Half the women had been lovers with each other at some time or another and were still working through old resentments. Most of them were political refugees of the 1970s. Several of them were either alcoholics or proselytizing twelve-steppers. In one scene they sat around the porch with a guitar, singing Holly Near songs and recounting their coming out stories.

The comic centerpiece was a twenty-three-year-old corporate-bimbo type in a glen plaid suit with miniskirt and high heels, page-boy hair, and Estee Lauder face. She was the much younger lover of one of the reunionees, and many other things she wasn't supposed to be: well groomed, attractive, and straight-seeming in voice and demeanor. She was also many of the things the writer believed must naturally follow from all the above: vapid, spoiled, rich, uninformed, rootless, and complacent.

Many of the story's biggest jokes were at this character's expense, the most pointed being the one in which she takes her turn in the Holly Nearfest and tells her coming out story. The rest of the coming out stories, as you might expect, were bathetic and trite. In contrast, the ditz character simply giggles ungratefully and says, "I don't know. I just came out"—thereby indicating that coming out these days is an unpremeditated nonevent, thanks to the old war-horses for whom it was, no doubt, an art form.

Recently, many poorly made lesbian films have embarrassed me, but this script was conspicuous because it embodied so much of what is wrong with the "lesbian community." The bimbo character was a caricature of lesbian youth as seen through the eyes of the ossified gerontocracy. The writer's message was clear: don't be young, don't accept beauty, don't trespass, don't be yourself; instead, be disgruntled and carping, self-deprecating in your dress and demeanor, avoid anything that passes for accomplishment or assimilation in the mainstream, be a real lesbian and sing along.

As a young lesbian, my answer is this: be original, and write something that is a profound, intelligent depiction of the human spirit in a lesbian milieu (à la Leslie Feinberg's *Stone Butch Blues*), or if you prefer comedy, at least produce something that is clever enough not to become a parody of itself.

If lesbians truly want *equal* rights and *equal* treatment, they should step into the real world, make a case for their humanity first, and, above all, learn to take a joke.

PAUL VARNELL

The following piece appeared in the *Windy City Times* on 31 August 1995.

THE LIMITS OF GAY IDENTITY

"I do not wish to contribute to gay groupiness."

—LEO BERSANI

"The American achievement is not the multicultural society, it is the multicultural individual.... Many things are possible in America but the singleness of identity is not one of them."

—LEON WIESELTIER

I want to argue that the notion of a "gay identity" is not a very useful one and that it can seriously mislead people in their effort to obtain clarity about themselves. But let us do all this a little more slowly.

The catch-term *identity* and its compounds (e.g., *sexual identity, personal identity, identity politics*) are if not omnipresent at least naggingly recurrent in the vogue lexicon of popular communication. And yet there is something very odd about their use. Everyone uses them as if they were very important and insightful and yet, at the same time, crystal clear and uncomplicated, even trivially obvious, attributes that seldom occur together.

Identity? What is it? What we are? All we are? What we mostly are? At some point we may begin to suspect that "identity" is the '90s way of talking about the "self."

In the '50s and '60s everyone spoke about the self. People were examining the inner self, looking for the true self, nurturing their self, etc. Although people confidently talked about "it," the more they tried to focus on it, the more elusive it got as layer after layer was peeled away and there seemed to be no core content.

"Identity" seemed a more fruitful route to self-knowledge. It was really there, safely outside, "objective." So it was not just empty psychobabble. Identity now takes on some of the same tasks as "self," claiming to answer such questions as "Who am I?" and "What makes me me?" or even "How am I to understand myself?" That is, to a potentially profound question, it provides a prepackaged, ready-to-wear, one-size-fits-all answer: a label. Call it sociobabble.

For most people, the answers are at hand: their race, or nationality, or ethnicity, or religious heritage, or even mode of earning a living. For gays it can seem a little more complicated because, for most of us, being gay is something we came to understand about ourselves after we had already developed some other identity or primary self-understanding such as one of the above.

Then, too, a "gay identity" appears to have developed as a defensive posture, an affirmative assertion forged under the pressure of hostility. There is some evidence—e.g., in Plato's *Symposium*—that although the Greeks were fully aware of homosexuality and homosexuals, sexual orientation was not a master category, not the primary category in which people who were gay thought of themselves.

But now that the identity is available as an option along with all the others, what are we to do with it? As *New Republic* literary editor Leon Wieseltier wrote last year in an essay to which this one is a modest pendant:

> The constant clamor for self-justification is a drain on American dignity. One must defend oneself, of course, if one is attacked for being a black, or a homosexual, or a woman, or a Jew, or a Catholic, but one must dream of being more than a defender of oneself.

No doubt. But what? Jewish gays and African-American gays may face that question more clearly because they often feel they have more than one identity and may feel pressured to choose one over the other. Increasingly, though, the answer they seem to be reaching is that they are both identities and that that is a kind of identity itself. But the relationship between the two contributions almost surely varies from person to person.

All the rest of us who are gay face the same sort of problem, if in a less intense way, and have access to the same solution. Not only are we gay, which has a heritage we can learn if we choose, but we also have other heritages, other identities we can draw on; how we combine them or draw upon them is up to us. Some people may experience dual or triple (or more) identities as a source of internal conflict, but they can also be of value as a source of creative tension, forcing people to go beyond either or any of the identities alone.

In an important sense, identity—who you are—can never be satisfactorily accounted for by the preexisting labels, because how anyone introjects or copes with them is necessarily individual: both the number one takes into account and the mutual adjustment among them. Identity, then, either generates an ascent into individuality—what makes a person identifiably himself—or risks sinking into an unreflecting torpor of absolute sameness with everyone else with the same identity.

Since in a modern society unreflecting torpor is not respectable and probably not even possible, each of us is stuck with creating our own identity. We can do that either well or badly, meaning either reflectively or unreflectively.

Entertaining questions here are: Is it not one's identity that is at work in shaping the reflecting and determining the decisions? If so, how can one get beyond one's existing identity? The short answer is, of course, try it and see.

However that may be, there is no doubt I am subtly altering my self-understanding by the things I (choose to) experience, the places I go, and books I read, the kinds of things I learn from all those, and their effect on how I think about things. Just as your "self" is what you put into it, your "identity" is what you make yourself into. And you alter it by adding new and different things.

It is entirely understandable that for young gays and lesbians, "Who am I" can translate into "What does this sexual orientation mean for me?" and results in a vigorous exploration of the gay subculture. But as diverting or absorbing as that subculture can be, it remains a subculture, not a culture.

The subculture can offer the real benefits of erotic fulfillment as well as positive personal reinforcement (which is what erotic fulfillment usually reduces to), but it can only *contribute* to an identity, it can hardly *be* an identity—unless, maybe, one's identity is as a person who seeks positive personal reinforcement.

Put in different language, someone whose identity is being gay is going to be a fairly limited person, and, happily enough, fairly rare. It is, after all, people's individuality, their differentness from ourselves, that makes them interesting to talk to, to get to know.

If all this is so, then while *gay* itself is a useful term, a "gay identity" is neither a desirable goal nor even a useful concept for talking about real people.

SECTION V

GAYNESS AND GOD

It's impossible to discuss anti-gay bigotry in America without discussing religion. Preachers routinely reassure their flocks that prejudice against gays has a scriptural basis; televangelists have reaped rewards by placing homosexuality at the head of their lists of sins. As *New York Times* columnist Frank Rich has noted, "the religious right has learned that gay-bashing . . . is the most productive fund-raising tool."

Generally, the queer establishment has responded to this hate-mongering either by mocking faith and branding religious gays as traitors, or by insisting that gays who are drawn to religion practice a specifically queer spirituality within the context of exclusively gay institutions. For instruction in such queer spirituality, gays are encouraged to turn to such books as Will Roscoe's *Queer Spirits: A Gay Men's Myth Book,* Mark Thompson's *Gay Soul: Finding the Heart of Gay Spirit and Nature,* and Nancy Wilson's *Our Tribe: A Lesbian Ecu-Terrorist Outs the Bible for the Queer Millennium,* all published in 1995.

In such an environment, membership in traditional religious bodies is anathema. Eric Marcus's splendid 1992 book *Making History: The Struggle for Gay and Lesbian Equal Rights* quotes

Kathleen Boatwright, a leader of the gay Episcopalian group Integrity, as saying that "the only thing dirtier than being a lesbian in a Christian community is being a Christian in the lesbian community." Indeed, despite such admirable church-based challenges to homophobia as Letha Dawson Scanzoni and Virginia Ramey Mollenkott's *Is the Homosexual My Neighbor?* (1978), Yale professor John Boswell's *Christianity, Social Tolerance, and Homosexuality* (1980), and the Rt. Rev. John Shelby Spong's *Living in Sin?* (1988), the queer establishment's failure to answer vigorously and responsibly the lies of anti-gay preachers—and to insist on the right of gays to a place at the communion tables of traditional churches, rather than offering up the predominantly gay Metropolitan Community Church as the sole institutional answer to every gay person's spiritual questions—has helped feed the growth of the Christian Coalition and has hampered progress toward equal rights and social acceptance within mainstream religious bodies.

But things are changing. In the 1990s, the movement to modify doctrines concerning homosexuality—a movement supported by such high-profile figures as Episcopal Presiding Bishop Edmond Browning and Anglican Archbishop Desmond Tutu—has gone into high gear in mainstream Protestant denominations, in which the presence of gay members (and even gay clergy) is openly acknowledged in an increasing number of congregations. The essays in this section, in which gay believers discuss their beliefs and their sexuality, are part of a process of change that has, among other things, thrown into sharp relief the counterproductiveness of the traditional gay-left approach to church-fostered prejudice. As I wrote in a 1994 *Advocate* column entitled "In Good Faith,"

> In its glory days the black civil rights movement looked for inspiration and guidance largely to dedicated spiritual leaders whose rhetoric was not about victimization, vengeance, separation, us versus them. Instead, these leaders drew on the deepest elements of their religious traditions to speak of love and hope and common humanity, and they called on men and women of all skin colors to be their best and bravest selves.
>
> This, it seems to me, is a big part of what the gay rights cause needs now—and some of its most promising leaders realize it. . . . [Many of us] have been so abominably treated in the name of God—by our family churches or by our parents—that we equate Christianity with hatred. Just as some Christians, moreover, generalize about gay people on the basis of what they see on the more sensational TV clips of Gay Pride Day marches, so gay people often think of all Christians as being like Robertson and Falwell.
>
> This is a shame because Christianity, properly understood, isn't about hate; it's about love. And so is homosexuality—a point that many Christians don't get. Yet more and more do get it, and as they do, their desire to do what's right is increasingly a force *for* us. For this reason I feel strongly that instead of bashing back at Christian gay bashers, we should be answering their charges with as much wisdom, dignity, and integrity as we can muster; instead of mocking faith and morality, we should make it clear that homosexuality is not inconsistent with faith and that morality, properly comprehended, demands not condemnation of gay people but respect for loving homosexual relationships.

This last sentence sums up the common theme of the essays brought together in this section.

RABBI YAAKOV LEVADO

Levado is the pseudonym of an Orthodox Jewish rabbi. This essay originally appeared in a 1993 issue of the Jewish intellectual journal *Tikkun*. The meanings of the Hebrew words used in this essay are generally clear from the context, though it may be useful to note that the *halacha* (Hebrew for *law*) refers to the legal portion of the Talmud and of post-Talmudic literature, and that a halachist is a student and interpreter of that law. *Hesed*, often translated as "steadfast love," is used in the scriptures to denote the perfect devotedness that can exist between husband and wife as well as that of God for his people.

GAYNESS AND GOD

I am an Orthodox rabbi, and I am gay. For a long while I denied, rejected, railed against this truth. The life story that I had wanted—wife, kids, and a family that modeled Torah and *hesed*—turned out to be an impossible fantasy. I have begun to shape a new life story. This essay is part of that life story and thus remains unfinished, part of a stream of consciousness rather than a systematic treatise.

It is hard to say how or when I came to know myself as a gay man. In the beginning, it was just an array of bodily sensations; sweaty palms and that excited sort of nervousness you feel around certain people occurred without awareness. The arrival of the hormonal hurricane left me completely dumbfounded. Just when my body should have fulfilled social expectations, it began to transgress them. I had no physical response to girls. But I was physically pulled, eyes and body, toward guys. I remember my head turning sharply once in the locker room for an athletic boy whom I admired. At the time, I must have noticed my body's involuntary movement, but it meant nothing to me. I understood nothing. How could I? I had no idea what it meant to be homosexual. *Faggot* or *homo* were words reserved for the boys hounded for being passive, or unathletic. None of this said anything about sexual attraction. There were no categories for this experience, no way to explain the strange muscle spasms, the warm sensation on my face, or the flutter in my chest. Not until years later, after countless repetitions of such events, did it slowly, terrifyingly, break through to my consciousness.

When other boys were becoming enraptured by girls, I found my rapture in learning Torah. I was thrilled by the sprawling rabbinic arguments, the imaginative plays on words, and the demand for meaning everywhere. *Negiah,* the prohibition to embrace, kiss, or even touch girls until marriage, was my saving grace. The premarital sexual restraint of the Halacha was a perfect mask, not only to the world but to myself.

My years in yeshiva were spectacular, in some measure because they were so intensely fueled by a totally denied sexuality. There were many *bachurim* (students) in the yeshiva whose intense and passionate learning was energized with repressed sexual energy. For me, the environment deflected sexual energy and generated it as well. The male spirit and energy I felt in yeshiva was both nourishing and frustrating. I do not know if I was alone among my companions or not. From those early years, I remember no signs by which I could have clearly read my gayness or anyone else's. I only know that I was plagued with stomachaches almost every morning.

Later, on one desperate occasion, beset with an increased awareness of my attraction to a fellow yeshiva student, I visited a sage, Rav Eliashuv, who lives in one of the most secluded right-wing Orthodox communities in Jerusalem. He was old and in failing health, but still taking visitors who daily waited in an anteroom for hours for the privilege of speaking with him for a few minutes.

Speaking in Hebrew, I told him what, at the time, I felt was the truth. "Master, I am attracted to both men and women. What shall I do?" He responded, "My dear one, then you have twice the power of love. Use it carefully." I was stunned. I sat in silence for a moment, waiting for more. "Is that all?" I asked. He smiled and said, "That is all. There is nothing more to say."

Rav Eliashuv's words calmed me, permitting me to forget temporarily the awful tensions that would eventually overtake me. His trust and support buoyed me above my fears. I thought that as a bisexual I could have a wider and richer emotional life and perhaps even a deeper spiritual life than is common—and still marry and have a family. For a long while I felt a self-acceptance that carried me confidently into rabbinical school. I began rabbinical training with great excitement and a sense of promise. At the center of my motivations were those powerful rabbinic traditions that had bowled me over in my early adolescence. I wanted more than anything else to learn and to teach Torah in its full depth and breadth. I finished rabbinical school, still dating and carefully avoiding any physical expression, and took my first jobs as a rabbi. There were many failed relationships with wonderful women who could not understand why things just didn't work out. Only after knocking my shins countless times into the hard wood of this truth was I able fully to acknowledge that I am gay.

It has taken a number of years to sift through the wreckage of "my life as I wanted it" to discover "my life as it is." It has taken more time to exorcise the self-hatred that feeds on shattered hopes and ugly stereotypes. I am still engaged in that struggle. I have yet to receive the new tablets, the whole ones, that will take their place in the Ark beside the broken ones. Rav Nachman of Bratzlav teaches that there is nothing so whole as a broken heart. It is in his spirit that I continue to try to make sense of my life.

Although much has changed in the past few years as I have accepted my gayness, much remains the same. I am still a rabbi, and I am still deeply committed to God, Torah, and Israel. My religious life had always been directed by the desire to be a servant of the Lord. None of that has changed. The question is an old one, merely posed anew as I strive to integrate being gay into my life. Given that I am gay, what is it that the God of Israel wants of me?

Of course, many will hear this as an illegitimate question—fallacious in thinking that the God of Israel can somehow accept and move beyond my gayness. Leviticus 18:23 instructs: "Do not lie with a male as one lies with a woman, it is an abhorrence." I do not propose to reject this or any text. For the present, I have no plausible halachic method of interpreting this text in a manner that permits homosexual sex.

As a traditionalist, I hesitate to overturn cultural norms in a flurry of revolutionary zeal. I am committed to a slower and more cautious process of change, which must always begin internally. Halacha, as an activity, is not designed to effect social revolution. It is a society-building enterprise that maintains internal balance by reorganizing itself in response to changing social realities. When social conditions shift, we experience the halachic reapplication as the proper commitment to the Torah's original purposes. That shift in social consciousness in regard to homosexuality is a long way off.

If I have any argument, it is not to press for a resolution, but for a deeper understanding of homosexuality. Within the living Halacha are voices in tension, divergent strands in an imaginative legal tradition that are brought to bear on the real lives of Jews. In order to know how to shape a halachic response to any living question, what is most demanded of us is a deep understanding of the Torah and an attentive ear to the people who struggle with the living question. Confronting new questions can often tease out of the tradition a *hiddush,* a new balancing of the voices and values that have always been there. There is no conclusive *psak halacha* (halachic ruling) without the hearing of personal testimonies, and so far gay people have not been asked to testify to their experience.

How can halachists possibly rule responsibly on a matter so complex and so deeply foreign, without a sustained effort at understanding? Whatever the halachic argument will be, we will need to know much more about homosexuality to ensure that people are treated not merely as alien objects of a system but as persons within it. Halachists will need to include in their deliberations the testimony of gay people who wish to remain faithful to the Torah. Unimagined halachic strategies, I believe, will appear under different conditions. We cannot know in advance the outcome of such an investigation. Still, one wonders what the impact might be if Orthodox rabbis had to face the questions posed by traditional Jews, persons they respect and to whom they feel responsible, who are gay.

There is one quasi-halachic issue I must address—that of choice. One of the mitigating factors in halachic discourse is the presence of free will in matters of law. A command is only meaningful in the context of our freedom to obey or disobey. Thus the degree of choice involved in homosexuality is central to the shaping of a halachic response. There is indeed a certain percentage of gay people who claim to exercise some volition in their sexual choices. But for the vast majority of gay people, there is no "choice" in the ordinary sense of the word. Gay feelings are hardwired into our bodies, minds, and hearts. The strangeness and mystery of sexuality is universal. What we share, gay or straight, is the surprising "queerness" of all sexual desire. The experience of heterosexuals may seem less outlandish for its being more common, but all sexual feeling is deeply mysterious, beyond explanation or a simple notion of choice.

The Halacha addresses activities, however, not sexual identities;

thus, in halachic Judaism there is no such thing as a gay identity—there are only sexual impulses to control. The tradition describes all sexual desire as *yetzer ha'ra* (evil impulse), rife with chaotic and destructive possibilities. Heterosexual desire is redeemed and integrated back into the system through a series of prescriptions and prohibitions that channel sexuality and limit its range of expression. Confined within marriage, giving and receiving sexual pleasure, even in nonprocreative ways, is raised to the level of *mitzvah*.

Homosexual desire, in contrast, is not seen as redeemable and thus remains an implacable *yetzer ha'ra* that needs to be defeated rather than channeled. In this argument, gay people are treated as people with a dangerous and destructive sexual desire which must be repressed. The spiritual task of a gay person is to overcome the *yetzer ha'ra* that prods one to have erotic relations with members of the same sex.

The unfairness of this argument begins with the recasting of homosexuals as heterosexuals with perverse desires. The Torah is employed to support the idea that there is only one sexuality, heterosexuality. God confirms heterosexual desire, giving heterosexuals the opportunity to enjoy love and companionship. With the impossibility of another sexuality comes the implicit assumption that gay people can "become" straight and marry and, indeed, should do so.

This has in fact been the ordinary state of affairs for many, if not most, gay men and women throughout history. I know a number of gay (or bisexual) men who have married and sustain relationships with their wives. Of those, most have had an affair at some point that did not end their marriage. Two gay rabbis I know were married and are now divorced, and a third remains happily married, surviving recurrent bouts of depression and emotional exhaustion. What disturbs me most in this sometimes heroic attempt at approximating the traditional ideal is the cost to the heterosexual spouse.

While in my first rabbinical post, I decided to come out to an older rabbi and seek his advice. He counseled me to find a woman and marry. I asked him if I was duty-bound to tell her about my attractions to men and my general sexual uninterest in women. He said no. I was shocked to hear that it was all right to deceive a woman who could very easily be damaged by such a marriage. It made no sense to me.

Surely some heterosexual women might be willing to marry a gay friend who could provide children and be a wonderful father.

There have been rare instances of gay women and men who have worked out marriages where the "uninterest" was mutual. I struggled for a number of years to find such a woman, gay or straight, with whom to begin a family. Sometimes I still torment myself to think that this is all possible, when it is not. I still feel ripped apart by these feelings—wanting a woman at the Shabbat table and a man in my bed. If I am judged for some failure, perhaps it will be that I could not choose the Shabbat table over the bed, either for myself or for the forlorn woman who, after dinner, wants the comfort of a man who wants her back.

Having rejected this option, the standard Orthodox position is to require celibacy. Many recent articles and responsa regard gay sex as indistinguishable from adultery, incest, or bestiality. The heterosexual is asked to limit sexuality to the marital bed, to nonrelatives, to human beings; the homosexual is asked to live a loveless life. I have lived portions of my adult life as a celibate clergyman. While it can have spiritual potency for a Moses or a Ben Azzai, who abandoned sexual life for God or Torah, it is not a Jewish way to live. Always sleeping alone, in a cold bed, without touch, without the daily physical interplay of lives morning and night—this celibate scenario is life-denying and, for me, has always led to a shrinking of spirit. What sort of Torah, what voice of God would demand celibacy from all gay people? Such a reading of divine intent is nothing short of cruel.

Many gay people now and in the past have been forced to purchase social acceptance and God's love through a denial of affection and comfort and, worse, a denial of self. Today many simply leave Judaism behind in order to salvage a sense of dignity and to build a life. This understanding of homosexuality leaves no sanctified option for gay people, no possibility of *keddusha* or *keddushin*.

I have come to understand my gayness as akin to my Jewishness: it is integral to my sense of self. I did not choose it, but it is mine. To try to escape it would be self-defeating. There is nothing left to do but celebrate it. Whether in or out of the given halachic rubric, I affirm my desire for a full life, for love, and for sexual expression. Given that I am gay and cannot be otherwise, and given that I do not believe that God would demand that I remain loveless and celibate, I have chosen to seek a committed love, a man with whom to share my life.

But so little of life is carried on in the bedroom. When I indeed find a partner, what sort of life do we build together? What is it that the God of Israel wants of me in regard to family and community?

Struggling with God and with Torah as a gay person was just the beginning. To be Jewish is to be grounded in the continuity of the Jewish people as a witness—a holy people, a light among the nations—a blessing to all the families of the earth. How does a gay person help to shape the continuity of the Jewish people? The carrying forth of the Jewish people is accomplished by marriage and procreation. It is both a tool of the Abrahamic covenant and its most profound meaning statement.

We are a people on the side of life—new life, more life, fuller life. The creation story invited the rabbis to read God's blessing of "be fruitful and multiply" as a command to have two children, a male and a female. Every Jewish child makes the possibility of the

Torah's promise of a perfected world more real, more attainable. Abraham and Sarah transmit this vision by having children. Often the portrayal of blessing includes being surrounded with many children. Childlessness is a punishment and curse in the tradition, barrenness a calamity.

Gay life does not prevent the possibility of producing or raising Jewish children, but it makes those options very complicated. Being gay means that the ordinary relationship between making love and having children is severed. This is a deep challenge to the structure of Judaism, since its very transmission is dependent on both relationship and reproduction. For Jews who feel bound by *mitzvot,* bound by the duty to ensure that life conquers death, the infertility of our loving is at the core of our struggle to understand ourselves in light of the Torah.

This problem, among others, lies at the root of much of the Jewish community's discomfort with gay people. To a people that was nearly destroyed fifty years ago, gay love seems irresponsible. Jews see the work of their lives in light of the shaping of a world for their children. By contrast, gay people appear narcissistic and self-indulgent. Gay people's sexuality is thus a diversion from the tasks of Jewish family and the survival that it symbolizes, and is perceived as marginal to the Jewish community because we are shirkers of this most central and sacred of communal tasks.

This challenge also has a moral chord that strikes deep into the problems of gay subculture. The tradition understood parenting as one of the major moral crucibles for human development. No judge could serve without first being a parent for fear that without the experience of parenting, one could grasp neither human vulnerability nor responsibility. Being heterosexual carries one down a path that demands years of selfless loving in the rearing of children. While not all straight couples have children, and some gay couples adopt them, the norm is shaped less by choice and more by biology. Yet if gay people do not ordinarily fall into monogamous coupling and childbearing, how do we find our place in the covenant? And what of the moral training that caring for children provides; how do we make up for that? Is there another job to be done that requires our service to God and to the Jewish people? Of all the problems entailed in gay sexuality, this one looms for me, both spiritually and emotionally.

Although there is no obvious biblical resource for this dilemma, there are biblical writers who struggled to address God's will in very new social circumstances. Isaiah was one such writer who bridged the worlds before and after the Exile. Some familiar passages have become charged for me with new meaning. In these verses Isaiah is speaking to his ancient Israelite community and trying to convince them that God's covenantal plan for Israel is larger than they think. The covenant begins with Abraham and Sarah but has become much more than a family affair. He speaks to two obvious outsider groups in chapter 56, the *b'nai ha'nechar,* the foreigners of non-Israelite birth, and the *sarisim,* the eunuchs:

> Let not the foreigner say,
> Who has attached himself to the Lord,
> "The Lord will keep me separate from His people";
> And let not the eunuch say,
> "I am a withered tree."

In the Talmud, a eunuch is not necessarily a castrated male, but a male who is not going to reproduce for various reasons (*Yevamot* 80b). Why does Isaiah turn his attention here to the foreigners and the eunuchs? In the chain of the covenantal family, the foreigner has no past and the eunuch no future. They both seem excluded from the covenantal frame of reference. It is this "exclusion" that the prophet addresses:

> For thus said the Lord:
> "As for the eunuchs who keep my sabbaths,

Who have chosen what I desire
And hold fast to My covenant—
I will give them, in My House
And within my walls,
A monument and a name
Better than sons or daughters.
I will give them an everlasting name
Which shall not perish.

The prophet comforts the pain of eunuchs with the claim that there are other ways in which to observe, fulfill, and sustain the covenant. There is something more permanent than the continuity of children provides. In God's House, the achievement of each individual soul has account. A name in the Bible is the path toward the essence, the heart of being. It is passed on to progeny. But there is another sort of a name, a name better than the one sons or daughters provide. The covenant is carried forward by those who live it out, in the present. Loyalty to the covenant is measured in God's House in such a way that even if one's name is not passed on through children an eternal name will nonetheless be etched into the walls. Isaiah offers a place to the placeless, an alternative service to the person who cannot be part of the family in other ways:

As for the foreigners
Who attach themselves to the Lord,
to be His servants—
All who keep the sabbath and do not profane it,
And who hold fast to my covenant—
I will bring them to my sacred mount
And let them rejoice in my house of prayer.
Their burnt offerings and sacrifices
Shall be welcome on My altar;
For My House shall be called

A House of prayer for all peoples."
Thus declares the Lord God,
Who gathers the dispersed of Israel:
"I will gather still more to those already gathered."

So inclusive is God's plan for the Israel in the world that any foreigner can join. The notion of conversion, so obvious to us now, was a striking innovation for the generation of Isaiah. Conversion is about rewriting the past. Like adoption, conversion redefines the meaning of parents and family. Birth and lineage are not discarded. The central metaphor for Israel is still family, but Isaiah and later tradition open up another avenue into the covenant. Those with no future are promised a future in the House of the Lord; those with no past are nevertheless included in Israel's destiny.

God can only require the doable. A foreigner cannot choose a different birth, or the eunuch a different procreative possibility. Gay people cannot be asked to be straight, but they can be asked to "hold fast to the covenant." God will work the story out and link the loose ends as long as we hold fast to the covenant.

Holding fast to the covenant demands that I fulfill the *mitzvot* that are in my power to fulfill. I cannot marry and bear children, but there are other ways to build a family. Adoption and surrogacy are options. If these prove infeasible, the tradition considers a teacher similar to a parent in life-giving and thus frames a way that the *mitzvah* of procreation can be symbolically fulfilled.

Holding fast to the covenant demands that I seek a path toward sanctity in gay sexual life. The Torah has much to say about the way people create *keddusha* in their sexual relationships. The values of marriage, monogamy, modesty, and faithfulness that are central to the tradition's view of holiness need to be applied in ways that shape choices and life styles.

Holding fast to the covenant means that being gay does not free one from the fulfillment of *mitzvot.* The complexities generated by a verse in Leviticus need not unravel my commitment to the whole of the Torah. There are myriad Jewish concerns, moral, social, intellectual, and spiritual, that I cannot abandon. Being gay need not overwhelm the rest of Jewish life. Single-issue communities are political rather than religious; religious communities tend to be comprehensive of the human condition. The richness of Jewish living derives in part from its diversity of attention, its fullness.

For gay Orthodox Jews, this imagination of engagement between ourselves and the tradition is both terribly exciting and depressing. Regretfully, the communities that embrace us, both gay and Jewish, also reject us. The Jewish community wishes that we remain invisible. The gay community is largely unsympathetic and often hostile to Judaism. There are some in the gay community who portray Judaism as the original cultural source of homophobia. More often, the lack of sympathy toward Jewish observance derives from the singlemindedness of gay activism. Liberation communities rarely have room for competing loyalties.

Gay synagogues have filled a void for many, providing a place of dignity in a Jewish community. This work is part of a movement toward a fuller integration in the larger Jewish community for which most gay Jews long. Gay-friendly synagogues may well point the way, modeling a community of families and singles, young and old, straight and gay that is in spirit much closer to my hopeful future imagination than anything yet.

Gay Jews who wish to be part of an Orthodox community will find very few synagogues in which there is some level of understanding and tolerance. Some gay Jews attend Orthodox services and remain closeted in their communities. It is crucial that Orthodox rabbis express a loving acceptance for known gays in their synagogues even if public legitimation is now impossible. Attacks on homosexuality from the pulpit are particularly painful to those who have remained connected to the traditional synagogue, despite the hardships.

I have hesitated until now to address the central halachic concerns of homosexuality. Real dialogue is necessary before such a process of responsa writing can begin. Still, it appears to many Orthodox Jews that in the case of homosexuality there is little use for dialogue in the face of such a clear biblical prohibition. A number of my colleagues and friends want very much to respond compassionately to gay people, but feel compelled to remain loyal to what they see as the unambiguous word of the Torah. Let me offer the possibility of an intermediate position to demonstrate that real listening may indeed give birth to new halachic strategies.

The Torah very specifically forbids anal intercourse between two men. If the Torah expressly forbids only this one form of sexual fulfillment, could we articulate a possible "halachic" form of gay loving that excludes anal intercourse but permits a loving physical and emotional relationship between two men or two women? After all, heterosexuality is not a free zone of activity for halachically committed Jews. For the sake of holiness, the Torah requires heterosexual couples to refrain from intercourse during menstruation. Why not offer such a sanctified option to gay men who wish to find acceptance in the halachic community?

For many gay men, this will not be a realistic choice. But until it becomes a real possibility, who knows who will agree to commit? Of course, this challenge to gay Jewish men will be sincere only if the halachic community then takes a lead in accepting the couples who commit in this covenantal fashion. (Lesbian women would be accepted without condition, because there is no Torah text that specifically prohibits their relationships.)

I offer this framework knowing that Orthodox Jews will protest that there are rabbinic prohibitions that invalidate it, and that many gay Jews will feel that it too severely limits the essence of gay lovemaking. Let it then simply demonstrate at least the beginnings of a language of discourse between the tradition as it now stands and the lives of gay people.

For the present, in regard to sexual behavior, I personally have chosen to accept a certain risk and violate the Halacha as it is presently articulated, in the hope of a subsequent, more accepting halachic expression. I realize that this is "civil disobedience." It is not the system itself which I challenge but its application to an issue that has particular meaning for me and for those like me. There is always the possibility that I am wrong. Ultimately, the halachic risks that I take are rooted in my personal relationship with God, Who I will face in the end. It is this faith that makes me both confident and suspicious of myself.

I have, admittedly, a rather privatized form of community. I am closeted and have chosen to write this essay in anonymity to preserve what is still most precious to me: the teaching of Torah and caring for my community of Jews. What concerns me most is neither rejection by the Orthodox community, nor the loss of my particular pulpit. Were I to come out, the controversy would collapse my life, my commitments, my identity as a teacher of Torah, into my gayness. Still, the secrecy and the shadowy existence of the closet are morally repugnant and emotionally draining. I cannot remain forever in darkness. I thank God that for the time being, the Torah still sheds ample light.

I have a small circle of friends, gay and straight, men and women with whom I share a sense of community. We are looking for other tradition-centered Jews who can help build a place that embraces both the Torah and gay people. Not a synagogue, not a building, but a place for all the dispersed who are in search of community with Israel and communion with God. In this place, this House of the Lord, now somewhat hypothetical and private (and soon, I pray, to be concrete and public), those of us who have withered in the darkness, or in the light of day have been banished, will discover our names etched upon the walls.

THOMAS H. STAHEL, S.J.

The following interview appeared in the Catholic magazine *America* in May 1993.

I'M HERE: AN INTERVIEW WITH ANDREW SULLIVAN

You are both Catholic and gay and open about both, and it would be helpful to others in the church to know how you bring those two parts of your life together, in view of official church teaching on homosexuality and also in view of your evident respect for the Catholic tradition.

Well, part of what I've found frustrating is the notion that I've made some public announcement that I was these two things—which is not true. The fact of the matter was that both those things were part of my life, as a human being, when I got this job. As a writer, I had written about both areas of my life. As a journalist, my first material—and I've always found this—is trying to understand oneself and one's life through telling these things. That's why I studied philosophy and theology and why I found myself drawn to writing about and wrestling with issues of sexuality. So it was what everybody else said, it was they that presented this matter as such.

It's very hard to know where to start in saying how you actually reconcile the two elements, and it is something profoundly personal and private. There were two things I didn't want to do, however. One, I did not want to lie about either. I did not feel that that was intellectually or spiritually worthy. And I did not want to make an issue of this with the church either. It was foisted upon me. I was asked the questions. As the editor of a public magazine, I was, to some extent, obliged to answer them.

It was not as if you wished to issue a challenge, then?

No, not at all. And I have not, in anything that I've written. I think I've been extremely respectful of the authority of the church—I mean, authority as it is understood in the church's complex notion. That's not what I wanted to do. I've never challenged the church. I've always attempted to understand its teachings on sexuality within the context of the teachings of the church on broader notions of sexuality and in general.

On the other hand, of course, I do try and live a life that is not in complete internal conflict. But I don't believe that any Christian or any person trying to live a life of faith expects a life which is not full of conflict. One of the things I've tried to resist is the temptation to resolve contradictions. There are some contradictions which cannot be resolved or explained away that have to be lived with. It would be, I think, an insult both to the intellectual coherence of a great deal of the church's teaching and to what I hope may be the moral integrity of my own and many other people's lives, to say that contradiction can easily be avoided.

There was a moment once in a talk I gave at the University of Virginia, on the politics of sexuality. At the end of the talk, a young kid, who must have been about nineteen, said, "I'm struggling with this. I'm gay, and I'm in the church, and I don't know what to do. Can you help me?" And I said, "No, I can't help you. I don't have the moral authority to help anybody." Undoubtedly the very fact of my existence, at some level, in the public area has provoked and prompted an enormous number of letters and an enormous amount of interest from people in exactly the same position—who want desperately to have a life that can be spiritually and morally whole. The church as presently constituted refuses to grapple with this desire.

I'm not being very coherent. If I were writing an article, I'd be more coherent.

Your argument, in any case, has to do with a contradiction that nevertheless cannot be avoided.

There is a basic contradiction. I completely concede that, at one level. At another level—and I confronted this, actually, with my first boyfriend, who was also Roman Catholic. When we had a fight one day, he said:

"Do you really believe that what we are doing is wrong? Because if you do, I can't go on with this. And yet you don't want to challenge the church's teaching on this, or leave the church." And of course I was forced to say I don't believe, at some level, I really do not believe that the love of one person for another and the commitment of one person to another, in the emotional construct which homosexuality dictates to us—I know in my heart of hearts that cannot be wrong. I know that there are many things within homosexual life that can be wrong, just as in heterosexual life they can be wrong. There are many things in my sexual and emotional life that I do not believe are spiritually pure, in any way. It is fraught with moral danger, but at its deepest level it struck me as completely inconceivable—from my own moral experience, from a real honest attempt to understand that experience—that it was wrong.

I experienced coming out in exactly the way you would think. I didn't really express any homosexual emotions or commitments or relationships until I was in my early twenties, partly because of the strict religious upbringing I had, and my commitment to my faith. It was not something I blew off casually. I struggled enormously with it. But as soon as I actually explored the possibility of human contact within my emotional and sexual makeup—in other words, as soon as I allowed myself to love someone—all the constructs the church had taught me about the inherent disorder seemed just so self-evidently wrong that I could no longer find it that problematic. Because my own moral sense was overwhelming, because I felt, through the experience of loving someone or being allowed to love someone, an enormous sense of the presence of God—for the first time in my life.

Within the love?

Yes.

And within the sexual expression of that love?

The mixture of the two, the inextricable mixture of the two. I mean, I felt like I was made whole.

Having made this discovery that you were whole for the first time, how then did you retain your respect and reverence for the church understood as a contrary tradition?

It's very curious, I think, because I've never felt anger toward the church. I know I'm weird in this regard.

Many gay people do feel anger.

Enormous anger, enormous. They've left. The depth of the pain that's been caused people—I mean, real pain—not only by the laity, but by the clergy too, is extraordinary. Honestly and truly, there are few subjects on which the church is now, by virtue of its teaching, inflicting more pain on human beings than this subject—real psychic, spiritual pain. I'm not sure why I don't feel anger. I have always, I think, assumed that I probably don't understand enough to experience anger, that the church was never meant to be a perfect institution, that it was grappling and finding and struggling to find its way toward the truth of its own doctrine, the truth of its own mission.

The official church teaching is at a loss to deal with homosexuality, in my view, because according to this official moral teaching homosexuality has no finality. Any comment?

It is bizarre that something can occur naturally and have no natural end. I think it's a unique doctrine, isn't it? The church now concedes—although it attempts to avoid conceding it in the last couple of letters—but it has essentially conceded, and does concede in the new Universal Catechism. . . .

Have you seen it?

I've read it in French, yes.

What does it concede?

That homosexuality is, so far as one can tell, an involuntary condition.

An "orientation"?

Yes, and that it is involuntary. The church has conceded this: Some people seem to be constitutively homosexual. And the church has also conceded compassion. Yet the expression of this condition, which is involuntary and therefore sinless—because if it is involuntary, obviously no sin attaches—is always and everywhere sinful! Well, I could rack my brains for an analogy in any other Catholic doctrine that would come up with such a notion. Philosophically, it is incoherent, fundamentally incoherent. People are born with all sorts of things. We are born with original sin, but that is in itself sinful—an involuntary condition but it is sin.

The analogy might be thought to be disability, but at the core of what disabled human beings can be—which means their spiritual and emotional life—the church not only affirms the equal dignity of disabled people in that regard but encourages us to see it and to take away the prejudice of not believing a disabled person can lead a full and integrated human life even though they cannot walk or they experience some other disability.

But the disability that we are asked to believe that we are about is fundamental to our integrity as emotional beings, as I understand it. Now, I have tried to understand what this doctrine is about, because my life is at stake in it. I believe God thinks there is a final end for me and others that is related to our essence as images of God and as people who are called to love ourselves and others. I am drawn, in the natural way I think human beings are drawn, to love and care for another person. I agree with the church's teachings about natural law in that regard. I think we are called to commitment and to fidelity, and I see that all around me in the gay world. I see, as one was taught that one would see something in natural law, self-evident activity leading toward this final end, which is commitment and love: the need and desire and hunger for that. That is the *sensus fidelium,* and there is no attempt within the church right now even to bring that sense into the teaching or into the discussion of the teaching.

You see it even in the documents. The documents will say, on the one hand compassion, on the other hand objective disorder. A document that can come up with this phrase, "not unjust discrimination," is contorted because the church is going in two different directions at once with this doctrine. On the one hand, it is recognizing the humanity of the individual being; on the other, it is not letting that human being be fully human.

Would you agree that the acknowledgment of this issue within Catholic family life will inevitably change the way the church expresses itself toward people who are professedly homosexual?

I would, probably. My family is an interesting example. My mother is a very devout Catholic. My sister is a devout and practicing Catholic. Both are now pillars of moral and emotional support for me, and for gay people in general. That, I think, is the authentically Catholic response. And the family is the key to broader change. I think that's how it will get resolved in society in general, because homosexuality—when you actually look at it in people whom you need and love—is a very different issue from when it's some abstract mode of being or some closeted, repressed mode of being, which is equally abstract. Once it is actually human—well, there are many sides to the Catholic temperament and sensibility, but one great strand is its ability to understand the human experience and empathize with it. That will overcome so much, I think.

Of course, there's "hate the sin, but love the sinner." But as we've said, it's no longer that. It's "accept the condition, and reject the conditioned." That's what it is.

As the church's present policy . . .

That's the present policy. But that will not hold, because it is intellectually incoherent. I have searched in vain for a truly coherent intellectual defense of the position that doesn't merely come down to "We're sorry."

Also, I think that the competence and the change in gay society as a whole, in American society as a whole, will trickle in. I think in a small way someone like me has an effect on people: Well, here's someone who looks like a real human being, who is responsible, who can do a job, who doesn't seem to be depraved or dysfunctional or disordered in any more than a usual sense. Do we really think this person merits this particular censure, so much that we could not tolerate being in the same march or organization or pew?

If you had been a consultor to New York's Cardinal John J. O'Connor, how would you have advised him to act with respect to gays seeking to march in the St. Patrick's Day parade? [This conversation took place two days after St. Patrick's Day.]

He's in an impossible position. He really is. I think there could have been a far clearer statement from the Cardinal that gay human beings are human beings and that the church fights for the dignity of every human being and fights for the dignity of every homosexual human being. He could have made that statement and distinguished it—however incoherently, but he could have distinguished it—from an endorsement of a particular political platform that approves something the church still believes is a sin.

Once, I remember, I was downtown late on a Sunday afternoon, and I wanted to go to Mass, and I was wearing a gay T-shirt. The question was whether I could go to Mass wearing this T-shirt. And I did, because as a gay person I am a human being, and the church says that. The way that the Cardinal Archbishop of New York behaved, I think, failed to make that important distinction—which, given the existence of bigotry, was an extremely unnerving stance.

Why would you have characterized his position as "impossible"?

Because the church's position is so incoherent. You can't really say, "We love gay people, but you can't be gay." You have to assume, if they're marching as gay people, that they practice. But of course the church is there defining gay people by a sexual act in a way it never defines heterosexual people, and in this the church is in weird agreement with extremist gay activists who also want to define homosexuality in terms of its purely sexual content. Whereas being gay is not about sex as such. Fundamentally, it's about one's core emotional identity. It's about whom one loves, ultimately, and how that can make one whole as a human being.

The moral consequences, in my own life, of the refusal to allow myself to love another human being were disastrous. They made me permanently frustrated and angry and bitter. It spilled over into other areas of my life. Once that emotional blockage is removed, one's whole moral equilibrium can improve, just as a single person's moral equilibrium in a whole range of areas can improve with marriage, in many ways, because there is a kind of stability and security and rock upon which to build one's moral and emotional life. To deny this to gay people is not merely incoherent and wrong, from the Christian point of view. It is incredibly destructive of the moral quality of their lives in general. Does that make sense? These things are part of a continuous moral whole. You can't ask someone to suppress what makes them whole as a human being and then to lead blameless lives. We are human beings, and we need love in our lives in order to love others—in order to be good Christians! What the church is asking gay people to do is not to be holy, but actually to be warped.

Technically, the church is asking gay people to live celibately.

Right. But let's take that for a minute. Celibacy for the priesthood, which is an interesting argument and one with which I have a certain sympathy, is in order to unleash those deep emotional forces for love of God. Is the church asking this of gay people? I mean, if the church were saying to gay people, "You are special to us, and your celibacy is in order for you to have this role and that role and this final end," or if the church had a doctrine of an alternative final end for gay people, then it might make more sense. It would be saying God made gay people for this, not for marriage or for children or for procreation or for emotional pairing, but He made gay people in order to—let's say—build beautiful cathedrals or be witnesses to the world in some other way. But the church has *no* positive doctrine on this at all. You see, that would be a coherent position at some level—that, for some mysterious reason, God made certain people with full sexual and emotional capability and required them to sublimate that capability into other areas of life.

So you don't really accept the analogy of homosexuality to a handicap?

Not really. There are various ways in which that analogy doesn't work. It's not a physical handicap, clearly. It's not as if there's a physical impediment. It's the possible analogy to a mental handicap that is more interesting—because that's the closest it comes to what one might call an "objective disorder." But in a mentally handicapped person, the acts that person commits under the influence of that handicap are not morally culpable. When an epileptic knocks someone out in the process of a fit, that act is not regarded as an intrinsic moral evil, as is understood of a homosexual act. The acts of a retarded person are morally blameless insofar as they are produced by their handicap. But with gay people, the condition is like a handicap, but its expression is an intrinsic moral evil!

In the strongest terms one can use, the argument is intellectually contemptible. It really is. It's an insult to thinking people.

If that's the worst possible construction that can be put on the church's present teaching, what is the best?

Well, the best is that human sexuality is procreative, inextricably procreative, and that human beings are somehow meant to be that way, and that any expression of their sexuality is related to *Human Life* [the title of Paul VI's 1968 encyclical]. It's part of a continuous doctrinal argument. Undoubtedly, the impulse behind that reasoning is not merely biological but is to protect and promote human well-being as much as possible.

Do you see homosexual love as procreative?

It can't be procreative.

Not in the technical sense, but in some metaphorical or otherwise more significant sense than the merely biological?

In terms of the other thing the church understands conjugal love to be about, insofar as it teaches one the disciplines of love, yes, it's procreative. Marriage in its broadest sense teaches us something, I think, about the love of God for man . . . that's part of it. The permanent commitment of one person to another teaches human beings—the church teaches—what love is. In that sense, the love of one man for another man, or the love of one woman for another woman, in that conjugal bond, teaches exactly the same thing.

There is also enormous capacity, I think, for gay people to adopt children. Again, the church does not see that, in its attempt to care about the unborn—it's never been so imaginative as to say, "If we are interested in adoption and caring for children"—which is the important other side of a pro-life stand—"here are all these people able to love." Why not put the potential with the need?

What has been your own experience of pastoral care within the Catholic Church? Granted the possibility of a difference between official teaching and sympathetic advice of a counselor or priest, have you been well treated?

Yes, in general. But I have to say that I find it increasingly difficult. Once I had lost, at one point, my prime confessor who knew me, it was hard for me to reconstruct it all for someone else for fear of rejection. You never know what you are going to get back. For a Catholic that sometimes is the great . . . I mean, I've heard stories about people who have been wounded, deeply, by brusque treatment, a complete inability to understand what this is about. But, personally, I have nothing but positive things to say.

My parish in Washington is the cathedral parish. I go there for Mass on Sunday, and the congregation must be about 25 percent gay—I mean, it's the mid-city. There is almost no ministry to gay people, almost no mention of the subject. It is shrouded in complete and utter silence, which is the only practical way they can find to deal with it. Partly, of course—and here I'm not speaking of this particular cathedral or any particular congregation—because of the *great* tragedy of the church in what it requires of its own gay clergy. I mean, this horrific bargain they have to strike, which is not only are they required to be silent about their own sexuality but the repression is so great, they cannot even bring themselves to speak about it. It would bring up so much emotion and difficulty that it's best not even to touch upon it.

This is not a defense of a non-celibate clergy. The gay priest, in a way, would be ideal. If the church were really true to its convictions, it would be perfectly happy with openly gay priests who were also openly celibate, because presumably celibacy is the only issue the church has with homosexuals. Maybe the church should say the final end of all gay people is the priesthood—explicitly rather than implicitly. That would be a final end.

But it doesn't. It's crippled by its own internal inconsistency.

I think that in every statement the church makes, given the forces within our society as a whole, it has to be extremely careful that its doctrines not be misunderstood—especially in this matter—for fear that it become an accomplice to all sorts of forces that, of all things, it really should not be an accomplice to. People are beaten up. People are killed, actually, for their sexual orientation—on the streets, in bars, in the military. Slurs are made. This is surely something the church should oppose.

It's amazing that these distinctions are not made. If the church believed in its own position, it would constantly be making these distinctions, saying, for example, "We can't accept an explicitly pro-sexual-activity cohort in the [St. Patrick's Day] march . . . but we do believe that gay men and women are human beings, that they have dignity, that they are to be protected, that bigotry against them is to be resisted, that violence against them is to be opposed at all levels." There are ways in which you can frame these questions. The church has an obligation to teach both—if it's going to teach this doctrine.

But, you see, I think the church, at the highest levels, does not believe this. I think that on this doctrine, more than many others actually, the church is suffering from a crisis of its own internal conviction. Because homosexuality is not a new subject for the

Roman Catholic Church. It is not a distant subject. It is at the very heart of the hierarchy, so every attempt to deal with it is terrifying. But the fact of the matter is, if the church is to operate in the modern world, the conspiracy of silence is ending. So something has to be said. And the something that has to be said has to be coherent, or it will be exposed, as incoherence is always exposed.

There is so much in the church's doctrine that could give us an ability—even within the current doctrine—to present it in a positive way. I think the inability to do so suggests that, on the part of the hierarchy, there's a problem.

What are the good and positive elements in the Catholic tradition that could lead us to a more coherent position?

Natural law! Here is something [homosexuality] that seems to occur spontaneously in nature, in all societies and civilizations. Why not a teaching about the nature of homosexuality and what its good is. How can we be good? Teach us. How does one inform the moral lives of homosexuals? The church has an obligation to *all* its faithful to teach us how to live and how to be good—which is not merely dismissal, silence, embarrassment or a "unique" doctrine on one's inherent disorder. Explain it. How does God make this? Why does it occur? What should we do? How can the doctrine of Christian love be applied to homosexual people as well?

Now it may be this search will turn up all sorts of options and possibilities. There may be all sorts of notions and debate about the nature of this phenomenon and what its final end might be. But that it *has* a final end is important. The church has to understand—people in the church have to understand—what it must be to grow up loving God and wanting to live one's life well and truly, as a human being, able to love and contribute and believe, and yet having nothing.

I grew up with nothing. No one taught me anything except that this couldn't be mentioned. And as a result of the total lack of teaching, gay Catholics and gay people in general are in crisis. No wonder people's lives—many gay lives—are unhappy or distraught or in dysfunction, because there is no guidance at all. Here is a population within the church, and outside the church, desperately seeking spiritual health and values. And the church refuses to come to our aid, refuses to listen to this call.

You know, I see something like the AIDS quilt. What an extraordinary and spiritual thing that was, and this was done by people who are denied any spiritual support. What has happened with AIDS is the most extraordinary event for so many people of my generation, who have seen many of our friends die. The spiritual dimension of this event is enormous, and the need for the church to provide some structure, some hope, some spiritual guidance and balm—and nothing! Virtually nothing.

The quilt was in Washington. It is made by families, many of them Catholic, mothers and fathers and sons and daughters, who found somehow in their own lives a way to sacramentalize the lives of their sons and daughters, and to go to the Mall and do it. That afternoon, I went to church. The Gospel was about the ten lepers who were cleansed and the one who came back to give thanks [Lk. 17:11–19]. This Gospel, on this day of all days—when I had read the names of my friends on a loudspeaker—with its notion of the double alienation of being a leper and a Samarian, like suffering a plague and being gay: It was too perfect.

The sermon was about modern leprosy and how it was being cured. The bidding prayers had no reference to AIDS whatsoever, whereas a quarter of the congregation had been stricken or had seen it directly in their own lives. What is the church for? Could it not see this?

For the first time, I went up to the priest afterward, and I said, "I just want you to know that I've just been to the quilt. It's here in Washington. It's the most extraordinary event. I came here to pray. I came for what the church is here for, to help me, and to help me understand this. And you said—with this Gospel—you said nothing! Don't you understand how that must feel?"

He said, "Well, we prayed for the sick."

"Sure," I said. "But isn't there anybody here who can witness to what is happening?"

"Well, you are a witness to it."

And I said, "Well, *you* should be the witness to it."

In other words, there are basic, human, spiritual needs among gays that the church refuses to minister to, uniquely among all human beings. Even to ask the question "How can we help you?" or "How can we inform your moral and emotional life?" That is the church's first duty to its members and to the world at large, and it's refusing to live up to it, to such an extent that people have to do it themselves. The quilt was a great cathedral, really, a spontaneous cathedral, but it was an indictment of the church's inability to deal with it.

Do you think the church's denial is hard-heartedness, or fear and confusion?

The latter. I'm not angry at the church, because I do not believe the church is an evil institution. I do not believe it wants to hate gay people. I think the church just cannot cope. It's like a family that cannot talk about this even though its own son or daughter is gay.

That's why I think the family is important here . . .

Yes. If the analogy is complete, nothing can be healed until this can be dealt with.

Maybe the healing will come precisely from the families who deal with the issue more directly at the level of human love.

Exactly.

One problem in that case is that the hierarchy, who are the authorities, do not have to deal with gay children the way your mother did.

Also it's incumbent upon gay Catholics, just as it is always incumbent upon the gay child, to say, "I'm here." There's a two-way street.

You know, I see so many ways in which people are trying to say that, but they are so fearful of the rejection that they can't say it. I listen to gay America, and I hear this great cry for spiritual help. It doesn't sound like that a lot of the time. It sounds like anger, or protest. Many of the movements are semi-religious. And look at their tenacity. Look at Dignity, look at what people are doing to insist upon the spiritual possibilities, despite the disincentives.

BRUCE BAWER

In 1994 I was invited by members of St. John's Episcopal Cathedral in Denver, Colorado, to give a Sunday evening talk. This was part of an effort to help straight parishioners to understand homosexuality and the issues surrounding it, and to make the cathedral more welcoming to gay parishioners. I gave the talk on 18 September 1994 to a large, diverse audience whose willingness to listen respectfully, ask blunt questions, and reexamine long-standing assumptions and prejudices proved inspiring.

LECTURE AT SAINT JOHN'S CATHEDRAL

As many of you undoubtedly know, to talk to straight people about being a gay person, and especially to talk to straight Christians about being a gay Christian, can be frustrating and painful. There's an incredible amount of misunderstanding and discomfort in our society surrounding the subject, and good people can say hurtful things without even realizing it. In approaching encounters such as this one, I find it helpful to remind myself that coming to understand and be comfortable with homosexuality can be a long and difficult process not only for most straight people but for most gay people, too. In fact it's the same process, except that for gays it's imperative—if we want to live emotionally whole and healthy lives—to try to understand and come to terms with homosexuality, because it's something that society has conditioned us to think of as a bad thing but which is inside us and integral to our identities. For straight people, it's something that you can choose not to think about. Unless, of course, the subject touches you closely because a close friend turns out to be gay, or your sibling, or your child.

I begin my book *A Place at the Table* with an anecdote about such a child—a teenager, actually. One day when I was in my mid-twenties I went into a bookstore in New York and saw a well-dressed, obviously well-loved and well-taken-care-of boy of about fifteen standing alone at the magazine rack. As soon as I saw him I felt a rush of awareness, a sense of intimate and absolutely certain knowledge that stunned me and that forced me to stop what I was doing. I stood there watching while he picked up and glanced at one magazine, then put it down and did the same with another, and another. I knew he wasn't interested in those magazines but was trying to work up the nerve to read something else. I stood there because I wanted to see if he'd work up that nerve.

He did. He picked up a copy of the *New York Native,* a gay tabloid. If he'd just paged idly through the other publications, he went at the *Native* with a thirst like that of someone who'd crossed a desert and stumbled on a flowing stream. I was proud of him. Because I'd known from the moment I saw him that he was gay, not because he displayed any stereotypical characteristics that might jump out at some of you but because there was something about him that resonated powerfully with me, that connected with my memories of myself at that age, that communicated a fear, a curiosity, a tentativeness, an intense aloneness that I recognized and identified with. In any event, I knew in that moment that he was gay and that he was beginning to realize that fact, and I knew also that there was nobody with whom he felt he could talk about this momentous discovery he'd made about himself. And so he'd come to this bookstore.

But what had he found? Standing there I could see some of the pictures in the *Native.* There were ads for strip clubs, for drag shows, for leather bars, for escort services and phone sex, all of them illustrated with photographs of near-naked men, some of them in leather, some of them simulating sadomasochistic sex acts, and so forth. This wasn't the sort of thing I'd been looking for at that boy's age, and it wasn't anything that I or most of my gay friends could identify with, and I suspected that boy wasn't looking for that sort of thing either. He was confused, and such images could only aggravate his confusion. I know that in his shoes, looking at those pictures, I would've said to myself: "But that isn't *me.*" I worried that he might be thinking, "Well, if that's what it means to be gay, then I guess I must not be gay." Or, "Well, I'm gay, so I guess I'd better try to become like that." Or, "Well, I'm gay, but I refuse to become like that, so I guess the only alternative is to repress it and marry."

The irony of it all was that there I was, standing there. I could've explained things to him. I could've told him that gay life is a spectrum just as straight life is. Yes, there are gay men who are into S&M or cross-dressing, gay men who are very promiscuous. And there are also straight men into all those things, too. But most gay people are in most ways pretty much like most straight people. The main difference is that they're virtually invisible. They're essentially silent about being gay; so that the basically mainstream-oriented majority of gay people don't contribute very much to the public image of—or the public dialogue about—what it means to be gay. The image is formed, rather, and the "gay" end of the dialogue largely carried out, by that very visible and extreme segment of the gay population. Standing there behind that boy, I realized what a bad thing it was that that was the case. Because by being silent I was powerless to help him, to correct the images formed in his mind by those pictures in the *Native.* If I dared to speak to him, he might think I was trying to pick him up—and that thought would probably terrify the hell out of him. I wished at least that I might be able to hand him a book that might help him to understand who he was. But there wasn't such a book. That's why I eventually wrote one.

There's a line in *Shadowlands,* the movie about C. S. Lewis: "We read in order to know we're not alone." One of the loneliest things you can be in this world is a young person who's begun to realize that he or she is gay, who doesn't have any idea what that might mean in terms of his or her future, who doesn't know what to do about it, and who has nobody in his or her life—no parent or teacher or clergyperson—with whom he or she feels that the subject can be safely raised without fear of estrangement, rejection, condemnation. That's why the boy went to that bookstore and stood at that magazine rack and worked up his courage to read the *Native.*

Many gay readers have responded very strongly to that anecdote. When I handed the manuscript of the book in to Simon & Schuster, my editor sent copies of the first twenty or so pages around the company. In the next few days, she said, virtually every gay man at Simon & Schuster came into her office and said to her, "That boy was *me.*" And in the six months since this book was published, I've met several gay men who have said the same thing to me: "That boy was me." They don't mean it literally, of course; they simply mean that they identified with that loneliness, that need to understand and be understood.

A couple of straight readers have protested to me that they had similar experiences at that age, sneaking a look at *Playboy* or whatever. But that's different, and it points to the real difference between growing up gay and growing up straight. A straight kid is surrounded by images of what it means to be straight, surrounded by potential role models. His parents, his parents' friends, the couples on TV shows and in movies, the relationships that are sung about on the radio and MTV, the family situations in the stories and books that he's given to read in school. His inner sense of himself, of his sexual identity, is reflected all around him in a spectrum of images of which *Playboy* is only one extreme. For a gay kid, things are utterly different. It's not easy to explain how different it is, and how it feels. To be a gay kid in most families is to grow up very confused. It's to find an utter contradiction between your very powerful but unarticulated inner sense of who you are and the notions of who you are that are communicated to you by your parents and other people in your life and in fact by the whole world. It's to look around and see all these images of men and women sharing their lives together and being intimate, and to feel an utter lack of identification with those images. From infancy onward, your parents assume you're straight. It's expected that when you reach a certain age you'll want to start dating someone of the opposite sex; everybody asks what kind of girl you like, and if you have a girlfriend. And somehow, even if you haven't figured it out yet and connected who you are with that funny word *gay,* it all feels wrong, as if somehow you'd been set down on the wrong planet.

For too many gay kids, there's no one in their lives to make them feel *right.* Try to imagine what it feels like to be a gay kid of thirteen, say, who's struggling to understand his feelings when he's surrounded by things like an ad I saw in the *New York Times* a week or two ago. It's an ad for "Partnership for a Drug-Free America" and it shows a boy of about thirteen who's preparing to snort a line of cocaine. The caption reads, "It used to be, at thirteen, little boys became interested in little girls." To a thirteen-year-old boy who's started to become interested in other boys, this ad is one more message that tells him there's something wrong with him, that he just doesn't fit in. Nobody meant any harm with this ad, of course; it's trying to do good. That's the whole point: we send these messages out without even realizing it. Just two or three nights ago, I saw a TV commercial for a movie called *Blue Sky* in which one character said to another, "You are the reason that men like women in the first place." My point isn't that references to heterosexuality should be banned or censored, and it's certainly not that gay men don't like women. It's just that we could be more sensitive to the consequences on gay kids of this steady stream of media and pop-culture signals that tell them over and over, with very few exceptions, that all men fall in love with women and all women with men, period.

As the House of Bishops' new pastoral study document, "Continuing the Dialogue," observes, "Our society . . . acculturates all youth to presume they are heterosexual. Advertising, movies, romance novels, and virtually all of our educational programs (secular and religious) presume heterosexuality. For most of those adolescents who are homosexual, the already difficult adolescent experience becomes a nightmare."

A novelist named Robb Forman Dew has just come out with a memoir entitled *The Family Heart,* about how she felt and what she learned after her son came out to her in 1991 when he was a sophomore at Yale. After talking to him over a period of weeks and months, and after meeting the parents of other gay kids, and hearing about the problems and the suicides of some of them, she came to realize that "gay children grow up alone" and that "parents' assumptions of the heterosexuality of their sons and daughters . . . are a threat to their children's lives." She also came to be very angry at Dr. Spock and other child-care "experts" who don't mention the very real possibility that any parent's kids might grow up to be gay, and don't talk about how to deal with that. Mrs. Dew writes, "I find their irresponsibility shocking; they might have saved lives."

Every day gay kids all over the country come out to their parents. Every day gay kids commit suicide because they've been rejected by their parents, or are terrified that they will be. And it's all so unnecessary. There's no need for them to go through the loneliness and confusion they experience. The only reason this happens to them is that there's still so much discomfort, confusion, rage, insecurity, unconscious prejudice, automatic disdain, and condescension on the part of a lot of straight people when it comes to homosexuality. When most parents think of homosexuality, if they think of it at all, they think of it as something "out there" that their kids have to be protected from. But the fact is that if your son, say, turns out to be gay, it's not because of something or someone out there that infected him or recruited him. It's because of something *inside* him that he's likely been aware of, in some way, from a very early age; and because neither his parents nor his teachers have ever prepared him for this or explained to him what this feeling might be, he feels incredibly alienated, different, weird. It's probably taken him years to put a name to this feeling, and perhaps years more to work up the nerve to mention it to anybody.

Though homosexuals as ordinary people in daily life remain almost invisible, homosexuality as an "issue" has been all over the media. It's a staple on the daytime talk shows. The news media cover gay news much more extensively than they did a few years ago. Some straight people have learned a good deal; some people's prejudice has diminished or even, in some cases, dissolved. But there's still an incredible amount of misinformation and discomfort. Some people are tolerant, but not yet *accepting.* They don't like the idea of gay people being as open about their lives as straight people are. Deep down, they may suspect that someone close to them is gay, but they simply don't want to think about it. Until those people move beyond prejudice, or beyond a grudging tolerance, the lives of their gay children or friends or siblings will continue to be more difficult and more lonely than they have to be.

Public discussion of the subject of homosexuality has been controlled mostly by ideological extremes—the extreme gay left and the extreme anti-gay right—and the debate between these two extremes has shed more heat than light. There are those who, in the name of God, go out there and tell lies about what it means to be gay. Not only do they tell lies; the whole way in which they discuss the subject is a lie. They have a lexicon of words that a lot of people who mean well have unconsciously taken up—and even to think about the subject in such terms is to distort it utterly.

They speak of homosexuality as being a "choice," when it isn't. They speak of the "gay lifestyle," as if all gay people lead the same kind of life. They speak of gays "promoting" and "advocating" homosexuality and "recruiting" young people into it, which makes no more sense than advocating being left-handed or recruiting people into having blue eyes. They speak of gays "shoving a homosexual agenda down their throats"; wanting to live your life honestly and to be respected is not an agenda.

This kind of rhetoric politicizes the subject of homosexuality, dehumanizes it, makes it easier to put out of one's mind that we're talking about people's lives. Homosexuality is described as a threat to the family. Yet those who attack homosexuality and gay rights in the name of "the family" are precisely those whose kids, if they turn out to be gay, are most likely to end up as runaways, prostitutes, drug addicts, suicides. It's anti-gay rhetoric, *not* homosexuality, that's a threat to the family. Some people say gays want "approval." No. You can approve or disapprove of an act; you can't approve or disapprove of a fact. In my book I speak of acceptance—meaning, accept the simple fact that this exists, and that it is what it is and not what some hateful people say that it is, and that certain understandings and adjustments must of necessity and out of a concern for justice follow from that acceptance.

The phrase "moral equivalence" comes up a lot. Perhaps the cruellest single comment that I've had as a consequence of my book was made by a former editor of mine. I quit his publication several years ago when he refused to run a very tame review that I'd written of the movie *Longtime Companion,* which was about several gay male couples' experiences with AIDS. When a reporter called him for an explanation, he said: "Bawer's review was striking a total equivalence between a heterosexual couple in love and a homosexual couple in love. I think that's not convincing. I haven't come across it." Well, I have. I've lived it. Love *is* the same, gay or straight; a lot of people just don't see that, or don't want to. They feel a strong compulsion to see the personal lives and feelings of gay people as being somehow different from their own. They say, in effect, "You can be my friend, you can work for me, you can belong to my church—but your life by definition is tinged with sinfulness in a way that mine is not." When they think about sex in their own lives, they place it, quite properly, in the context of their loving relationships; when they think about sex in gay people's lives, they often isolate the sex from the life in which it occurs and the love of which it is an expression, and they call it "sexual behavior" or "conduct" or "practice." Imagine such terms being applied to the sexual component of your own loving committed relationships and try to understand how demeaning it is to be thought of and talked about that way.

The whole thing comes down to a basic fact: homosexuality is a naturally occurring variation in sexual orientation. It may not be natural to most individuals, but it is, like left-handedness, the natural condition of a significant minority. Homosexual people are as capable of love as heterosexuals and need deep, committed human attachment in the same way that heterosexuals do. Sexual activity is not the only element in such relationships, but it's an important part of them. The bishops' study document quotes a 1958 document in which the Lambeth Conference describes the role of sex in marriage. "Sexual intercourse," it says, "is not by any means the only language of earthly love, but it is, in its full and right use, the most intimate and the most revealing; it has the depth of communication signified by the Biblical word so often used for it, 'knowledge'; it is a giving and receiving in the unity of two free spirits which is in itself good (within the marriage bond) and mediates good to those who share it." This is as true of a loving, committed union between two homosexuals as it is of one between two heterosexuals. Homosexuals are created in such a way that the only kind of marriage in which this kind of bond can truly exist for them is a homosexual marriage. In fact, what sexual orientation is ultimately about is not sexual capability or sexual pleasure—because many straight people are capable of having and receiving pleasure in homosexual sex under certain circumstances, and many homosexual people are capable of having and receiving pleasure from heterosexual sex under certain circumstances. Sexual orientation is essentially about how an individual loves; it's about the kind of unity of two free spirits that a given individual is, by his or her intrinsic nature, capable of forming.

To my mind, these truths lead inexorably to a recognition that the only Christian way for the church to respond to the fact of homosexuality and the identicality of homosexual love and commitment to heterosexual love and commitment is to bless gay unions and to allow the ordination of openly gay clergy.

It's taken me a long time to arrive at this place. I'm a product of a denominationally mixed marriage. My mother was baptized in the Southern Baptist Church; my father was raised as a Roman Catholic. As a child, I attended a Lutheran Sunday school for several years, which was chosen mainly because it was around the corner from our home. We weren't a regular churchgoing family, but I said my prayers every night with great conviction. And I did so right up until the night before the day that I realized I was gay—or perhaps I should say the day I accepted consciously that I was gay. I stopped cold and didn't pray again for nearly ten years. Why? Because everything I had ever been taught made me believe that you couldn't be gay *and* Christian. The moment I realized that I was gay, I also realized that it was an essential part of me and that there was nothing wrong with it. In fact, that realization was such an extraordinarily positive and beautiful experience, it was about wholeness and self-knowledge and truth and the possibility of love, and I couldn't imagine believing in any God that would ask me to deny these things. So instead I rejected Christ.

Thankfully, that wasn't the end of it. Years later I fell in love with someone who had been brought up in a Seventh-day Adventist faith community and had left that church after realizing he was gay. Together he and I found our way to the Episcopal Chuch, and it was our love that served as the vehicle of the Holy Spirit. It wasn't until then that I was able to understand to the depths of my being what it means to say, "God is love." For me, those three words bring everything together; they make sense of it all for me. Yet there remains a tension for me, as for all gay Christians, because while our committed relationships seem for us to reflect God's love more truly than anything else in our lives, the church as a human institution continues to suggest that the very aspect of us that makes that love possible is profane in the eyes of God. A priest can bless our cat or our apartment, but he can't bless our relationship with each other.

Last year Andrew Sullivan, the openly gay editor of the *New Republic* and a practicing Roman Catholic, gave an interview to the Catholic magazine *America* about being gay and Catholic. He describes how difficult his coming out was because of the teachings of his faith. But he goes on to say that "as soon as I actually explored the possibility of human contact within my emotional and sexual makeup—in other words, as soon as I allowed myself to love someone—all the constructs the church had taught me about [homosexuality] seemed just so self-evidently wrong that I could no longer find it problematic. Because my own moral sense was overwhelming, because I felt, through the experience of loving someone or being allowed to love someone, an enormous sense of the presence of God—for the first time in my life." I identify very, very strongly with that.

Sullivan says of the Roman Catholic Church that "it defines gay people by a sexual act in a way it never defines heterosexual people, and in this the church is in weird agreement with extreme gay activists who also want to define homosexuality in terms of its purely sexual content. Whereas being gay is not about sex as such. Fundamentally, it's about one's core emotional identity. It's about whom one loves, ultimately, and how that can make one whole as a human being." Indeed, he says, "the moral consequences, in my own life, of the refusal to allow myself to love another human being were disastrous. They made me . . . frustrated and angry and bitter. It spilled over into other areas of my life. Once that emotional blockage is removed, one's whole moral equilibrium can improve, just as a single person's moral equilibrium in a whole range of areas can improve with marriage, in many ways, because there is a kind of stability and security and rock upon which to build one's moral and emotional life. To deny this to gay people is not merely incoherent and wrong, from the Christian point of view. It is incredibly destructive of the moral quality of their lives in general. Does that make sense? These things are part of a continuous moral whole. You can't ask someone to suppress what makes them whole as a human being and then to lead blameless lives. We are human beings, and we need love in our lives in order to love others—in order to be good Christians! What the church is asking gay people to do is not to be holy, but actually to be warped."

Many heterosexual Episcopalians have come to recognize that there's something good, and dare I say holy, in the loving committed relationships of gay people. Yet many of those same straight Episcopalians have a residual discomfort with the whole business, and a residual attachment to old ways of thinking about things, that keeps them from following through logically on their increased understanding of gay people and relationships. They accept homosexuality as a constitutive, unchangeable, intrinsic characteristic, yet they can't bring themselves to countenance the adjustment of conventions and institutions in such a way as to truly acknowledge the existence of homosexuality and make a real, full, and equal place for homosexuals who seek to lead whole Christian lives. And the tension between the ability of many heterosexual church members to perceive what's fair and right and their attachment to old ways of thinking can give rise to resentments, can make them feel as if gay people are causing trouble, pushing their private lives in other people's faces, trying to destroy things that are familiar and precious. I know that some straight Episcopalians look at homosexuals and think: "How much do these people want? Why can't they leave well enough alone?" They worry that the Episcopal Church is being turned from a church into a social-services organization, and that gay people are less concerned about their responsibilities as Christians than about their rights as members of an institution. Many of these people get tired of hearing about sensitivity to gays and lesbians.

I certainly know that I get tired of talking about it. But there's still much to be talked about, because to a large extent when gays and straights talk about these things we're still speaking two different languages. You and I, if you're straight, can hear a sermon and have two very different experiences of it—because it may contain a phrase or a line of argument that doesn't trouble you because it conforms to a truth about your life, but that makes me feel excluded because it implicitly rejects a truth about my life. This sort of disjunction can be especially pronounced at ceremonies like weddings and funerals. For me, at least, my happiness at the wedding of straight friends is always mixed with a constant awareness of the difference between the church's view of my relationship and its view of theirs. From the moment that couple walks back up the aisle together, they're viewed as a couple by the church and the state. Their relationship is official. From that moment on, they take for granted a universal acceptance of their membership in each other that to a gay person in a loving relationship seems beyond one's wildest hopes. Yes, there are gay people who have wedding ceremonies, and some Episcopal priests are even willing to perform them. But it's not the same; the church and state don't recognize it, and neither do most Episcopalians. Think about how often you're asked to check a box on an official form: "single," "married," "divorced," "widowed." In my heart I'm married; on the dotted line and in the list of my church's members, I'm single. That's not wholeness.

The Episcopal Church, in short, is our family. And it's a tolerant family. And some members of it are loving in their acceptance. But the family itself isn't yet fully accepting.

The usual way of defending this lack of acceptance is to turn to Scripture. Of course the Bible has been used to justify slavery and polygamy, among other things, because there are passages in which those practices are treated as acceptable. Also, while Christ taught us to love our enemies rather than make war on them, and taught us also not to store up treasures on earth, you don't see members of the religious right protesting outside military bases or the houses of millionaires with placards bearing those quotations the way they protest at every Gay Pride Day march with signs bearing quotations from Leviticus and Romans and the handful of other Biblical passages that supposedly condemn homosexuality. Few things have been more widely taken out of their historical and textual context and more dishonestly and maliciously misused than those passages. First of all, exact translation of them is difficult, if not impossible, because most of the ancient words pertaining to sex roles and sexual identity have no exact modern equivalents. This makes sense, since ancient societies had different sex roles than ours does, had different understandings of sexual relations, and had no concept of sexual orientation. Some ancient cultures had male temple prostitutes, for example, and publicly recognized man–boy relationships, and the terms used to refer to those roles and relationships in certain New Testament passages have often been mistakenly translated as "homosexual." As the House of Bishops' study document says, "The biblical views about sexuality are thoroughly enmeshed in cultural and historical circumstances. . . . Sexual mores are governed or influenced by various taboos and concerns about ritual purity. . . . Procreation and the continuation of the people are, understandably, important concerns." Another concern was that the Israelites distinguish themselves from the Canaanites, whose social and religious practices included all sorts of things, including homosexual relations.

A concern for ritual purity informs Leviticus 18:22, which reads: "You may not lie with a man as with a woman; it is an abomination." This, as the bishops' document notes, occurs "in a context of teaching about ritual and moral holiness," along with passages that forbid eating pork or wearing a garment containing more than one material or sowing fields with two different kinds of seed. These injunctions were laid aside by early Christians; yet two thousand years later people still quote Leviticus 18:22 against homosexuality.

Genesis 19, the story of Sodom, is also used against gays. Sodom is destroyed because the men of Sodom attempt to gang-rape two angels, not known to be angels, who have been taken in as guests by Lot. Most serious biblical scholars agree that the homosexual element, however much it might turn the heads of certain readers, is not the point of the story. It's not about homosexuality; it's about a breach of hospitality, which was a sacred trust in biblical times. It's obscene, in any event, to suggest that a story of an attempted violent gang rape is intended to convey to us God's view of a loving committed relationship between two men or two women.

Similarly, Paul's reference in Romans to how "God gave [the Gentiles] up to dishonorable passions," exchanging "natural" sexual relations for "unnatural," is not a judgment on homosexual orientation, or even on homosexual acts per se; rather, Paul uses the debauched life at Rome, which included homosexual relations, to support an argument for Christianity and God's natural order and against Roman paganism and what they saw as unnatural. Of course the ancients, Paul included, didn't understand that there are some people for whom homosexuality is natural; he assumes the Gentiles to be people for whom heterosexuality is natural but who give themselves up to something which for them is unnatural. In any event, the ultimate point of this passage, which many people hurl at gays, is precisely that people shouldn't use such passages to judge others, but rather as aids in examining their own morality—"for," as Paul says, "in passing judgment on another you condemn yourself." (Romans 3:10)

Jesus himself said nothing directly about homosexuality, though the bishops' study document cites his quotation of the line in Genesis saying that "a man shall leave his father and mother and be joined to his wife, and the two shall become one flesh." Yet Christ wasn't insisting here that all men must marry women—he didn't—rather, he was replying to a question about divorce by making the point that marriage should be regarded as indissoluble. Indeed, while Jesus never condemned homosexuality, he was very blunt in forbidding divorce. As the Bishops note in their document, "Perhaps the most obvious discontinuity we currently live with in the area of sexual relationships is the practice of divorce and remarriage, which stands in the face of Jesus's explicit prohibition against both the dissolution of and the contracting of subsequent marriages."

Christians who reject the ordination of homosexuals or the blessing of committed homosexual relationships, even though they accept that it is better for some marriages to end in divorce, have to ask themselves honestly if they're taking these positions because they've read their Bibles and feel morally compelled by what they've read to take these positions—or if they've gone to their Bibles to find or fabricate scriptural support for a pre-existing prejudice or discomfort, an attachment to the familiar, a fear of something that just seems too radical or alien or outrageous.

For the fact is that when you listen to some Christians talking about homosexuality, and then turn to the gospels, you find an absolute divergence in tone and emphasis. When Christ talks about good and evil, he doesn't focus on sex. It's clear from his preaching and his example that for Christ morality means being kind, gentle, responsible, considerate, and generous of spirit. It means being willing to rethink your assumptions, reject your traditions, and act boldly in the cause of God. As Christians we're very diverse, but we share two things: our baptism and our moral obligation to the Summary of the Law, which tells us to love God and to love our fellow human beings. And tied up in the pairing of those two loves is a recognition of human love as a reflection of divine love—and implied in that recognition, it seems to me, is an obligation to honor and to take joy in the love that other people bear for each other. Christianity is all about the struggle to get beyond your prejudices and to look into the eyes of the scruffiest, smelliest, most ornery and obnoxious stranger and to see God and to feel love. To say that someone is straight or gay is to say that they've been made to love in this or that way. Not to embrace that love and recognize a commitment based upon it is to condemn love, to demand that certain people live without love, and nothing could be more un-Christian.

How can we live this out in the Episcopal Church? How can we be more inclusive? Well, first of all, we must recognize what inclusivity is and isn't about. Inclusivity in the Episcopal Church isn't an open-ended accommodation of all human beliefs, dispositions, moral commitments, and needs for ritual. Certain things are required of all members: that they be baptized; that they acknowledge the scriptural authority of the Bible *and* that they read it intelligently, thoughtfully, and critically; that they attend to the importance of tradition, including the creeds, prayer book, and catechism, while recognizing the fallibility of all human institutions and interpretations; and that they employ and respect the human faculty of reason, which includes bringing to bear on Scripture and tradition the lessons learned from real-life experience, the illuminations yielded through scientific discoveries, and the information provided by social and historical research. Inclusivity is about agreeing to differ within an informed framework, and to strive corporately toward the justice and respect for individual dignity we promise one another in our baptismal vows. That said, here are a few specifics. The idea, first of all, should not be to accept gay people as gay people, but as Christians who happen to be gay. Avoid an "us" and "them" mentality, a special-interest mentality. Instead of thinking in terms of "welcoming gays and lesbians into the parish family," think in terms of welcoming people into the parish without regard to their sexual orientation. And also of making sure that gay people who are already members of the parish family, but who keep their homosexuality to themselves, feel free to be as open about their sexual orientation as straight people are about theirs. In any case think of all the members of the congregation as individuals, some of whom are in the natural order of things going to be gay—are going to be individuals who have the same capacity to love, the same need for relationships, the same human dignity.

Not long ago I read a memoir by James Ferry, an Anglican priest in Canada whose bishop defrocked him for being gay. He had the support of many people in his congregation. For me, the saddest line in the book was something that one of those people said to him after he learned that a small group of parishioners was going to complain to the bishop about his homosexuality if he didn't resign first. That night he was going to preach at the local Metropolitan Community Church, which is a mostly gay denomination. When he mentioned this to that parishioner, she said kindly, "You'll be with your own people tonight. I'm so glad." She didn't mean to hurt him, but she did. Because she didn't understand that to him, his sexual orientation didn't determine who his "own people" were; his parish family were his "own people." That woman loved and respected him as a priest and friend, but for her, his homosexuality still made him different in some way, made him a member of some other group. That's the kind of thinking that we have to be aware of in ourselves, and that we have to learn to get beyond.

Part of this has to do with what's said from the pulpit. Many clergy who have the best intentions toward homosexuals nonetheless give sermons that presume the congregation's heterosexuality, addressing parishioners in a way that assumes they're married to, or will be or have been married to, someone of the opposite sex, and using the word *family* to mean nothing other than a man and a woman and their children, if any. Many clergy will deliver sermons that specifically and positively address gay issues but will then in the next sermon go back to saying things that unintentionally make gay people feel excluded. One of the more moving experiences I've ever had in church took place several years ago in the company of a conflicted young gay friend of mine, who'd grown up in the parish I now belong to but who'd left it as a child—and, at the time I attended that service with him, had recently become involved in a committed relationship that he felt had cut him off from God, even though it felt to him intensely holy. The preacher at that service was Paul Moore, Jr., who was then the bishop of New York. It was the day of the solemnity of the conversion of Saint Paul, and the bishop talked about his own road to Damascus, about the experience that had made him accept his vocation and become a priest. As an Army nurse in World War II, he treated men whose shattered bodies were the most horrifying sights imaginable. He realized afterwards that when he'd looked into those men's eyes, he'd been looking into the eyes of God. For, he told us, "that's where God resides: in the flesh, in the corrupt, imperfect flesh, in the flesh of everybody around you—your closest friend, the homeless man on the curb, your husband, your wife, your lover." Yes, that was the word he used, *lover.* And when he said it, I turned to my young spiritually tormented friend, and I saw that his eyes were full of tears, because with that one word, *lover,* the bishop had included him, embraced him, and acknowledged the holiness that he himself felt to be present in his committed relationship but that the church, as an institution, refused to recognize.

There are a number of ways in which various churches have shown their inclusivity. Their parish bulletins or service announcements acknowledge anniversaries not only of heterosexual marriages but of gay unions. They publish newspaper ads that include sentences such as "Men and women of all sexual orientations are invited to participate in the life of our church." They offer counseling to gay couples of the same kind that they offer to straight couples.

And, of course, in some churches the clergy bless gay unions. Most don't, of course. And to be gay and to sit in the church week after week beside your partner of five or ten or thirty years and hear announcements of weddings and to know that the two of you can't be married in the church is to be reminded that you're *not* really full, equal members. As a heterosexual you take for granted that you can walk into a church as a couple, hold hands in the pew if you're moved to do so, introduce each other to other members as "my husband" or "my wife" and not have to steel yourself waiting to see how people will react, whether they'll even speak to you. Of course the priest will marry you; of course the congregation will accept you as a couple, a family, as two people who belong to each other. For gay people in the church, that's not yet a reality.

Then there's the question of ordination. In 1991 the church's Commission on Human Affairs recommended "that the Church be open to ordaining gay men and lesbians otherwise qualified who display the same integrity in their sexual relationships which we ask of our heterosexual ordinands. We recommend this because we consider the opening of the ordination process to gays and lesbians a matter of justice when justice should no longer be denied. . . . Explicitly opening the ordination process in this way is desirable to clear the Church of the taint of hypocrisy, since the presence of gay men and lesbians among the clergy is no secret." The report also mentioned "the irrational fear and hatred of gay men and lesbians rampant in our society" and said, "We cannot effectively advocate civil rights for gay men and lesbians in society at large if we appear to deny such rights within our fellowship."

I would add that permitting the open ordination of openly gay men and women would make a big difference to the emotional health, pastoral effectiveness, and spiritual integrity of clergymen and women who happen to be gay. A disproportionate number of the letters I've received about my book have been from gay Episcopal and Anglican priests, some of whom are married and who say that I'm the first person they've ever told about their homosexuality; some of whom are in committed gay relationships—who have beautiful, loving domestic lives that they're compelled to keep secret from everybody except a small circle of highly trusted friends. And some gay priests feel that it would be such a risk to attempt to live in a committed relationship, or haven't found anybody, understandably, willing to live in such secrecy, that they've pursued sex lives—not emotional relationships, but fleeting sexual encounters—furtively, guiltily, in inappropriate places and with inappropriate strangers. The torment and loneliness in which all those gay priests live, and the deep sense of guilt over the duplicity forced upon them by the church's "don't ask, don't tell" approach to gay clergy, are indescribable. What impressed me so powerfully about the letters I've received from those priests, however, is the strength of their faith, their sense of pastoral duty, and their love for the people that they serve.

I'll close with a quote from the bishops' pastoral study document:

> Understanding develops through prayer, Scripture study, worship, life in a community, mission, and in confrontation with the realities of history. Such realities of history include the many critical questions Church and synagogue have had to face at other historical crossroads. In reality, theology is generally done in response to questions raised either inside or outside the community of believers that come to challenge the current understanding of the faith.
>
> The Jerusalem Church early faced the issue of whether and how to overcome the religious barrier between Jew and Gentile . . . so that the latter might be admitted to the Christian community without first being circumcised. . . .
>
> Galileo's and then Darwin's theories forced the Church to review and revise the theological understanding of their time about the nature of the world. They required serious and painful adjustments which in some ways we are still working through. Today's questions are also painful and raise issues with which the Church would rather not deal. . . . What is clear is that challenges are not new, that the function of theology is to grapple with such challenges, and that the questions being asked of the Church today, like some of those of yesterday, may result in new insights and a deeper and more comprehending faith.

Amen.

SECTION VI

FAMILY VALUES

To many people on the far right, the term *family values* signifies one thing above all: "no gay rights." The signs brandished by young Republicans at the 1992 Houston convention said it all: "Family rights forever, gay rights never."

How should gay people react to rhetoric that paints them as a threat to families? If you ask the queer establishment, the proper response is to say dismissively, "Why should we care what *they* think?" Or, even better, to reply aggressively, "Yes, we *are* a danger." Typical of this kind of approach is the following passage from an article by Michael Swift in the *Gay Community News:*

> We shall sodomize your sons, feeble emblems of your masculinity. We shall seduce them in your schools, in your dormitories, in your gymnasiums, in your locker rooms, in your sports arenas, in your seminaries, in your youth groups, in your army bunkhouses, wherever men are with men together. Your sons shall become our minions and do our bidding. They will be recast in our image.

This passage is plainly the work of someone attempting to sow mischief, to enkindle fear. I quote it not from its original place of publication but from the *Congressional Record* of March 24, 1993.

On that day, Swift's words were cited on the House floor by Republican Congressman Mel Hancock, who, having proposed an amendment that would inhibit AIDS education and responsible counseling of gay teens, effectively used the gay activist's remarks in support of the argument that gay people are a threat from which children need to be protected. Thus does gay-left rhetoric serve the purposes of anti-gay crusaders.

Until recently it has fallen mostly to straight people—notably, to members of the organization Parents and Friends of Lesbians and Gays (PFLAG)—to send out the message that most gay people belong to families, that the bond between loving gay partners is identical to that between a loving husband and wife, and that it's not homosexuality but the denial of marriage rights to gay people that represents a rejection of true family values. Gay people who have tried to communicate this message have often been maligned by gay-left folk who see any effort to explain homosexuality as an apology. Fortunately, however, responsible and conspicuous challenges by gay writers to the reigning misapprehensions about homosexuality and the family have multiplied during the 1990s. Notable among these challenges was Jonathan Rauch's essay "A Pro-Gay, Pro-Family Policy," published in the *Wall Street Journal* on 29 November 1994. In the essay, Rauch proposed a "principled, pro-family but not anti-gay position":

> "No," family advocates might say, "we are not anti-gay. We are pro-responsibility. We welcome open homosexuals who play by the rules of monogamy, fidelity and responsibility. And we frown upon heterosexuals and homosexuals who do not play by those rules.
>
> "We believe that marriage and fidelity are crucial social institutions that channel lust into love and caprice into commitment. We believe faithful relationships are not only good for children but help keep men settled and help keep the burdens of caring for one another off society's shoulders. And we support extending these norms to all Americans, gay and straight.

> "We do not insist that homosexuals 'change,' which is impossible, or that they live lives of lovelessness and despair; we do ask that they—and heterosexual Americans—settle down into patterns of responsibility. We believe in the general universality of family values. We embrace all who embrace those values, without regard to sexual orientation."
>
> Here is a fully consistent and staunchly pro-family position, one whose benefits are manifold. It elevates family values to genuine universality. It separates the real issue (responsibility vs. license) from the phony one (straight vs. gay). It hurts radical activists by putting them in the position of arguing for license rather than for toleration of minorities. . . .
>
> This view doesn't require family advocates to like homosexuality, but it does require them to accept the importance of settled relationships for homosexuals. No easy sell, perhaps, but consider the alternative. More non-fringe, non-radical homosexuals emerge into public view every day. As the stereotype of the homosexual as antisocial deviant crumbles, a party or faction that tolerates gay-baiting rhetoric in the name of "family values" makes "family values" look more and more like common bigotry.

Or, as I wrote in an op-ed article for the *Chicago Tribune*, "Family values . . . are not irreconcilable with gay equal rights—they're among the best arguments *for* gay rights."

ANDREW SULLIVAN

This, the earliest piece included in the present book, appeared in the *New Republic* on 28 August 1989, when Sullivan was still in his twenties and was not yet the editor of that magazine.

HERE COMES THE GROOM: A (CONSERVATIVE) CASE FOR GAY MARRIAGE

Last month in New York, a court ruled that a gay lover had the right to stay in his deceased partner's rent-control apartment because the lover qualified as a member of the deceased's family. The ruling deftly annoyed almost everybody. Conservatives saw judicial activism in favor of gay rent control: three reasons to be appalled. Chastened liberals (such as the *New York Times* editorial page), while endorsing the recognition of gay relationships, also worried about the abuse of already-stretched entitlements that the ruling threatened. What neither side quite contemplated is that they both might be right, and that the way to tackle the issue of unconventional relationships in conventional society is to try something both more radical and more conservative than putting courts in the business of deciding what is and is not a family. That alternative is the legalization of civil gay marriage.

The New York rent-control case did not go anywhere near that far, which is the problem. The rent-control regulations merely stipulated that a "family" member had the right to remain in the apartment. The judge ruled that to all intents and purposes a gay lover is part of his lover's family, inasmuch as a "family" merely means an interwoven social life, emotional commitment, and some level of financial interdependence.

It's a principle now well established around the country. Several cities have "domestic partnership" laws, which allow relationships that do not fit into the category of heterosexual marriage to be registered with the city and qualify for benefits that up till now have been reserved for straight married couples. San Francisco, Berkeley, Madison, and Los Angeles all have legislation, as does the politically correct Washington, D.C., suburb, Takoma Park. In these cities, a variety of interpersonal arrangements qualify for health insurance, bereavement leave, insurance, annuity and pension rights, housing rights (such as rent-control apartments), adoption, and inheritance rights. Eventually, according to gay lobby groups, the aim is to include federal income tax and veterans benefits as well. A recent case even involved the right to use a family member's accumulated frequent-flier points. Gays are not the only beneficiaries; heterosexual "live-togethers" also qualify.

There's an argument, of course, that the current legal advantages extended to married people unfairly discriminate against people who've shaped their lives in less conventional arrangements. But it doesn't take a genius to see that enshrining in the law a vague principle like "domestic partnership" is an invitation to qualify at little personal cost for a vast array of entitlements otherwise kept crudely under control.

To be sure, potential DPs have to prove financial interdependence, shared living arrangements, and a commitment to mutual caring. But they don't need to have a sexual relationship or even closely mirror old-style marriage. In principle, an elderly woman and her live-in nurse could qualify. A couple of uneuphemistically confirmed bachelors could be DPs. So could two close college students, a pair of seminarians, or a couple of frat buddies. Left as it is, the concept of domestic partnership could open a Pandora's box of litigation and subjective judicial decision-making about who qualifies. You either are or are not married; it's not a complex question. Whether you are in a "domestic partnership" is not so clear.

More important, the concept of domestic partnership chips away at the prestige of traditional relationships and undermines the priority we give them. This priority is not necessarily a product of heterosexism. Consider heterosexual couples. Society has good reason to extend legal advantages to heterosexuals who choose the formal sanction of marriage over simply living together. They make a deeper commitment to one another and to society; in exchange, society extends certain benefits to them. Marriage provides an anchor, if an arbitrary and weak one, in the chaos of sex and relationships to which we are all prone. It provides a mechanism for emotional stability, economic security, and the healthy rearing of the next generation. We rig the law in its favor not because we disparage all forms of relationship other than the nuclear family, but because we recognize that not to promote marriage would be to ask too much of human virtue. In the context of the weakened family's effect upon the poor, it might also invite social disintegration. One of the worst products of the New Right's "family values" campaign is that its extremism and hatred of diversity has disguised this more measured and more convincing case for the importance of the marital bond.

The concept of domestic partnership ignores these concerns,

indeed directly attacks them. This is a pity, since one of its most important objectives—providing some civil recognition for gay relationships—is a noble cause and one completely compatible with the defense of the family. But the way to go about it is not to undermine straight marriage; it is to legalize old-style marriage for gays.

The gay movement has ducked this issue primarily out of fear of division. Much of the gay leadership clings to notions of gay life as essentially outsider, anti-bourgeois, radical. Marriage, for them, is co-optation into straight society. For the Stonewall generation, it is hard to see how this vision of conflict will ever fundamentally change. But for many other gays—my guess, a majority—while they don't deny the importance of rebellion twenty years ago and are grateful for what was done, there's now the sense of a new opportunity. A need to rebel has quietly ceded to a desire to belong. To be gay and to be bourgeois no longer seems such an absurd proposition. Certainly since AIDS, to be gay and to be responsible has become a necessity.

Gay marriage squares several circles at the heart of the domestic partnership debate. Unlike domestic partnership, it allows for recognition of gay relationships, while casting no aspersions on traditional marriage. It merely asks that gays be allowed to join in. Unlike domestic partnership, it doesn't open up avenues for heterosexuals to get benefits without the responsibilities of marriage, or a nightmare of definition litigation. And unlike domestic partnership, it harnesses to an already established social convention the yearnings for stability and acceptance among a fast-maturing gay community.

Gay marriage also places more responsibilities upon gays: it says for the first time that gay relationships are not better or worse than straight relationships, and that the same is expected of them. And it's clear and dignified. There's a legal benefit to a clear, common symbol of commitment. There's also a personal benefit. One of the ironies of domestic partnership is that it's not only more complicated than marriage, it's more demanding, requiring an elaborate statement of intent to qualify. It amounts to a substantial invasion of privacy. Why, after all, should gays be required to prove commitment before they get married in a way we would never dream of asking of straights?

Legalizing gay marriage would offer homosexuals the same deal society now offers heterosexuals: general social approval and specific legal advantages in exchange for a deeper and harder-to-extract-yourself-from commitment to another human being. Like straight marriage, it would foster social cohesion, emotional security, and economic prudence. Since there's no reason gays should not be allowed to adopt or be foster parents, it could also help nurture children. And its introduction would not be some sort of radical break with social custom. As it has become more acceptable for gay people to acknowledge their loves publicly, more and more have committed themselves to one another for life in full view of their families and their friends. A law institutionalizing gay marriage would merely reinforce a healthy social trend. It would also, in the wake of AIDS, qualify as a genuine public health measure. Those conservatives who deplore promiscuity among some homosexuals should be among the first to support it. Burke could have written a powerful case for it.

The argument that gay marriage would subtly undermine the unique legitimacy of straight marriage is based upon a fallacy. For heterosexuals, straight marriage would remain the most significant—and only legal—social bond. Gay marriage could only delegitimize straight marriage if it were a real alternative to it, and this is clearly not true. To put it bluntly, there's precious little evidence that straights could be persuaded by any law to have sex with—let alone marry—someone of their own sex. The only possible effect of this sort would be to persuade gay men and women who force themselves into heterosexual marriage (often at appalling cost to themselves and their families) to find a focus for their family instincts in a more personally positive environment. But this is clearly a plus, not a minus: gay marriage could both avoid a lot of tortured families and create the possibility for many happier ones. It is not, in short, a denial of family values. It's an extension of them.

Of course, some would claim that any legal recognition of homosexuality is a de facto attack upon heterosexuality. But even the most hardened conservatives recognize that gays are a permanent minority and aren't likely to go away. Since persecution is not an option in a civilized society, why not coax gays into traditional values rather than rail incoherently against them?

There's a less elaborate argument for gay marriage: it's good for gays. It provides role models for young gay people who, after the exhilaration of coming out, can easily lapse into short-term relationships and insecurity with no tangible goal in sight. My own guess is that most gays would embrace such a goal with as much (if not more) commitment as straights. Even in our society as it is, many lesbian relationships are virtual textbook cases of monogamous commitment. Legal gay marriage could also help bridge the gulf often found between gays and their parents. It could bring the essence of gay life—a gay couple—into the heart of the traditional straight family in a way the family can most understand and the gay offspring can most easily acknowledge. It could do as much to heal the gay–straight rift as any amount of gay rights legislation.

If these arguments sound socially conservative, that's no accident. It's one of the richest ironies of our society's blind spot toward gays that essentially conservative social goals should have the appearance of being so radical. But gay marriage is not a radical step. It avoids the mess of domestic partnership; it is humane; it is conservative in the best sense of the word. It's also practical. Given the fact that we already allow legal gay relationships, what possible social goal is advanced by framing the law to encourage those relationships to be unfaithful, undeveloped, and insecure?

PAUL VARNELL

This column appeared in the *Windy City Times* on 21 May 1992.

FAMILY VALUES: OURS AND THEIRS

One of the most entertaining—if possibly apocryphal—anecdotes about Mahatma Gandhi is the one in which some foreign journalist is interviewing Gandhi and asks him, "What do you think of Western civilization?" The story goes that Gandhi looked thoughtful for a moment, then brightened up and said, "Why, I think it sounds like an excellent idea!"

Unbidden, that old story comes to mind when one hears claims made for "traditional values" or "family values," especially when those terms are uttered as slogans by fundamentalist religious groups or opportunistic politicians.

The marked failure of "family values" to have any meaning beyond the polemical seemed particularly clear in a recent California news item. Last Easter some gay demonstrators protested the apparently homophobic teachings of the Rev. Glen Cole, the pastor of a fundamentalist mega-church in Sacramento. According to the valuable reportage of Marghe Covino, a young fourteen-year-old church member named E. J. Byington went over to the demonstrators and told them that it was fine for them to be protesting and that, contrary to what Rev. Cole taught, he himself saw nothing wrong with them.

Later that day, Byington was beaten with a strap by a twenty-one-year-old cousin in the Marine Corps and thrown out of his home by the aunt with whom he was staying. The aunt claimed that young Byington had disgraced her, ruined her business, and that she could never go back to that church again. Nor would the aunt let Byington take his clothes or his bicycle with him when she expelled him.

With friends like that, "family values" scarcely needs enemies. But we must make as clear as possible that many of the partisans of "family values" have little interest in preserving families. The current polemical use of the term is largely devoid of positive meaning and is primarily a way of attacking (a) gays—for simply existing, much less seeking equal rights; (b) women—for wanting the same opportunities as men; and (c) human sexuality—for so relentlessly resisting legal or doctrinal control.

The natural reaction by some people has been to take a condescending or dismissive view of "the family"—or "nuclear family." Yet the family has survived over centuries, in a variety of social, political, and economic circumstances. It survived attempts to eliminate it by both early Christianity and early Communism. And it seems likely to survive now because it serves some necessary social functions better than any of the obvious alternatives. Those of us, therefore, who wish the family well may have a particular stake in opposing the "family values" rhetoric to the extent that by its simplistic understanding of what is at issue, it serves to inhibit the clear and careful thinking that needs to go into the work of helping authentic family values survive and flourish.

Seldom, in fact, do the proponents of "family values" elucidate what values they have in mind. And that must be part of their intention, for if they did, most people would recognize the inappropriateness of the term for attacking gays.

Part of our task, then, is unpacking the concept of "family values" to show that according to any reasonable content for the term, it contains nothing anti-gay. Most of us, if we reflect on our upbringing, would think of things like mutual support, empathic understanding, a genuine concern for our well-being, mutual trust, and a reciprocal willingness to teach and learn.

Parents and Friends of Lesbians and Gays has made a start at this already by demonstrating that parents and gay children can love and support each other. In a recent press release, P-FLAG's Paulette Goodman pointed out, "We simply want our children protected from discrimination. . . . It is only fair that they have the right to live together and receive the benefits of committed relationships. . . . We stand with our children in their fight for the respect and dignity that we believe is the birthright of all human beings."

Fundamentalists and their political spokesmen sometimes speak as if gays and lesbians, by their very existence, somehow threaten the survival of "the family." It may be true that it is not easy currently to maintain a well-functioning family. But gays and lesbians are not the reason. Rather, the challenges have been economic, technological, medical, even political: the educational emancipation of women made them dissatisfied with earlier limitations placed on them; the birth control pill increased the opportunities for sexual variety and complicated emotional sequelae; inflation raised the cost of living along with maintaining a family and educating children; increased access to the mass media led to awareness of the variety of social and cultural values; and enhanced personal mobility separated people from their family and neighborhood and the prolonged social control they exercised. It is hard to see how our simply living our lives could have any impact on families coping with those problems.

Sometimes the argument goes that if you are not supporting "the family" you are hurting it—i.e., if you are not part of the solution, you are part of the problem. But that is an example of ideologically outdated social collectivism, and we can comfortably reject it.

A variant of the argument was used by the Catholic archbishop of San Francisco in opposing that city's domestic partners ordinance. Since there is an unlimited supply of marriage rights, he could not argue that our getting married would deprive anyone else of the right to marry. He argued instead that letting gays form legal relationships would cheapen traditional marriage, lessening its value for heterosexuals. That seemed to reduce to the notion that if you get a piece of apple pie, that will make my piece of apple pie seem less valuable and appealing. Put that way, it is the argument of an eight-year-old.

And that, ultimately, is the point. Every time the "family values" people make an argument, it sounds good only so long as it goes unexamined. If we respond in a knee-jerk fashion, taking the opposite side on every issue from them, we will fail to use our greatest strength, which is to show that they do not believe the very values they purport to uphold, and that we ourselves are much more the bearers of "family values" carefully explained and rightly understood. We need only speak up.

JAMES P. PINKERTON

Pinkerton, a former deputy assistant to President George Bush for policy planning, also worked in the Reagan White House and in the four Republican presidential campaigns from 1980 to 1992. He is a lecturer at the George Washington University. The author of *What Comes Next: The End of Big Government—and the New Paradigm Ahead,* he lives with his wife and children in northern Virginia. This op-ed article appeared in *New York Newsday* on 3 June 1993.

CONSERVATIVES: DON'T BASH GAY MARRIAGE

From Hawaii, best known for surfing, suntanning and hula dancing, comes news that could be the Pearl Harbor of social issues in the 1990s—gay marriage.

In a ruling last month, Hawaii's Supreme Court held that "marriage is a basic civil right" for same-sex couples, too. Other litigation will surely follow elsewhere—the American Civil Liberties Union is on the case.

Conservatives face a choice: having fought the leftist politics of gay liberation, do they now fight the conservative instinct to form families? The right may choose to act as if all gays belong to

Queer Nation. But if they do so, they will alienate the vast majority of gays who seek to join the mainstream.

The most explosive opponent of gay politics is Sen. Jesse Helms (R-N.C.). He led the fight last month against Roberta Achtenberg's nomination to be an assistant secretary of housing and urban development. His reason? She's a "damn lesbian." This helped Helms get on the national news, but hurt the GOP. Consider the consequences.

First, Achtenberg was confirmed. She's now free to pursue her agenda, able to slough off future criticism as merely more lesbian-bashing. Second, the GOP's image as the party of homophobes is reinforced. That may be the goal of some conservatives, but it's hard to call that a winning strategy for the party—look at the 1992 elections. Other Republicans of a more libertarian, live-and-let-live bent had better speak up, lest Helms be seen as speaking for the party. Remember, gays are organizing, fundraising, and voting. And they have friends and family. If the issue is abetting intolerance, silence = death for the GOP.

Principles are worth fighting for. There was a legitimate case to be made against Achtenberg as an inexperienced, left-wing ideologue. Unfortunately, that case wasn't made; or, if it was, it was buried under the fusillade of personal epithet. The vast majority of Americans, who don't really care what Achtenberg does at home, dismissed the whole thing as just another unpleasant Washington incident.

What should conservatives think about gay marriage? The best answer comes from Ross Perot, who dismisses all social issues with his refrain: "I don't have time to talk about it, I'm too busy trying to rebuild the job base of this country!" However, Andrew Sullivan, the gay conservative editor of the *New Republic,* argues that the institution of gay marriage would actually advance the conservative cause: "It would foster social cohesion, emotional security, and economic prudence."

Sullivan echoes George Gilder, the visionary conservative author. In "Men and Marriage," Gilder maintains that marriage is conservatizing because it lengthens time horizons beyond immediate gratification. "Men need marriage," he writes. Society does, too, because we all have an interest in getting males to settle down. Gilder calls it "converting barbarians into useful citizens." Admittedly, Gilder is talking about heterosexual relationships, but the same logic applies to everyone. Doesn't the social order consist of all of us? Doesn't everyone have a stake in it?

Experts—not to mention gays themselves—are increasingly sure that homosexuals are born that way. If so, it's counterproductive to make them fugitives inside the legal system. We have enough real problems to worry about.

Lincoln had a better idea: You conquer your political opponents by making them your friends. The first Republican president also knew he had to focus on one challenge at a time. The news that economic growth was an anemic 0.9 percent for the first quarter, combined with rising gold prices, is an early warning that all of us—straight and gay alike—are sinking into the quicksand of Carter-esque stagflation. To pull ourselves out, we're going to need all the friends we can get. If the real battle is against taxes and bureaucracy, conservatives should not open up a second front against potential allies.

DAVID LINK

This essay appeared in the August/September 1993 issue of *Reason.*

I AM NOT QUEER

There were fourteen of us at the family dinner table, representing four generations. We were at my sister's house just outside of Victorville, part of a growing community in southern California's high desert, about two hours east of Los Angeles. It was a little above thirty degrees outside, and the sky was a clear window on a million stars.

My sister and parents, as well as a number of my uncles and aunts, had moved here partly because of the affordable housing, partly because they are golfers and their neighborhood is built around a lovely golf course, and partly because it is the kind of quiet community that is the antithesis of the city none of them ever liked. They are endlessly satisfied with the distance they have put between themselves and Los Angeles. In most of these details, I am very different from my family.

Still, I come up to visit them often. They are my family, and I enjoy spending time with them. But they are also something else to me: they are my ground. A large part of the country is made up of people like them, people who do not often get involved in the political rhetoric I am used to—the rhetoric of the media, of academic debates, of the centers of power. People like my family, suburban, churchgoing people, are consumed with the day-to-day details of their lives and have little time for things like the big picture, the effect society has on individuals, the law. I have always been drawn to big-picture issues.

But in the small things, the family rituals, I share a great deal with them. My family is located squarely at the heart of the middle class, and so am I. In that way among others, I am much like them. And here among these people I loved, having one more in a lifetime of family dinners, I noticed something that struck a chord in me, not because it was unusual, but because it was so very usual that it went without any comment at all. As I looked around the table, I realized that of the fourteen people busily loading their plates and talking, five of us were gay.

And no one cared.

The cast of characters was for the most part as familiar to me as the photographs on the walls of my apartment. My grandmother and parents were there, as were my sister and brother-in-law. Two of my seven uncles were with us: one sat next to his wife, while the other was there with his longtime male lover. My sister's stepson, Rick, had brought his girlfriend. Early in the evening Rick's brother had called to let us know he would be there, too. When he arrived, he introduced us to the young man he had brought along as his date. Since in my family there is always enough food, my sister set another place at the table for the additional guest with little fuss. The fact that he and his date were the same sex was no big deal.

Just before dessert, my Aunt Ann and Uncle Fred dropped by. Even among my family—who, with rare exceptions, are conservative Republicans—these two have always been especially conservative. I have long been uneasy with both major parties, but I am a registered Democrat, and I sometimes espouse Democratic party positions I don't wholly support so that Fred and I will have something to argue about. The never-ending political debates between Fred and me are a family tradition as predictable as turkey on Thanksgiving, and Ann is always there to chide me with some argument Fred might have forgotten. Our debates are usually loud and intense; whatever the details, we both care deeply about politics. Because of our political passions I have long felt a special kinship with Fred and Ann, and they have always felt close to me. Most of the rest of the family discusses politics only reluctantly.

In making her greetings to everyone, Ann, as usual, saved a special zeal for my uncle's lover. He is one of those people who came into the family's enthusiastic embrace easily. While my family generally accepts all comers, in the natural course of things some are more loved than others. My uncle's lover was a favorite from the start.

This domestic picture will be an affront to some people who are homosexual. I have long been aware that the family I come from is not like the families many lesbians and gay men were brought up in and had to escape, the families that the notorious Mad Pats at the Republican convention thought they could use as a weapon against lesbians and gay men. While that strategy backfired badly, it remains true that because of the disquiet the Mad Pats exploit, many gay people are unable to have the kind of relationship with their families that I have.

That said, I bring my family up for a very specific reason. They are not alone. They and hundreds of thousands of families like them are too often absent in the discussion about gay rights—not as weapons against gay people, but as their imperfect allies. The public discussion of homosexuality tends to take place at the extremes; since the loudest objections come from radical conservatives, the opposition tends to be equally intense, equally extreme. While this makes for symmetry, the fervor on both sides sometimes excludes people like my family who have a more moderate interest in the issue. Those people, who are neither particularly articulate nor especially inflamed, feel as if they have no place in the ring.

I think these families and family members should be acknowledged. They are people of good faith who, while they are not champions of gay rights, have found a way to respect and accept their lesbian and gay relatives as well as they can. In some ways, that kind of unexpressed but lived support is more important than all the manifestos and blood-boiling demonstrations.

Those families and those children can have the relationships they have because the way was paved by giants, lesbians and gay men who took what for the time was a radical position in a wholly uncomprehending world: that they should be accepted in their entirety, regardless of their sexual orientation. The almost unbelievable bravery of Harry Hay and the other men and women who can be counted as founders of the gay rights movement helped to change the way we think about people who are homosexual.

New giants are in the making, younger ones: Roberta Achtenberg, the first open lesbian to serve in high government office; Michelangelo Signorile, the champion of "outing"; Rich Jennings of Hollywood Supports, continuing the work he began in the Gay and Lesbian Alliance Against Defamation; and hundreds of others. They have stepped into the world their predecessors helped create, ready to carry on that work.

But there are different styles of activism. A number of high-profile lesbians and gay men now proudly call themselves "queer." This is particularly true in the gay press. Many have joined Signorile and given life to radical groups like Queer Nation; some seem to be most satisfied when they can make others most uncomfortable.

I am one of those who feel uncomfortable.

There is no shortage of lesbians and gay men who adopt this in-your-face attitude toward the world at large. But what is it supposed to accomplish?

In part, identifying as queer is a way of disarming the epithet. When minorities embrace the words used against them, they mitigate, to some extent, the use of the words as weapons. But that strategy has never been fully successful. African-Americans once tried to defuse the word *nigger* in a similar way. But despite their best intentions, the word never lost its force as an epithet, as any member of the Ku Klux Klan can attest. *Nigger* still pierces, still causes harm.

A second reason for lesbians and gay men to identify themselves as queer is to exercise some control over their position in the world. Rather than having a name imposed, the group chooses its own. Even if the group chooses a name that already exists, it is still a form of empowerment, or at least it feels that way. Whatever its value, though, this tactic has the potential to try the public's patience. Minority groups are not like nations or states; they do not have a unified government that can decide once and for all what the country and its people will be called. As group members debate, the jury is still out in editorial rooms across the country about whether to use *African-American* or *black*.

It is in this context that I have wrestled with myself over whether, as a gay man, I am queer. I have decided that I am not. *Queer* is the word of the other, of the outsider. I do not feel as if I am outside anything due to my sexual orientation.

The generations of lesbians and gay men who lived in the time leading up to the Stonewall riots in 1969 were radicals by definition. They said out loud what at the time was unsayable—that sexual orientation should not matter. While sexual orientation is obviously a difference among people, people are different in a multitude of ways. Hair color is a more obvious difference than sexual orientation, since it is immediately visible. But we did not create a systematic hierarchy of preferred over less-preferred and non-preferred hair color, granting blonds and brunettes rights that are unavailable to redheads, requiring people who choose to marry to find a mate whose hair color is different from theirs, or the same. Hair color is one of thousands of differences that can be noticed but carries no legal or normative weight.

Since the pioneering sex studies in Germany early in this century, those arguing for equality for lesbians and gay men have asserted that sexual orientation is not a sickness or a pathology, that it is another neutral difference that should be treated neutrally. For most of the century, mainstream society disagreed, saying that sexual orientation was a difference that mattered and would be treated by the law as if it mattered.

Since Stonewall, though, the law has made considerable strides toward neutrality. The ultimate goal was equality, the elimination of the laws that treated homosexuality and heterosexuality differently. Bit by bit that equality is being recognized. As Barney Frank has observed, recent movements like that in Colorado explicitly to deny equality to lesbians and gay men have arisen in part because of growing tolerance. Colorado for Family Values, which backed the Colorado initiative, wants to return to the inequality its members are comfortable with because it feels that inequality slipping away. If the gay rights movement had not had its successes, CFV would not be necessary.

Like members of CFV, those who want to identify themselves as queer are capitalizing on the significance of the difference between heterosexuals and homosexuals. Some have been outspoken in their focus on this difference.

But to say that lesbians and gay men are different from heterosexuals is no more than a tautology. The game of definitional difference can be played on a number of axes. In addition to being gay, I am also male, of Italian background, and Catholic; I practice law and write for a living, am reasonably well educated, and am thirty-nine years old. To some extent, each of these is as important to my identity as my sexual orientation. Therefore, I could identify myself at any given moment as a gay man, a male, an Italian (or, more broadly, a Caucasian), a Catholic, a baby-boomer, a lawyer, or a writer, and I would be telling the truth.

By choosing one group, however, I would also be leaving out a great deal. I am no more male than I am Italian or Catholic or lawyer or writer or homosexual. All fit together in some way that adds up to me. Therefore, while I do claim membership in all of those groups, and while some are more important to me than others, it would be too easy to lose sight of the whole if I were to grant one group special status as the group I identify with. Each is an adjective about me; none is me.

Each of us belongs to a lot of groups, many of which overlap. Any individual could draw a Venn diagram of the dozens or hundreds of groups he or she belongs in, and the intersection of all those circles would be a group of one. The poet Maya Angelou has made this point explicitly: "In my work, in everything I do, I mean to say that we human beings are more alike than we are unalike, and to use that statement to break down the walls we set between ourselves because we are different. I suggest that we should herald the differences, because the differences make us interesting, and also enrich and make us stronger. [But] the differences are minuscule compared to the similarities. That's what I mean to say."

Experiences of love and loss, trust, betrayal, jealousy, injustice, joy and pain, comfort, rage—all these are points at which we can touch one another as people because they are experiences every one of us shares. One of the jobs of the artist has been to explore those touching points, to bring us together from our varied and diverse particulars into a single place where we can recognize something we have in common.

Hamlet, for example, is a Dane, a heterosexual, and a male, but he is also the embodiment of something that transcends all human categories, the human problem of indecision. The particulars of his story are interesting and relevant, but in his very particular story we can also find something universal. Generations of individuals who have encountered this ambivalent hero have seen something of themselves on the stage. Anyone who has ever had to choose a restaurant or a video knows on a trivial level how hard it is to decide to act. And everyone knows how difficult the larger decisions are—what profession or job to enter, where to live, whom to trust or to love. Hamlet's truth about the difficulty of decision defies gender and race and sexual orientation and everything else.

Balancing our similarities and differences is the juggling act of identity. The current focus on the ways lesbians and gay men differ from heterosexuals simply reinforces the walls between us and leaves no gate. In this, lesbians and gay men dishonor the success of those whose work has so much changed the world.

A generation ago, I could not have had the dinner with my family that I did. What my family and I have in common would have been destroyed by a single difference. To maintain a relationship with them, the burden would have been on me to lie. In my family, those days are gone. The five gay men who were at that family table could be honest, and we were not penalized for our honesty. And the family as a whole benefited by remaining intact, by keeping all of the bonds between us alive. We could find some reassurance in our similarities while taking advantage of the differing viewpoints each brings to the family's dynamic.

That is only one measure of what the very loose phrase *gay rights* means. It is my understanding that the goal of the gay rights movement all along was to allow lesbians and gay men to live their lives irrespective of their sexual orientation, not superrespective of it. This was difficult to do when heterosexuals focused—sometimes obsessively—on homosexuality. Lesbians and gay men know their sexual orientation is a part of their makeup, but it isn't any more important to them than a heterosexual's sexual orientation is to him or her. Sex is certainly a part of an ordinary life, but most people—lesbians and gay men included—spend more time watching TV than doing the nasty.

By identifying as queer, lesbians and gay men do exactly the same thing that the most virulent homophobes do: they make their sexual orientation hyper-important, more important than any single factor should be in a complex human personality. Equally important, by marking ourselves as outsiders, we deny what we have in common with others.

Lesbians and gay men in the past were radicals because they had no other choice. That is no longer true. Because of decades of radical work, millions of people are able to view homosexuality now within the context of ordinary human variations and, like my family, pay it no mind. This goal has clearly not been achieved everywhere, but we are far enough along the road that openly homosexual people can choose to avoid a radical identity.

Some lesbians and gay men may decide to follow the path of the sexual outlaws, determined to be the outsider. This pose has long been a kick for the young, straight or gay. But in adopting that pose in today's world, lesbians and gay men are making a free choice. In that they will be less like the gay sexual outlaw John Rechy proclaimed himself to be and more like Madonna. Whatever else can be said about Madonna, she has made her own choices and not let anyone else dictate what part her sexuality plays within her identity. As a gay man in the '60s, Rechy did not have that choice.

Making an identity has always been difficult. The superficial advantage of group identification is that it offers a prefabricated self. Choosing an identity off the rack saves a great deal of time and hard emotional exploration. The downside, of course, is that an off-the-rack identity was designed for the mass market; it does not have the individual in mind. Thus, some people who are homosexual find that they are criticized for not being "gay enough," for departing from the party line in certain instances, for not wearing their gay identity properly. But that is because, unlike the tailor-made identity, one bought in the current department store of identities will only come close to the actual proportions of its wearer. The small gaps and sags may be tolerable, but the purchaser must know he or she is buying something manufactured for millions. And like all uniforms, it comes with expectations.

For the most part, homosexuality is no longer outside the law. While there are certainly laws that still need to be changed—some dramatically—the strategy for change may need to be rethought. Confrontations were required in the early days because a majority of people were simply dead to the problems faced by lesbians and gay men. Confrontations are less necessary now and in some cases are probably harmful.

That is because confrontation is a strategy for those who are not being heard. Lesbians and gay men do not want to argue with the heterosexual majority because we like arguing; the point is to persuade a majority that the law is unfair when it treats homosexuals differently from heterosexuals and to get those who disagree to change their minds. That is how the First Amendment is supposed to work. Confrontation is a last resort. It is dramatic, extreme, a battering ram to knock down a door that will not open. It is the antithesis of persuasion.

But in most cases, the doors of discussion are open. After all of the work that has been done, particularly in the last two or three decades, most people are aware that lesbians and gay men have a grievance and most people will listen, even though many will not agree. This progress can be seen in the way the recent March on Washington was covered by the media. A similar march in 1987—which drew, even by the conservative estimate of the National Park

Service, about 300,000 people—was given cursory coverage in most media outlets and was initially ignored by some, including both *Time* and *Newsweek*. Six years later, the same kind of event, with God knows how many participants, was judged worthy of banner headlines, cover stories, ample air time, and considerable pre- and post-march attention. The task is no longer getting people to acknowledge that lesbians and gay men exist; the task is to change the minds that can be changed.

Radicals, however, continue to believe they are not being heard at all. They treat the world as if it were populated only by their polar opposites. This is as true of the religious radicals as it is of the gay radicals. Both sides hurl images out of their own personal horror movies into the debate. The campaigns in Colorado and Oregon were not so much about homosexuality and religion as they were about sado-masochism and the Spanish Inquisition. Grotesque images of chained and (barely) leather-garbed San Francisco parade participants were pitted against the sour faces of paranoid preachers and the bruised bodies of gay bashers' victims. No matter which side you talked to, the end of the world was imminent.

Supporters of the ban on open lesbians and gay men in the military use a similar strategy. The military's argument is a simple one: Removing the ban will destroy our armed forces. The prejudice against lesbians and gay men is so powerful, it is argued, that heterosexual service members will ignore their too-fragile military discipline, violence and chaos will be unstoppable, and the country will be left defenseless.

Most people are aware that such apocalyptic thinking is self-dramatization in a world that adores indulgence. There is no winning with the extremists. It should be clear by now that the Mad Pats of the world will never accept open homosexuality. But they do not need to. No political issue is ever settled finally. There are no public questions whose resolution will command

100 percent of the population. Politics takes place in the middle of the bell curve.

The people who can be persuaded are going to be like my family. Grand theories about justice and social change will not do the trick with them, and visions of the apocalypse leave them cold. They do not much care for theories. They respond to what is in front of them, to what they can see and feel. They are not interested in how lesbians and gay men are different from them—that much is obvious. They want to know about the common ground. Lives become connected not through difference but through similarity. Connected lives become interesting because of difference, but they do not initially connect at that level. Remember the first stages of love, where so much time is devoted to revelations such as, "Oh, you like Rocky and Bullwinkle too."

There are many more people yet to make those connections with. The task is finding where the connections can be made. Sexual orientation is no longer so all-important that it overrides everything else about a person. My family used to think that. They do not anymore. My gay uncle and his lover are just like the rest of my family, sexual orientation aside. The news is that sexual orientation can be set aside. Being gay makes my uncle and his lover interesting, but other things make them interesting too.

Some lesbians and gay men, especially the artists, may balk at the implication that in certain ways they are quite ordinary. To a generation brought up to worship individuality, this is anathema. But there are many things that make each of us unique. Sometimes it is very nice to share small and common things, to just watch TV with someone or talk about sports, or help a sister making cookies in the kitchen. It is on those ordinary battlefields that what is left of this war can be won.

It is a great burden to make your life always and everywhere extraordinary. Homosexuality used to be that kind of a burden.

But homosexuality no longer makes anyone extraordinary by default. Perhaps the new radicals regret the loss of that sort of specialness and are trying to reconstruct it. But what lesbians and gay men have lost in forced distinctiveness, they have gained in options. They do not have to approach politics only from the outside; there are gay lobbyists and elected officials as well as street protesters.

The battle for gay rights has not left the streets and the books, but it is now being waged inside millions of private homes too. The assumption that heterosexuals are irretrievably opposed to gay rights is unfair, one more stereotype that hinders this debate. Heterosexuals of good faith have every right to find such an assumption as offensive as lesbians and gay men have ever found any stereotype about them, and for the same reasons.

I am not a queer, because I do not have to be one. I am not that different from most people in this country. As a gay man who is other things besides, I stand the best chance of finding a connection with someone, of starting a conversation, of changing a mind. That exposure is one of the fundamental principles of coming out: Reality undermines the fears that invisibility permits and opens the possibility of dialogue. It is in those plain and often tentative encounters that I and millions of others can make our contributions.

It is unfair that the burden is still on lesbians and gay men. Events like the March on Washington are still necessary; persuasion is a reality we cannot wish away. But this residue of injustice cannot be compared to the injustice those who came before us faced. The world is listening now because of what those pioneers did, and to assume anything less is to deny the achievements of my heroes, those men and women whose work in a hostile world gave me the gift of a family I love. Those men and women were radical so I would not have to be.

STEPHEN H. MILLER

This essay appeared in the 14 January 1994 issue of *Frontiers,* a gay newspaper published in Los Angeles.

HONEY, DID YOU RAISE THE KIDS?

A headline on the coveted front page of the *New York Times* blared out, "County in Texas Snubs Apple Over Unwed-Partner Policies." The story, which had percolated through the gay press before it was discovered by "the paper of record" and the rest of the national media, concerned the now infamous decision by Williamson County, Texas, to deny Apple Computer a tax abatement to build an $80 million office complex just north of Austin.

The deal, with the promise of 1,500 or more high-tech, high-wage jobs, was originally nixed over Apple's policy of granting unmarried partners of its employees—whether heterosexual or homosexual—the same health benefits conferred on spouses. Following intense arm-twisting by Texas Gov. Ann Richards, the county commission changed its mind—but clearly not its heart.

According to the *Times* account, the county's straight-laced commissioners felt Apple's policy undermined "traditional family values" and should not receive taxpayer support. The county "was not founded on same-sex lovers and live-in lovers," one opponent proclaimed. "It goes to what kind of morals you want to set for your community," argued another.

The typical take on all this is that virulent anti-gay bigotry is on a roll. "It's remarkable that in these economically difficult times, this blatant prejudice would prevail over smart business decisions," concluded William Rubenstein, director of the ACLU's Lesbian and Gay Rights Project. Now I wouldn't for one instant question that the good folks of Williamson County are deeply homophobic and homo-ignorant, but something else is also evident in their actions—something that the gay movement would do well to consider if it hopes to start winning political victories outside major urban centers.

Some employers, such as Lotus Development Corp., provide benefits to gay partners but not to unmarried heterosexuals. But Apple, like most city governments that have established domestic partner benefits, grants them to unmarried straight employees as well. What's wrong with that? Nothing, say those who view marriage as a stifling, patriarchal institution that should be undermined—regardless of whether children are involved. But plenty is wrong with it, in light of overwhelming evidence about the effect of family breakups that leave kids without fathers who provide financial support and act as paternal role models.

"As long as women continue to have relationships with, and continue to bear the children of, men who do not marry them, men will continue to be absent fathers," William Raspberry, a black columnist, wrote last month in his syndicated column. "The breakdown of family really does . . . lead to a culture whose rules of behavior are established by unsocialized adolescent males."

While the situation is most familiar in terms of the underclass African-American family (two-thirds of black births are now to single women), family breakdown should not be seen as a racial issue. Scholar Charles Murray noted these facts on the op-ed page of the *Wall Street Journal* last October: At the beginning of the 1970s some 6 percent of white births were illegitimate; in 1991 the figure was 22 percent. With the current growth trend implying a 40 percent illegitimacy rate by the year 2000, the prospect for a huge white underclass is looming.

It is not only conservatives who share this view. Liberal, pro-gay columnist Richard Cohen hailed Murray's warning, declaring a host of social pathologies—including crime, drugs, poverty and hopelessness—as "a clear consequence" of illegitimacy. "Without mature males as role models (not to mention disciplinarians)," Cohen wrote, about 1.2 million American children annually are "growing up unsocialized—prone to violence, unsuitable for employment and thus without prospect or hope." He added, "It's clear that the American taxpayer is losing patience."

Which brings us back to Apple. A corporate policy which appears to condone relationships without responsibility does threaten social stability, based on child-rearing within coherent families. Again, I don't doubt the effect of anti-gay bigotry in Williamson County, but linking benefits for gay partners who are not allowed to be married with benefits for heterosexuals who don't want to make a commitment puts the gay rights movement in the position of appearing to oppose all bedrock values—and plays directly into the hands of the religious right, which argues that the "gay agenda" is to destroy the moral foundation of Western civilization!

Alas, an otherwise positive goal—supporting child-rearing within stable families—is now bound up with the rest of the right wing's cultural program in all its exclusionary mean-spiritedness. But instead of exposing the sophistry of lumping gay rights (which would expand the range of families) with real anti-family phenomena such as unwed teen mothers and deadbeat dads, gay activists champion partner benefits for all. When New York state's top court, in response to a suit by gay rights groups, upheld the right of gay survivors to take over rent-stabilized apartments when a lover dies, activists rushed to point out that the decision also covered unmarried men and women living together—as if that made the decision "better."

How much more constructive it would be if our movement, while pushing for full marriage rights, stopped making alliances with cultural leftists favoring benefits for unwed heteros. As David Boaz advocates in the January 1994 issue of *Liberty,* a libertarian journal, workers should be told "if you want the benefits of marriage, get married; but if the state won't let you get married, we'll be more progressive." Benefits, he asserts, should not be seen "as one more goodie to hand out," but "as a way of remedying an unfairness, not to mention retaining valued employees."

He's right. Domestic partnership benefits should be a stop-gap measure for gays and lesbians until we achieve full marriage rights (based on legally recognized commitments). And, with legislators in Minnesota and elsewhere now introducing bills to specifically prohibit recognition of same-sex marriages (even if validated in other states), that fight is just beginning.

JONATHAN RAUCH

This essay appeared in the *Windy City Times* on 31 March 1994.

MORALITY AND HOMOSEXUALITY

On February 24, the *Wall Street Journal* ran a curious ramble on homosexuality ("Morality and Homosexuality"). The twenty-one theologians and scholars who wrote it purported to "articulate some of the reasons for the largely intuitive and pre-articulate anxiety of most Americans regarding homosexuality." They then presented an article that demonstrated no reasons at all. It was, in fact, one of the better demonstrations to date of the poverty of the emerging "thoughtful" anti-gay position.

The authors take the view that homosexuality is sinful, unnatural, "contrary to God's purpose." This is, of course, a flat moral claim, which one simply takes or leaves. But taking it leads them to a cruel and untenable position. Gay people should be expected to exercise "discipline of restraint" by not engaging in "homogenital behavior." In other words, homosexuals should be celibate or should fool heterosexuals into marrying them.

This is an astonishing demand. Homosexuality is not about what you do in bed, it is about whom you fall in love with. The authors assert that issues of human sexuality should not be viewed as mere "matters of recreation or taste," and of course they are right. I know of no homosexual who regards his love as a "matter of recreation or taste," any more than heterosexuals do. Human beings need food, they need shelter, they need love; love is a constitutive human need. That is why homosexuals view the social repression of their love not as the discouragement of a whimsical vice but as an act of scalding inhumanity.

To prescribe such repression without impeccable reasons is at best obtuse, at worst savage. "Morality and Homosexuality" tries to find reasons. It conspicuously fails.

The article deplores homosexuality as a form of license, bracketing it with "permissive abortion, widespread adultery, easy divorce." This is not, of course, an argument against homosexuality; it is an argument against license. Between homosexuals, legal marriage is forbidden and open commitment is stigmatized. No wonder, then, that license flourishes among gay people. If the authors of "Morality and Homosexuality" want to ask gay people to live responsibly in committed, stable relationships, then that is reasonable. But they oppose all gay relationships as immoral, and they loathe gay marriage. It is not wantonness which offends them; it is homosexuality.

They affirm the importance of marriage and family. So do I; so do most gay people, some radical activists notwithstanding. But again, the defense of family implies no coherent argument of any kind about homosexuality. How, precisely, is homosexuality a threat to "husband, wife and children, joined by public recognition and legal bond"? If some small percentage of the population forms same-sex relationships, how is that the downfall of the family? Divorce, illegitimacy and adultery are enemies of family. Homosexuality is not. It is a rare human trait of no great importance except to those who possess it.

Then come vague and muttered intimations that "civilization itself depends on the making" of "certain distinctions." One assumes that these intimations are vague and muttered because the presumed argument—that acceptance of a few homosexuals will ruin civilization—is plausible on its face. Now, it is possible that acceptance of homosexuality, like any other social change, may have some ill effects on society. So did the adoption of the automobile. But if the authors believe that the social damage done in accepting homosexuals will be so great as to outweigh any benefits to gay people and to society, it behooves them to show why. They do not.

Unable to point to any plausible mechanism by which homosexuals will destroy society or the family, the authors mumble about "seduction and solicitation" of the young, "predatory behavior," and so on. If the insinuation is that some more people may turn out to be gay in a society where homosexuality is accepted, that claim is both speculative and inconsequential. We do not torment left-handed people even if doing so would make a few more of them right-handed. We let people be as they are, provided they do no harm.

"Morality and Homosexuality" shows no harm. It merely assumes harm. By gliding unctuously from praise of cherished norms—family, civilization, self-control—to vague insinuations against an enemy group, it recalls a standard technique of anti-Semites, who praise patriotism, community and national security, and then proceed as if it were obvious that Jews threaten those things.

It is good that the writers of "Morality and Homosexuality" feel the need to find *reasons* for their dislike of homosexuality. From the point of view of sensible gay people, the substitution of anti-gay arguments for anti-gay sneers is one hopeful sign. Another is the sight of twenty-one theologians and scholars reaching for reasons to dislike homosexuality but grasping only straws.

DAVID BOAZ

Boaz, a graduate of Vanderbilt University, is executive vice president of the Cato Institute, a libertarian think tank in Washington, D.C. He previously served as editor of *New Guard* magazine and executive director of the Council for a Competitive Economy. An expert on such issues as the failure of big government, the politics of the baby-boom generation, drug prohibition, and educational choice, Boaz has written on those subjects and others in such publications as the *New York Times,* the *Washington Post,* the *Wall Street Journal, National Review, Liberty,* and the *Washington Blade.* He is the editor of *Left, Right, and Babyboom: America's New Politics; Assessing the Reagan Years; The Crisis in Drug Prohibition;* and *Liberating Schools: Education in the Inner City;* and coeditor of *Market Liberalism: A Paradigm for the 21st Century* and *The Cato Handbook for Congress.* The following essay appeared on the op-ed page of the *New York Times* on 10 September 1994.

DON'T FORGET THE KIDS

As conservatives gear up for the fall elections, many are pinning their hopes on attacking gay rights. Self-styled "pro-family" groups, seeking to build on the success of five local and state anti-gay initiatives in 1993, have been working to get similar measures on the November ballots in several states.

These organizations are correct in saying that America faces some real social problems, and that many can be attributed to the deterioration of families. What is upsetting, however, is the extent to which they focus on gay issues almost to the exclusion of the real problems.

Children need two parents, for financial and emotional reasons. Children in fatherless homes are five times as likely to be poor as those in two-parent families. Single mothers also find it difficult to control teenage boys, and such boys have made our inner cities a crime-ridden nightmare. Conservatives have taken note of this problem, and many of them have correctly indicted the welfare state. But with a few exceptions—notably Dan Quayle—they seldom put a high enough priority on condemning single parenthood.

And they pay almost no attention to the effects of divorce—every year more children experience divorce or separation than are born out of wedlock. These children are nearly twice as likely as those from intact families to drop out of high school or to receive psychological help.

Conservatives overlook this because they are too busy attacking gay men and lesbians. Consider the leading conservative journals. The *American Spectator* has run ten articles on homosexuality in the past three years, compared with two on parenthood, one on teen-age pregnancy, and none on divorce. *National Review* has printed thirty-two articles on homosexuality, five on fatherhood and parenting, three on teenage pregnancy, and just one on divorce.

The Family Research Council, the leading "family values" group, is similarly obsessed. In the most recent index of its publications, the two categories with the most listings are "Homosexual" and "Homosexuals in the Military"—a total of thirty-four items (plus four on AIDS). The organization has shown some interest in parenthood—nine items on family structure, thirteen on fatherhood, and six on teen pregnancy—yet there are more items on homosexuality than on all of those issues combined. There was no listing for divorce. (Would it be unfair to point out that there are two items on "Parents' Rights" and none on "Parents' Responsibilities"?)

As for the Christian Coalition, despite Executive Director Ralph Reed's vow not to "concentrate disproportionately on abortion and homosexuality," its current *Religious Rights Watch* newsletter contains six items, three of them on gay issues. The July issue of the American Family Association's newsletter, *Christians & Society Today*, contains nine articles, five of them on homosexuality.

Cobb County, Ga., a major battleground in the conservatives' culture war, is a microcosm of this distorted focus. In 1993 the county commission passed a resolution declaring "gay life styles" incompatible with community standards. Cobb County is a suburb of Atlanta; its residents, eighty-eight percent white, are richer and better educated than the national average. Yet it had a twenty percent illegitimacy rate in 1993, and there were two-thirds as many divorces as marriages. Surely the 1,545 unwed mothers and the 2,739 divorcing couples created more social problems in the county than the 300 gay men and women who showed up at a picnic to protest the county commission's assault on their rights.

When teen-age girls wear sexually explicit T-shirts, when teen-age boys form gangs to tally their sexual conquests, when eighth graders watch twice as much television as their European counterparts, when ten-year-olds on bicycles dart in front of my car at 1 A.M., when students take guns to class—where are the "family values" conservatives, and why aren't they calling on parents to take their responsibilities more seriously?

Perhaps they fear that making an issue of divorce would alienate middle-class supporters—including divorced conservatives. Perhaps they fear that putting welfare at the top of their agenda would seem racist, or worry that calling for parental responsibility would be a hard sell politically. They may be right, but that's no excuse for ducking crucial family issues. Their scapegoating of gay men and lesbians may get them some votes and contributions, but it's not going to solve any of American families' real problems.

DAVID BOAZ

The following essay appeared in the *New York Times* on 4 January 1995.

DOMESTIC JUSTICE

New York's new governor, George Pataki, plans to reverse Mario Cuomo's policy of granting health benefits to the domestic partners of all unmarried state employees. Mr. Pataki is part of a rising political tide that includes Gov. Pete Wilson of California, who said in vetoing his state's domestic partnership bill that "government policy ought not to discount marriage by offering a substitute relationship that demands much less."

That's legitimate, but it overlooks that there are two kinds of domestic partnerships—heterosexual and same-sex. Although the most vocal opposition to domestic partnerships is aimed at gay couples, giving them benefits doesn't undermine marriage. Rather, it remedies the injustice that homosexuals can't marry the people with whom they share their lives, and it creates financial incentives for stable relationships. Is this not the goal we seek in encouraging marriage?

Giving domestic partnership benefits to unmarried heterosexual couples, on the other hand, does undermine marriage. They give people who can marry all the financial benefits of a legal union without demanding commitment. "If two heterosexuals are going to shack up together, then they ought to get married," said the Rev. Charles Bullock, who fought successfully to overturn a partnership law in Austin. "If they're not going to make that commitment to each other, why should the city?"

Although the voters' shift to the right in 1994 has imperiled domestic partnership laws, the trend toward giving benefits remains strong in the workplace—most recently at Microsoft, Time Inc., and Capital Cities/ABC. Even Coors, perhaps America's most famously conservative company, is studying the issue.

But many politicians, upset by rising illegitimacy and divorce rates, say that such policies fly in the face of concern about family stability. As Senator Trent Lott, Republican of Mississippi, said in seeking to overturn the District of Columbia's domestic partnership law, "We must begin to take a stand for the family."

Gay leaders haven't helped themselves in this debate. They invariably urge that heterosexual couples be included in legislation and corporate policies. Many have even denounced the traditional family as a stifling, patriarchal institution, thereby fueling a middle-class backlash.

Gay leaders would be better off making a pro-family case, playing up their commitment to their partners and their desire for a legal union. This argument has found sympathy in the private sector. In 1992 Stanford University extended benefits to domestic partners of homosexuals (but not heterosexuals) because "their commitment to the partnership is analogous to that involved in contemporary marriage," said Barbara Butterfield, a university vice president.

Governments invariably get this wrong, while businesses usually get it right. Every city that has adopted domestic partnership laws has included both same-sex and heterosexual couples, and in almost every case more heterosexuals than homosexuals have filed for partnership status.

But many private organizations—including Stanford, Montefiore Medical Center, Lotus Development Corporation and the Public Broadcasting Service—have extended benefits only to same-sex couples. Most of these companies have said that if homosexual couples are allowed to legally marry, these policies would be ended—which is as it should be.

"This policy discriminates against heterosexuals who choose not to marry," an embittered heterosexual employee at Lotus said. Exactly. And that's a point that Governor Pataki and sensible gay activists ought to be able to agree on: commitment should be encouraged, while relationships without commitment should not expect social recognition or financial benefits.

BRUCE BAWER

The following column appeared in the *Advocate* on 15 November 1994.

THE FOLKS NEXT DOOR

A charge heard frequently these days is that some "assimilationist" or "straight-acting" gays are endeavoring to secure equal rights for themselves by selling out "gay-acting" or "nonconformist" gay people—including drag queens and leathermen—with whom straight America is uncomfortable.

This allegation always bemuses me. Leaving aside the question of whether such a plot is actually afoot, how, I wonder, can anyone believe that John and Jane Q. Public are more comfortable with "straight-acting" gays than with "gay-acting" ones? On the contrary, nothing's more disconcerting to some folks than a gay man or woman who, by failing to conform to stereotype, confounds any attempt to define neat, safe boundaries between the "worlds" of gay and straight. Gay or not, entertainers like Richard Simmons and the late Paul Lynde owe their appeal largely to people's eagerness to have their stereotypes affirmed, their condescension certified. With every word and gesture, such celebrities reinforce the comfortable notion that a homosexual is somebody odd, amusing, flamboyant, ridiculous, and, of course, tragically sad and lonely deep down. A person you can recognize at a hundred paces and whom you would probably never see in your own neighborhood anyway.

What makes many straight people uncomfortable by contrast is any image of gay life and love that seems too ordinary, too familiar. Years ago when I enthusiastically reviewed *Prick Up Your Ears,* the film about gay playwright Joe Orton, I didn't hear a peep of complaint from my editors at the reactionary *American Spectator,* for that movie gave a picture of gay life that they were comfortable with. It showed gays as weird, alienated, grubby, marginal, fundamentally unhappy, and destined for tragic ends. The showdown came, rather, over a few positive sentences I wrote about *Longtime Companion,* which dared to show gay men in steady jobs and fulfilling relationships. To many people that's the revolutionary image.

This way of thinking is by no means confined to right-wingers. Take James Wolcott, who in a 1989 issue of *Vanity Fair* ridiculed David Leavitt's novel *Equal Affections* for presenting "a gay version of that nice young couple down the block." Gays, Wolcott made it clear, should be "sexual outlaws." That review was an early salvo in what has since become an assault on "gays next door" by straight liberals who often don't see how offensive they're being. Consider an editorial in the *New York Times* that appeared in June on the morning of the Stonewall 25 march. After declaring support for gay rights, the editorial criticized "gay moderates and conservatives" for seeking "to assure the country that the vast majority of gay people are 'regular' people just like the folks next door." *Like* the folks next door? Look again, *Times* editors: Many of us *are* the folks next door. Similarly, in a recent issue of the *Los Angeles Times Magazine,* Joe Morgenstern described gay moderates as "a small army of gays who just want to be ordinary Americans." Correction: Most of us *are* ordinary Americans.

It's not ghetto-bound nonconformist gays, then, but ordinary gays next door that many people find threatening. Why? Because next door to them means next door to their kids. Gays next door means the possibility of a gay man or lesbian as their kid's home-room teacher or the family doctor or the minister at their church or the friendly neighbor whose lawn their teenage son mows every weekend. Heaven knows Junior will never know or want to be like an Allen Ginsberg or a Truman Capote or a Quentin Crisp, but—*horrors!*—what about that lawyer next door who happens to be gay? He's somebody they could actually imagine Junior liking and identifying with. Good Lord, deliver us!

A lot of straight people, then, who are entertained by drag queens camping it up in West Hollywood, "open-minded" about an aging beat poet coupling with somebody else's kid in the East Village, and fully supportive of the rights of gays on Castro Street feel deeply threatened by the thought of two gay men in suits coming out of the house next door to them in Scarsdale or San Bernardino or Walnut Creek and picking up the morning newspaper off the porch on their way to work. As Christopher Isherwood wrote in 1948, "Homosexual relations frequently are happy. Men [and women!] live together for years and make homes and share their lives and their work, just as heterosexuals do. This truth is particularly disturbing and shocking even to 'liberal' people, because it cuts across their romantic, tragic notion of the homosexual fate." Exactly. If gays in America are ever to achieve equal rights, we must make it our business to overcome not only outright reactionary bigotry, which seeks to drive us back into the closet, but also this kind of lingering, often liberal discomfort, which—intentionally or not—insidiously demands that we know our place. Let's get out the word: Our place is wherever we want it to be.

JONATHAN RAUCH

The following essay appeared in a 1996 issue of the *New Republic* .

WHO NEEDS MARRIAGE?

Whatever else marriage may or may not be, it is certainly falling apart. Half of today's new marriages will end in divorce, and far more costly still (from a social point of view) are the marriages that never happen at all, leaving mothers poor, children fatherless and neighborhoods chaotic. With a sense of timing worthy of Neville Chamberlain, at just this moment homosexuals are pressing to be able to marry, and Hawaii's courts are moving toward letting them do so. I'll believe in gay marriage in America when I see it, but if it gets as far as being even temporarily legalized in Hawaii, then the uproar about this final insult to a besieged institution will be deafening.

Whether gay marriage makes sense—and, for that matter, whether straight marriage makes sense—depends on what marriage is actually for. Oddly enough, at the moment secular thinking on this question is shockingly sketchy. Gay activists say: Marriage is for love and we love each other, therefore we should be able to marry. Traditionalists say: Marriage is for children, and homosexuals do not (or should not) have children, therefore you should not be able to marry. That, unfortunately, pretty well covers the spectrum. I say "unfortunately," because both views are wrong. They misunderstand and impoverish the social meaning of marriage.

I admit to being an interested party; I am a homosexual, and I want the right to marry. In fact, I want more than the right, I want the actual marriage (when Mr. Wonderful comes along, God willing). Nevertheless, I do not want to destroy the most basic of all social institutions, backbone of the family and bedrock of civilization. It is not enough for gay marriage to make sense for gay people; if they ask society to recognize and bless it, it should also make sense from society's broader point of view.

So what is marriage for?

AGAINST LOVE

In its religious dress, marriage has a straightforward justification. It is as it is because that is how God wants it. Depending on the religion, God has various things to say about who may marry and what should go on within a marriage. Modern marriage is, of course, based upon traditions that religion helped to codify and enforce. But religious doctrine has no special standing in the world of secular law and policy, with all due apologies to the "Christian nation" crowd. If we want to know what and whom marriage is for in modern America, we need a sensible secular doctrine.

At one point, marriage in secular society was largely a matter of business: cementing family ties, providing social status for men and economic support for women, conferring dowries, and so on. Marriages were typically arranged, and "love" in the modern sense was no prerequisite. In Japan today there are remnants of this system, and it works surprisingly well. Couples stay together because they view their marriage as a partnership: an investment in social stability for themselves and their children. Because Japanese couples don't expect as much emotional fulfillment as Americans do, they are less inclined to break up. They also take a somewhat more relaxed attitude toward adultery. What's a little extracurricular love, provided that each partner is fulfilling his or her many other marital duties?

In the West, of course, love is a defining element. The notion of lifelong love is charming, if ambitious, and certainly love is a desirable element of marriage. It cannot, however, be the defining element in society's eyes. You may or may not love your husband, but the two of you are just as married either way. You may love your mistress, but that certainly does not make her your spouse. Love helps make sense of marriage from an emotional point of view, but it is not terribly important, I think, in making sense of marriage from the point of view of social policy.

If blessing love does not define the purpose of secular marriage, what does? Neither the law nor secular thinking provides a very clear answer to this question. Today marriage is almost entirely a voluntary arrangement whose contents are up to the people making the deal. There are few if any behaviors that automatically end a marriage. If a man beats his wife—which is about the worst thing he can do to her—he may be convicted of assault, but his marriage is not automatically dissolved. Couples can be adulterous (or "open") yet still be married, so long as that is what they choose to be. They can be celibate, too; consummation is not required. All in all, it is an impressive and also rather astonishing victory for modern individualism that so important an institution should be so bereft of formal social instruction as to what should go on inside of it.

Secular society tells us only a few things about marriage. Among them are the following: First, marriage happens only with the consent of the parties. Second, the parties are not children. Third, the number of parties is two. Fourth, one is a man and the other a woman. Within those rules, a marriage is whatever anyone says it is. So the standard rules say almost nothing about what marriage is for.

AGAINST TRADITION

Perhaps it doesn't matter what marriage is for. Perhaps it is enough simply to say that marriage is as it is, and should not be tampered with. This sounds like a crudely reactionary position. In fact, however, of all the arguments against reforming marriage, it is probably the most powerful.

I'll call it a Hayekian argument, after the great libertarian economist F. A. Hayek, who developed this line of thinking in his book *The Fatal Conceit.* In a market system, the prices generated by impersonal forces may not make sense from any one person's point of view, but they encode far more information than even the cleverest person could ever gather. In a similar fashion, human societies evolve rich and complicated webs of nonlegal rules in the forms of customs, traditions and institutions. Like prices, the customs generated by societies may often seem irrational or arbitrary. But the very fact that they are the customs which have evolved implies that there is a kind of practical logic embedded in them which may not be apparent from even a sophisticated analysis. And the web of custom cannot be torn apart and reordered at will, because once its internal logic is violated it falls apart. Intellectuals, like Marxists or feminists, who seek to deconstruct and rationally rebuild social traditions will produce not better order but merely chaos. Thus hallowed social tradition should not be tampered with except in the very last extremity.

For secular intellectuals who are unhappy with the evolved framework for marriage and who are excluded from it—in other words, for people like me—this Hayekian argument is very troubling. It is also very powerful. Age-old stigmas on illegitimacy and out-of-wedlock pregnancy were crude and unfair to women and children. On the male side, shotgun marriages were, in an informal way, coercive and intrusive. But when modern societies began playing around with the age-old stigmas on illegitimacy and divorce and all the rest, whole portions of the social structure just caved in.

So the Hayekian view argues strongly against gay marriage. It says that the current rules for marriage may not be the best ones, and they may even be unfair. But they are all we have, and once you say that marriage need not be male–female, soon marriage will stop being anything at all. You can't mess with the formula without causing unforeseen consequences, possibly including the implosion of the institution of marriage itself.

But I demur. There are problems with the Hayekian position. The biggest is that it is untenable in its extreme form and unhelpful in its milder version. In in its extreme form, it implies that no social reforms should ever be undertaken. Indeed, no social laws should be passed, because they will interfere with the natural evolution of social mores. One would thus have to say that because in the past slavery was customary in almost all human societies, it should not have been forcibly abolished. Obviously, neither Hayek nor his sympathizers would actually say this. They would point out that slavery violated fundamental moral principles and was scaldingly inhumane. But in doing so, they do what must be done if we are to be human: they establish a moral platform from which to judge social rules. They thus acknowledge that abstracting social debate from moral concerns is not possible.

If the ban on gay marriage were only mildly unfair and if the social costs of changing it were certain to be enormous, then the ban could stand on Hayekian grounds. However, if there is any social policy today that has a fair claim to being scaldingly inhumane, it is the ban on gay marriage. As conservatives tirelessly and rightly point out, marriage is the most fundamental institution of society. To bar any class of people from marrying as they choose is an extraordinary deprivation. When, not so long ago, it was illegal in parts of America for blacks to marry whites, no one could claim this was a trivial disenfranchisement. Granted, gay marriage raises issues that interracial marriage does not; but no one can argue that the deprivation itself is a minor one.

To outweigh such a serious claim and rule out homosexual marriage purely on Hayekian grounds, saying that bad things might happen is not enough. Bad things might always happen. Bad things happened as a result of legalizing contraception, but that did not make it the wrong thing to do, and in any case good things happened also. It is not at all clear, on the merits, that heterosexual marriage would be eroded by legalizing homosexual marriage. On the contrary, marriage might be strengthened if it were held out as the norm for everybody, including homosexuals.

Besides, it seems doubtful that extending marriage to, say, another three or five percent of the population would have anything like the effects that no-fault divorce has had, to say nothing of contraception and the sexual revolution. By now, the "traditional" understanding of marriage has been tampered with by practically everybody in all kinds of ways. It is hard to think of a bigger affront to tradition, for instance, than allowing married women to own property independently of their husbands, or allowing them to charge their husbands with rape. Surely it is a bit unfair to say that marriage may be reformed for the sake of anyone and everyone except homosexuals, who must respect the dictates of tradition.

Faced with these problems, the milder version of the Hayekian argument says, not that social traditions shouldn't be tampered with at all, but that they shouldn't be tampered with lightly. Fine, and thank you. In this case, no one is talking about casual messing around, or about some lobby's desire to score political points; the issue is about allowing people to live as grown-ups and full citizens. One could write pages on this point, but I won't. I'll set human rights claims to one side, and in return ask the Hayekians to recognize that appeals to blind tradition and to the risks inherent in social change do not, a priori, settle anything in this instance. They merely warn against frivolous change. If the issue at hand is whether gay marriage is good or bad for society as well as for gay people, there is no avoiding a discussion about the *purpose* of marriage.

AGAINST CHILDREN

So we turn to what has become the standard view of marriage's purpose. Its proponents would probably like to call it a child-centered view, but a more accurate description would call it an anti-gay view, as will become clear. Whatever you call it, it is certainly the view that is heard most often, and in the context of the debate over gay marriage it is heard almost exclusively. In its most straightforward form, it goes as follows (I quote from James Q. Wilson's fine book *The Moral Sense*):

> A family is not an association of independent people; it is a human commitment designed to make possible the rearing of moral and healthy children. Governments care—or ought to care—about families for this reason, and scarcely for any other.

Wilson speaks about "family" rather than "marriage" as such, but one may, I think, read him as speaking of marriage without doing any injustice to his meaning. The resulting proposition—government ought to care about marriage almost entirely because of children, and scarcely for any other reason—seems reasonable. It certainly accords with our commonsense feeling that marriage and children go together. But there are problems. The first, obviously, is that gay couples may have children, either through adoption or (for lesbians) by using artificial insemination. I will leave for some other article the contentious issue of gay adoption. For now, the obvious point is that if the mere presence of children is the test, then homosexual relationships can certainly pass it.

You might note, correctly, that heterosexual marriages are more likely to wind up with children in the mix than homosexual ones. When granting marriage licenses to heterosexuals, however, we do not ask how likely the couple is to have children. We assume that they are entitled to get married whether they end up with children or not. Understanding this, conservatives often then make an interesting further move. In seeking to justify the state's interest in marriage, they shift from the actual presence of children to the anatomical possibility of making them. Hadley Arkes, a law professor and prominent opponent of homosexual marriage, makes the case this way:

> The traditional understanding of marriage is grounded in the "natural teleology of the body"—in the inescapable fact that only a man and a woman, and only two people, not three, can generate a child. Once marriage is detached from that natural teleology of the body, what ground of principle would thereafter confine marriage to two people rather than some larger grouping? That is, on what ground of principle would the law reject the claim of a gay couple that their love is not confined to a coupling of two, but that they are woven into a larger ensemble with yet another person or two?

What he seems to be saying is that where the possibility of natural children is nil, the meaning of marriage is nil. If marriage is allowed between members of the same sex, then the concept of marriage has been emptied of content except to ask whether the parties love each other. Then anything goes, including polygamy. This reasoning presumably is what anti-gay activists have in mind when they claim that once gay marriage is legal, marriage to pets will follow close behind.

Arkes and his sympathizers have here made two mistakes, both of them instructive. To see them, break down the Arkes-type claim into two components:

1. Two-person marriage derives its special status from the anatomical possibility that the partners can create natural children; and
2. Apart from (1), two-person marriage has no purpose sufficiently strong to justify its special status. That is, absent justification (1), anything goes.

The first proposition is peculiar, because it is wholly at odds with the way society actually views marriage. Leave aside the insistence that natural, as opposed to adoptive, children define the importance of marriage. The deeper problem, apparent right away, is the issue of sterile heterosexual couples. Here the "anatomical possibility" crowd has a problem, for a homosexual union is, anatomically speaking, nothing but one variety of sterile union, and no different even in principle: a woman without a uterus has no more potential for giving birth than a man without a vagina.

It may sound like carping to stress the case of barren heterosexual marriage; the vast majority of newlywed heterosexual couples, after all, can have children and probably will. But the point here is fundamental. There are far more sterile unions in America than homosexual ones. The "anatomical possibility" crowd cannot have it both ways. If the possibility of children is what gives meaning to marriage, then a post-menopausal woman who tries to take out a marriage license should be turned away at the courthouse door. What's more, she should be hooted at and condemned for stretching the meaning of marriage beyond its natural basis, and so reducing the institution to frivolity. People at the Family Research Council or Concerned Women of America should point at her and say, "If she can marry, why not polygamy? Why not marriage to pets?"

Obviously, the "anatomical" conservatives do not say this, because they are sane. They instead flail around, saying that sterile men and women were at least born with the right-shaped parts for making children, and so on. As they struggle to include sterile heterosexual marriages while excluding homosexual ones, their position is soon revealed to be a nonposition. It says that the "natural children" rationale defines marriage when homosexuals are involved, but not when heterosexuals are involved. When the parties to union are sterile heterosexuals, the justification for marriage must be something else. But what?

Now arises the oddest part of the "anatomical" argument. Look at proposition (2) above. It says that, absent the anatomical justification for marriage, anything goes. In other words, it dismisses the idea that there might be some other compelling reasons for society to sanctify marriage above other kinds of relationships. Why would anybody want to make this move? I'll just hazard a guess: to exclude homosexuals. Any rationale that justifies sterile heterosexual marriages can also apply to homosexual ones. For instance, marriage makes women more financially secure. Very nice, say the conservatives. But that rationale could be applied to lesbians, so it's definitely out.

The end result of this stratagem is perverse to the point of being funny. The attempt to ground marriage in children (or the anatomical possibility thereof) falls flat. But having lost that reason for marriage, the anti-gay people can offer no other. In their fixation on excluding homosexuals, they leave themselves no consistent justification for the privileged status of *heterosexual* marriage. They thus tear away any coherent foundation that secular marriage might have, which is precisely the opposite of what they claim they want to do. If they have to undercut marriage to save it from homosexuals, so be it!

If you feel my argument here has a slightly Thomist ring, the reason, of course, is that the "child-centered" people themselves do not really believe that natural children are the only, or even the overriding, reason society blesses marriage. In the real world, it's obvious that sterile people have every right to get married, and that society benefits by allowing and, indeed, encouraging them to do so. No one seriously imagines that denying marriage to a sterile heterosexual couple would strengthen the institution of marriage, or that barring sterile marriages would even be a decent thing to do. The "natural children" people know this perfectly well, and they admit it implicitly when they cheerfully bless sterile unions. In truth, their real posture has nothing at all to do with children, or even with the "anatomical possibility" of children. It is merely anti-gay. All it really says is this: the defining purpose of marriage is to exclude homosexuals.

This is not an answer to the question of what marriage is for. Rather, it makes of marriage, as Richard Mohr aptly puts it, "nothing but an empty space, delimited only by what it excludes—gay couples." By putting a non-rationale at the center of modern marriage, these conservatives leave the institution worse off than if they had never opened their mouths. This is not at all helpful.

If one is to set hypocrisy aside, one must admit that there are compelling reasons for marriage other than children—reasons that may or may not apply to homosexual unions. What might those reasons be?

ROGUE MALES AND AILING MATES

For the record, I would be the last to deny that children are one central reason for the privileged status of marriage. Rather, I gladly proclaim it. When men and women get together, children are a likely outcome; and, as we are learning in ever more unpleasant ways, when children appear without two parents, all kinds of trouble ensues. Without belaboring the point, I hope I won't be accused of saying that children are a trivial reason for marriage. They just cannot be the only reason.

And what are the others? I can think of several possibilities, such as the point cited above about economic security for women (or men). There is a lot of intellectual work to be done trying to sort out which are the essential reasons, and which incidental. It seems to me that the two strongest candidates are these: settling males, and providing reliable caregivers. Both purposes are critical to the functioning of a humane and stable society, and both are much better served by marriage—that is, by one-to-one lifelong commitment—than by any other institution.

Wilson writes, in *The Moral Sense,* of the human male's need to hunt, defend, and attack. "Much of the history of civilization can be thought of as an effort to adapt these male dispositions to contemporary needs by restricting aggression or channeling it into appropriate channels," he says. I think it is probably fair to say that civilizing young males is one of any society's two or three biggest problems. Wherever unattached males gather in packs, you see no end of trouble: wildings in Central Park, gangs in Los Angeles, football hooligans in Britain, skinheads in Germany, fraternity hazings in universities, grope-lines in the military, and (in a different but ultimately no less tragic way) the bathhouses and wanton sex of gay San Francisco or New York in the 1970s.

For taming males, marriage is unmatched. "Of all the institutions through which men may pass—schools, factories, the military—marriage has the largest effect," Wilson writes. A token of the casualness of current thinking about marriage is that the man who wrote those words could, later in the very same book, say that government should care about fostering families for "scarcely any other" reason than children. If marriage—that is, the binding of men into couples—did nothing else, its power to settle men, to keep them at home and out of trouble, would be ample justification for its special status.

Of course, women and older men don't generally travel in marauding or orgiastic packs. But in their case the second rationale comes strongly into play. A second enormous problem for society is what to do when someone is beset by some sort of burdensome contingency. It could be cancer, a broken back, unemployment, or depression; it could be exhaustion from work or stress under pressure. If marriage has any meaning at all, it is that when you collapse from a stroke, there will be at least one other person whose "job" is to drop everything and come to your aid; or that when you come home after being fired by the postal service, there will be someone to persuade you not to commit a massacre.

All by itself, marriage is society's first and, often, second and third line of support for the troubled individual. Absent a spouse, the burdens of contingency fall immediately and sometimes crushingly upon people who have more immediate problems of their own (relatives, friends, neighbors), and then upon charities and welfare programs that are expensive and often not very good. From the broader society's point of view, an unattached person is an accident waiting to happen. Married people are happier, healthier, and live longer; married men have lower rates of homicide, suicide, accidents, and mental illness. In large part, the reason is simply that married people have someone to look after them, and know it.

Obviously, both of these rationales—the need to settle males, the need to have people looked after—apply to sterile people as well as fertile ones, and apply to childless couples as well as to ones with children. The first explains why everybody feels relieved when the town delinquent gets married, and the second explains why everybody feels happy when an aging widow takes a second husband. From a social point of view, it seems to me, both rationales are far more compelling as justifications of marriage's special status than, say, love. And both of them apply to homosexuals as well as to heterosexuals.

Take the matter of settling men. It is probably true that women and children, more than just the fact of marriage, help civilize men. But that hardly means that the settling effect of marriage on homosexual men is negligible. To the contrary, being tied into a committed relationship plainly helps stabilize gay men. Even without marriage, coupled gay men have steady sex partners and relationships that they value, so they tend to be less wanton. Add marriage, and you bring to bear a further array of stabilizing influences. One of the main benefits of publicly recognized marriage is that it binds couples together not only in their own eyes but also in the eyes of society at large. Around the partners is weaved a web of expectations that they will spend nights together, go to parties together, take out mortgages together, buy furniture at Ikea together, and so on—all of which helps tie them together and keep them off the streets and at home. ("It's 1 A.M.; do you know where your husband is?" Chances are you do.) Surely that is a very good thing, especially as compared to the closet-gay culture of furtive sex with innumerable partners in parks and bathhouses.

The other benefit of marriage—caretaking—clearly applies to homosexuals, with no reservations at all. One of the first things many people worry about when coming to terms with their homosexuality is, "Who will take care of me when I'm old?" Society needs to care about this, too, as the AIDS crisis has made horribly clear. If that crisis showed anything, it is that homosexuals can and will take care of each other, sometimes with breathtaking devotion—and that no institution can begin to match the care of a devoted partner. Legally speaking, marriage creates kin. Surely, society's interest in kin-creation is strongest of all for people who are unlikely to be supported by children in old age and who may well be rejected by their own parents in youth.

Gay marriage, then, is far from being a mere exercise in political point-making or rights-mongering. On the contrary, it serves two of the three social purposes that make marriage so indispensable and irreplaceable for heterosexuals. Two out of three may not be the whole ball of wax, but it is more than enough to give society a compelling interest in marrying off homosexuals.

Moreover, marriage is the *only* institution that adequately serves these purposes. People who are uncomfortable with gay marriage—including some gay people—argue that the benefits can just as well be had through private legal arrangements and domestic-partnership laws. But only the fiduciary and statutory benefits of marriage can be arranged that way, and therein lies a world of difference. The promise of one-to-one lifetime commitment is very hard to keep. The magic of marriage is that it wraps a dense ribbon of social approval around each partnership, then reinforces commitment with a hundred informal mechanisms from everyday greetings ("How's the wife?") to gossipy sneers ("Why does she put up with that cheating bastard Bill?"). The power of marriage is not just legal but social. It seals its promise with the smiles and tears of family, friends, and neighbors. It shrewdly exploits ceremony (big, public weddings) and money (expensive gifts, dowries) to deter casual commitment and to make bailing out embarrassing. Stag parties and bridal showers signal that what is beginning is not just a legal arrangement but a whole new stage of life. "Domestic partner" laws do none of these things. Me, I can't quite imagine my mother sobbing with relief as she says, "Thank heaven, Jonathan has finally found a domestic partner."

I'll go further: far from being a substitute for the real thing, "lite" marriage more likely undermines it. Marriage is a deal between a couple and society, not just between two people: society recognizes the sanctity and autonomy of the pair-bond, and in exchange each spouse commits to being the other's caregiver, social worker, and policeman of first resort. Each marriage is its own little society within society. Any step that weakens this deal by granting the legal benefits of marriage without also requiring the public commitment is begging for trouble.

From gay couples' point of view, pseudo-marriage is second best to the real thing; but from society's point of view, it may be the worst policy of all. From both points of view, gay marriage—

real social recognition, real personal commitment, real social pressure to shore up personal commitment—makes the most sense. That is why government should be wary of offering "alternatives" to marriage. And, one might add, that is also why the full social benefits of gay marriage will come only when churches as well as governments customarily bless it: when women marry women in big church weddings as mothers weep and priests, solemnly smiling, intone the vows.

AGAINST GAY DIVORCE

So gay marriage makes sense for several of the same reasons that straight marriage makes sense; fine. That would seem a natural place to stop. But the logic of the argument compels one to go a twist further. If I am right, then there are implications for heterosexuals and homosexuals alike—not entirely comfortable ones.

If society has a strong interest in seeing people married off, then it must also have some interest in seeing them stay together. For many years that interest was assumed and embodied in laws and informal stigmas that made divorce a painful experience. My guess is that this was often bad for adults but quite good for children, though you could argue that point all day. In any event, things have radically changed. Today more and more people believe that a divorce should be at least a bit harder to get.

I'm not going to wade into the debate about toughening the divorce laws. Anyway, in a liberal society there is not much you can do to keep people together without trampling their rights. The point that's relevant here is that, if I'm right, the standard way of thinking about this issue is incomplete, even misleading. The usual argument is that divorce is bad for children, which is why we should worry about it. I wouldn't deny this for a moment. Some people advocate special counseling or cooling-off periods for divorcing couples with children. That may well be a good idea. But it should not be assumed that society has no interest in helping childless couples stay together, also—for just the reasons I've outlined. Childless couples, of course, include gay couples. In my opinion, if one wants to shore up the institution of marriage, then one had better complicate divorce (if that's what you're going to do) for all couples, including gay ones and childless heterosexual ones. Otherwise you send the message that marriage can be a casual affair if you don't happen to have children. Gay spouses should understand that once they are together, they are *really* together. The upshot is that gay divorce should be every bit as hard to get as straight divorce—and both should probably be harder to get than is now the case.

Another implication follows, too. If it is good for society to have people attached, then it is not enough just to make marriage available. Marriage should also be *expected*. This, too, is just as true for homosexuals as for heterosexuals. So if homosexuals are justified in expecting access to marriage, society is equally justified in expecting them to use it. I'm not saying that out-of-wedlock sex should be scandalous or that people should be coerced into marrying or anything like that. The mechanisms of expectation are more subtle. When Grandma cluck-clucks over a still-unmarried young man, or when Mom says she wishes her little girl would settle down, she is expressing a strong and well-justified preference—one that is quietly echoed in a thousand ways throughout society, and that produces subtle but important pressure to form and sustain unions. This is a good and necessary thing, and it will be as necessary for homosexuals as heterosexuals. If gay marriage is recognized, single gay people over a certain age should not be surprised when they are subtly disapproved of or pitied. That is a vital part of what makes marriage work.

Moreover, if marriage is to work, it cannot be merely a "lifestyle option." It must be privileged. That is, it must be understood to be better, on average, than other ways of living. Not mandatory, not good where everything else is bad, but better: a general norm, rather than a personal taste. The biggest worry about gay marriage, I think, is that homosexuals might get it but then mostly not use it. Unlike a conservative friend of mine, I don't think that gay neglect of marriage would greatly erode what remains of the bonding power of heterosexual marriage (remember, homosexuals are only a tiny fraction of the population). But it would certainly not help, and in any case it would denude the benefits and cheapen the meaning of homosexual marriage. And heterosexual society would rightly feel betrayed if, after legalization, homosexuals treated marriage as a minority taste rather than as a core institution of life. It is not enough, I think, for gay people to say we want the right to marry. If we do not use it, shame on us.

FURTHER READING

Section I

BRUCE BAWER, "Leaving the Comfort Zone." *The Advocate,* 21 March 1995.

——— "No Truce for Bruce." *Ten Percent,* November/December 1994. A study of the gay-press reception of *A Place at the Table.*

——— *A Place at the Table: The Gay Individual in American Society.* Simon & Schuster, 1993; Touchstone (paperback), 1994. "This book is a reflection on the theme of homosexuality. I have written it because the current debate on homosexuality and gay rights has generated a lot more heat than light."

——— "Radically Different." *New York Times Book Review,* 5 November 1995. A review of Urvashi Vaid, *Virtual Equality.*

——— "What *A Place at the Table* Really Says." *Harvard Gay and Lesbian Review,* 1:3, Summer 1994. Response to David Bergman's "A Place for the Rest of Us," an attack on *A Place at the Table* that appeared in the spring 1994 issue of the same journal.

PAUL BERMAN, "Democracy and Homosexuality." *New Republic,* 20 December 1993. A straight writer's review essay about several new books on gay politics and culture. It adds up to a succinct history of the post-Stonewall gay rights movement, with an emphasis on the counterproductiveness of revolutionary ideology and rhetoric and a recognition that the new era of activism by gay moderates and conservatives represents a key turning point.

WAYNE R. DYNES, "Queer Studies: In Search of a Discipline." *Academic Questions,* Fall 1995.

ERIC MARCUS, *Making History: The Struggle for Gay and Lesbian Equal Rights.* HarperCollins, 1992. A fascinating collection of profiles of gay rights heroes, gay and straight, who aren't on the queer left, including Dear Abby, Episcopal bishop John Shelby Spong, and a PFLAG founder.

DANIEL MENDELSON, "Virtual Reading." *Out,* November 1995. A review of *Virtual Equality* and of Andrew Sullivan's *Virtually Normal.*

STEPHEN H. MILLER, "Who Stole the Gay Movement?" *Christopher Street,* issue 218, October 1994. An account of the gay left's attacks on gay moderates, libertarians, and conservatives.

JIM THOMAS, "It's Not Too Late to Retool Our Movement." *Saint Louis Lesbian and Gay News-Telegraph,* August 1993. A call for "real responsibility in genuine community."

PAUL VARNELL, "The Trouble with Activists." *Windy City Times,* 21 October 1993. "We need to recruit a new generation of activists with emotional health, jobs, computer skills, and—frankly—charm." Varnell's "Observer's Notebook" column appears weekly in the *Windy City Times* and other journals.

The *New York Native*'s "Stonewalling" column, written under the pseudonym "Thomas J. Jackson," has for years provided informed critical commentary on the activities of gay-left political leaders and organizations.

Section II

BARRY GOLDWATER, "The Gay Ban: Just Plain Un-American." *Washington Post,* 10 June, 1993.

——— "Job Protection for Gays." *Washington Post,* 13 July 1994.

CHRISTOPHER KEITH, "Letter from a Gay Libertarian Republican Political Activist." *Christopher Street,* issue 167. A "rugged individualist" affirms his gayness, Christianity, and belief in the family.

MARVIN LIEBMAN, *Coming Out Conservative.* Chronicle Books, 1992. A prominent conservative's story of a life in the closet. Liebman's monthly column, formerly called "Conservatively Speaking" and now called "Independently Speaking," has appeared in many local gay newspapers since 1993.

——— "Letter to William F. Buckley, Jr." *National Review,* 9 July 1990.

——— "What Next? The Gay and Lesbian Community—and Republicans?" *Washington Blade,* 4 June 1993.

Stephen Macedo. "The New Natural Lawyers." *The Harvard Crimson,* 29 October 1993. A law professor criticizes the weak conservative "natural law" argument against homosexuality. "Public policics and proposals that—in the name of family values—fix their scornful attention on gays and lesbians . . . embody a double standard of permissiveness toward straights and censoriousness toward gays."

STEPHEN H. MILLER. "Election Reflections." *New York Native,* 21 November 1994. Observations on the 1994 GOP landslide.

ANDREW SULLIVAN, *Virtually Normal.* Knopf, 1995. "This is not a book about how a person deals with his or her sexuality. It is a book about how we as a society deal with that small minority of us which is homosexual . . . an attempt to think through the arguments on all sides as carefully and honestly as possible."

PAUL VARNELL, "Fighting—or Luring—the Right." *Windy City Times,* 16 June 1994.

——— "On Conservative Homophobia." *Windy City Times,* 6 April 1995.

Section III

BRUCE BAWER, "Let There Be Light." *New York Triangle,* 21 June 1994.

——— "Voters Reject a Straight Ticket." *New York Newsday,* 22 September 1994, p. A38. On the widespread support for Karen Burstein, a lesbian candidate for statewide office in New York.

STEPHEN H. CHAPMAN, "The Real Agenda in the Campaign Against Gay Rights." *Chicago Tribune,* 3 February 1994.

JONATHAN RAUCH, "In Defense of Prejudice." *Harper's,* May 1995. A libertarian case against speech codes and for the tolerance of diverse opinions, including those that Rauch—who is gay and Jewish—considers racist, sexist, anti-Semitic, or homophobic.

——— "Words Aren't Violence." *New York Times,* 26 June 1993.

PAUL VARNELL, "How to Create Tolerance." *Windy City Times,* 16 December

1993. An argument for gay involvement in mainstream community groups and for strategic thinking on the part of gay activists. "Gays will become more tolerated (maybe even affirmed) only when we begin to participate in block clubs and neighborhood associations, when we join local business groups, when we become active in our local church or civic betterment group—when we actually contribute something to them."

——— "The Wave of the Future." *Windy City Times*, 12 January 1995. Takes note of young people's increasing tolerance of gays.

Section IV

BRUCE BAWER, "The Bisexual Moment?" *New York Native,* 4 September 1995.

DANIEL MENDELSOHN, "Embracing Between the Bombs." *Nation,* 19 September 1994. Review of Monette's *Last Watch of the Night.* Praises some aspects of the book but chides Monette for his "self-indulgence" and his "refusal to depersonalize" his experience.

STEPHEN H. MILLER, "Exclusionary Diversity." *New York Native,* 12 December 1994. Miller's weekly "Culture Watch" columns, which pay particular attention to instances of radical feminist hostility toward gay males, appear regularly in the *Native.*

——— "Male-Bashing *in Extremis.*" *New York Native,* 7 February 1994. Critique of anti-male rhetoric by gay comedienne Kate Clinton, the Lesbian Avengers, et al.

——— "The 'Parity' Racket." *Windy City Times,* 27 October 1994. Critique of demands for inequitable "gender parity" in gay political organizations.

——— "A Parting of the Ways: Critiquing 'Lesbigay' Culture." *Christopher Street,* issue 212, April 1994. Criticizes the idea of a single "lesbigay" culture on the grounds that "men and women have vastly different behavioral patterns and psychological dynamics."

——— "White Guys Can't Vote?" *Newsday,* 1 July 1993. Criticizes lesbian leaders of gay organizations for "bashing gay white men."

MICHELANGELO SIGNORILE, "Unsafe Like Me." *Out*, October 1994. A gripping plea for sexual responsibility.

ANDREW SULLIVAN, "Washington Diarist." *New Republic,* 21 February 1994.

Credits the film *Philadelphia,* much maligned in the gay press, for portraying "a homosexual emphatically as a member of a heterosexual family."

PAUL VARNELL, "Gay, Bi, Trans, Drag, Etc." *Windy City Times,* 28 July 1994.

Section V

BRUCE BAWER, "The Gentlemen's Club." *Advocate,* 14 November 1995. "Anyone who knows the Episcopal Church knows it's swarming with gay clergy."

——— "In Good Faith." *Advocate,* 13 December 1994, p. 80.

——— "Why I Wrote *A Place at the Table.*" *Outlook* (Integrity/New York), April 1995.

MARCUS J. BORG, "Homosexuality and the New Testament." *Bible Review,* December 1994. In a Christian journal read by many fundamentalists, a New Testament scholar writes that "the prohibition of homosexual behavior is embedded in an ancient legal code that Christians typically see as no longer in force."

JOHN BOSWELL, *Christianity, Social Tolerance, and Homosexuality: Gay People in Western Europe from the Beginning of the Christian Era to the Fourteenth Century.* University of Chicago Press, 1980. A crucial book that has helped many readers reconcile their Christianity and homosexuality.

Continuing the Dialogue: A Pastoral Study Document of the House of Bishops to the Church as the Church Considers Issues of Human Sexuality. Forward Movement Publications, 1995. A document issued by the Episcopal Church in 1994.

LOUIE CREW, "Closetry and Ordination." *Outlook* (Integrity/New York), March 1995. The founder of the gay Episcopal group Integrity writes that "we need to ordain no more closet priests. . . . Dr. King used to say, 'There comes a time when those who go to the back of the bus deserve the back of the bus.' "

JAMES FERRY, *In the Courts of the Lord.* Crossroad, 1994. A gay Anglican priest's account of his defrocking.

CHARLES C. HEFLING, JR., ed., *Our Selves, Our Souls and Bodies.* Cowley, 1996. An excellent collection of essays about homosexuality and Episcopal theology and community. Among contributors are the distinguished theologians Rowan Williams, L. William Countryman, and Owen Thomas.

JACOB MILGROM, "Does the Bible Prohibit Homosexuality?" *Bible Review,* December 1993. A Jewish biblical scholar argues that "the Biblical prohibition is addressed only to Israel," that "Lesbianism is not prohibited in the Bible," and that "if [male Jewish gays] are biologically or psychologically incapable of procreation, adoption provides a solution."

LETHA DAWSON SCANZONI and VIRGINIA RAMEY MOLLENKOTT, *Is the Homosexual My Neighbor? A Positive Christian Response.* HarperCollins, 1994. Revised and updated edition of a book by two Protestant women, one straight and one gay.

JOHN S. SPONG, "A Statement of Koinonia." *Living Church,* October 1994. A statement signed by several Episcopal bishops maintaining that "those who declare themselves to be gay or lesbian persons, and who do not choose to live alone, but forge relationships with partners of their choice that are faithful, monogamous, committed, life giving, and holy are to be honored. . . . God is indeed present in their life together."

ANDREW SULLIVAN, "The Catholic Church and the Homosexual." *New Republic,* 28 November 1994.

PAUL VARNELL, "Dragging Christianity Along." *Windy City Times,* 3 December 1992. Discusses ministers in mainstream denominations who have expressed sympathy for various aspects of gay rights.

——— "God 1, Homophobes 0." *Windy City Times,* 14 March 1991. Examines reports by committees of the Methodist, Episcopal, and Presbyterian churches that indicate movement toward acceptance of homosexuality.

——— "Religious Complicity in Gay-Bashing." *Windy City Times,* 9 April 1992.

Section VI

BRUCE BAWER, "Linking Gay Rights and Family Values." *Chicago Tribune,* 11 October 1994. "Family values . . . are not irreconcilable with gay equal rights—they're among the best arguments *for* gay rights."

——— "The Marrying Kind." *Advocate,* 18 September 1995.

——— "Mom, I Have to Tell You . . ." *Washington Post,* 23 May 1994. A review of Robb Forman Dew, *The Family Heart.*

JOHN BOSWELL, *Same-Sex Unions in Premodern Europe.* Villard, 1994.

STEPHEN H. CHAPMAN, "Gay Moms, Gay Marriage: A Better Way." *Chicago Tribune,* 1 December 1994.

ROBB FORMAN DEW, *The Family Heart: A Memoir of When Our Son Came Out.* Addison-Wesley, 1994. A sensitive account of a mother's response to her son's homosexuality.

ERIC MARCUS, "They're Not Telling the Truth." *Newsweek,* 21 September 1992. A gay writer's attack on anti-gay stereotypes and an account of his own domestic life.

RICHARD D. MOHR, "The Case for Gay Marriage." *Notre Dame Journal of Law, Ethics & Public Policy,* 9:1 (1995). A detailed argument for the legal recognition of gay marriage.

——— "Recognize the Union of Two People," *Chicago Tribune,* 6 November 1993. A call for the legal recognition of gay marriage.

SCOTT PECK, *All-American Boy.* Scribners, 1995. Memoir of the gay son of Col. Fred Peck, commander of U.S. occupation forces in Somalia who testified before the Senate against lifting the ban on gays in the military.

JONATHAN RAUCH, "A Pro-Gay, Pro-Family Policy." *Wall Street Journal,* 29 November 1994.

PAUL VARNELL, "Equality and Gay Marriage." *Windy City Times,* 5 October 1989.

ACKNOWLEDGMENTS

Ever since the publication of *A Place at the Table* I've been collecting articles and op-ed pieces with the intention of compiling a book of this sort. But for the impetus to actually get the project under way I owe much to the encouragement of a group of friends and colleagues, most of whom I met with for a daylong conversation in Washington early in 1995, and with whom I have been engaged for some time now in an ongoing discussion of gay issues. Those friends and colleagues are David Boaz, Stephen Herbits, Stephen Macedo, Stephen H. Miller, James Pepper, Jonathan Rauch, Andrew Sullivan, and Paul Varnell. I am especially grateful to Stephen Herbits, whose inspiration it was to bring us together as a group and whose selfless service to this project has been an example to us all.

I'm indebted to my editor, Mitch Horowitz; to his assistant, Elena Vega; to Adam Bellow; and to my agent, Eric Simonoff, all of whom it has been a joy to work with. I wish to express my appreciation to my editor at the *Advocate*, Bruce Wright, for suggestions that improved several of my pieces included herein, and to Andrew Sullivan for his quick and skillful conversion of my

New York Public Library lecture into a *New Republic* cover story. I thank all the writers represented in this book for allowing their work to be included.

This book has also profited from the comments, criticism, and all-around moral support that I've received from these friends: Nancy Aidala, Jerome Andrews, Linda and David Attoe, Ron Bass and Carol Price, Carol Bawer, Nell and Ted Bawer, Joseph Bednarik, Daniel Blatt, David Bobbitt, Theodore Boukolos, Gloria and Will Brame, Tony Brooks, Patty Burger, Arlene Bullard, Chandler Burr, Kim Byham, Leo Carroll and Paul Lucre, Russell Clay and Stephanie Cowell, Barbara Crafton, Charlotte Davenport, Thomas DePietro and Dorothy Heyl, Tom Disch, Nick Dowen, Jack Finlaw and Greg Movesian, Carl French, Dante Germino, Judith Gillespie, Marsha and Aldo Greco, Michael Joseph Gross, Steve Gunderson and Rob Morris, Sara Hart, James Hatch, Geoffrey Heuchling and Kent Jeffreys, Timothy Holmes, Robert Hugh and Brian Mullaney, Gary Jansen, Kevin Ivers, Paul Jeromack, Harding Jones, Rob Kahn, Karen and Neil Kavey, Evelyn Kotch, "Yaakov Levado," Marvin Liebman, Michael Lind, David Link, James Loney-Wagner, James Lord, Hunter Madsen, Eric Marcus, Jorge Martin and Joshua Sherman, Abner Mason, Alane Mason, Robert McDowell, Brendan McEntee, Joshua McGaughey, Matthew McGaughey, Michael McGaughey and Craig Kettles, Timothy McGaughey, Robert McPhillips, Robert Meek, Daniel Mendelsohn, Gordon Micunis and Jay Kobrin, Jack Miller, Judith Milone, Frederick Morgan and Paula Deitz, Rebecca Ferrell Nickel and David Nickel, Thom Nickels, Richard T. Nolan and Robert Pingpank, Ray Olson, Walter Olson and Steve Pippin, Scott Palmer, Brice Peyre, Elaine Pfefferblit, David Plante, Michael Privitera, Gerardo Ramirez, Kirk Read, Sally Reed, Robert Rowland, Charles Rudesill, Richard Rue, the late Carol Saltus, Douglass Shand-Tucci, Michael Smith, Nelson Smith, Willard Spiegelman, Matthew Stadler, Carlos Stelmach, Bob Summer, Renato Sunico, Rich Tafel, Liz and Terry

Teachout, Rob Teir and Duane Rinde, Chip Teply, Paul Varnell, Ann Welton, Sarah Wenk, Judy White, Mel and Sally Whitehead, Robert E. Wright, Alice Zinnes, Harriet Zinnes, and Joanne Zyontz. The acknowledgments do not imply that any given person named above necessarily shares the views of any given contributor to this book.

For his abiding love, inspiration, and strong, unhesitating opinions I am everlastingly in debt to my partner, Chris Davenport.

PERMISSIONS

Bruce Bawer, "Notes on Stonewall" Reprinted by permission of the author.

Bruce Bawer, "The Road to Utopia" Reprinted by permission of the author.

Paul Varnell, "Memo to the Gay Movement" Reprinted by permission of *Windy City Times* © Sentury Publications, Inc. 1994.

Stephen H. Miller, "White Males: PC's Unseen Target" Reprinted by permission of the author.

John Weir, "Rage, Rage" Reprinted by permission of the author.

Bruce Bawer, "Truth in Advertising" Reprinted by permission of the author.

Carolyn Lochhead, "The Third Way" Reprinted by permission of the author.

Andrew Sullivan, "The Politics of Homosexuality" © Andrew Sullivan. Reprinted by permission of the author.

Paul Varnell, "Barry Goldwater vs. Pat Buchanan" Reprinted with permission of *The Windy City Times* © Sentury Publications, Inc. 1994.

Paul Varnell, "Why More Gay Conservatives?" Reprinted with permission of *Windy City Times* © Sentury Publications, Inc. 1994.

Paul Varnell, "Getting a Grip on Reality" Reprinted with permission of *Windy City Times* © Sentury Publications, Inc. 1994.

Paul Varnell, "What Homophobes Think" Reprinted with permission of *Windy City Times* © Sentury Publications, Inc. 1994.

Bruce Bawer, "Apocalypse? No" Reprinted by permission of the author.

John H. Berresford "A Gay Right Agenda" © John W. Berresford 1995. Reprinted by permission of the author.

Jonathan Rauch, "Thought Crimes" Reprinted by permission of the author.

Jonathan Rauch, "Beyond Oppression" Reprinted by permission of the author.

Mel Dahl, "No 'Special Rights' for Anybody" Reprinted by permission of the author.

Paul Varnell, "The Niceness Solution" Reprinted with permission of *Windy City Times* © Sentury Publications, Inc. 1994

Stephen H. Chapman, "If the Voters Are Angry, How Come They're So Tolerant?" © 1994. Copyrighted Chicago Tribune Company. All rights reserved. Used with permission.

Andrew Sullivan, "Sleeping with the Enemy" Reprinted by permission of the author.

Bruce Bawer, "Sex-negative Me" Reprinted by permission of the author.

Bruce Bawer, "Confusion Reigns" Reprinted by permission of the author

Bruce Bawer, "Canon Fodder" Reprinted by permission of the author

Norah Vincent, "Beyond Lebianism" Reprinted by permission of the author.

Paul Varnell, "Limits of Gay Identity" Reprinted with permission of *Windy City TImes.* © Sentury Publications, Inc, 1994

Rabbi Yaakov Levado, "Gayness and God: Wrestlings of an Orthodox Rabbi" Reprinted by permission of the author.

Thomas H. Stahel, S.J., "I'm here: An Interview with Andrew Sullivan" Reprinted by permission of Andrew Sullivan.

Andrew Sullivan, "Here Comes the Groom: A (Conservative) Case for Gay Marriage" Reprinted by permission of the author.

Paul Varnell, "Family Values: Ours and Theirs" Reprinted with permission of *Windy City Times.* © Sentury Publications, Inc. 1992.

James P. Pinkerton, "Conservatives: Don't Bash Gay Marriage" Reprinted by permission of the author.

David Link, "I Am Not Queer" Reprinted by permission of the author.

Stephen H. Miller. "Honey, Did You Raise the Kids?" Reprinted by permission of the author.

Jonathan Rauch, "Morality and Homosexuality" Reprinted by permission of the author.

David Boaz, "Don't Forget the Kids" © 1994 New York Times Company. Reprinted by permission.

David Boaz, "Domestic Justice" © 1995 New York Times Company. Reprinted by permission.

Jonathan Rauch, "Who Needs Marriage?" Reprinted by permission of the author.

Bruce Bawer, "The Folks Next Door" Reprinted by permission of the author.

The following pieces, which appear in this book for the first time, have been published here by arrangement with the authors:

David Link, "Why Outing Doesn't Work"

Daniel Mendelsohn, "Scenes From a Mall"

Bruce Bawer, "Lecture at Saint John's Cathedral

ABOUT THE EDITOR

BRUCE BAWER, who has been called "a literary essayist for the ages" (*Kirkus Reviews*), is the author of five books of literary and film criticism. His collection of poetry, *Coast to Coast* (1993), was cited in the *Dictionary of Literary Biography Yearbook* as "the finest first volume of poetry of the year." His book *A Place at the Table: The Gay Individual in American Society* was for many months a number-one bestseller in gay bookstores, was nominated for a Lambda Book Award, and was cited as a Notable Book of the Year by the *New York Times Book Review.* A former director of the National Book Critics Circle, Bawer has reviewed frequently for the *New York Times Book Review,* the *Washington Post Book World,* and the *Wall Street Journal,* and has contributed essays to the *New Criterion,* the *American Scholar,* the *Hudson Review,* the *Nation,* and *Newsweek.* His poems have appeared in *Paris Review* and *Poetry,* among many other journals. An active member of the Episcopal Church, Bawer lives in New York City with his partner, Chris Davenport.